Gillian Tett is an assistant editor at the *Financial Times* where she oversees the global coverage of the financial markets. In 2009 she won the British Press Award for Journalist of the Year. She often appears on high-profile discussion programmes such as *Today* and she lectures widely. She has a PhD in social anthropology from Cambridge University. *Fool's Gold* won Financial Book of the Year at the inaugural Spear's Book Awards.

Selected as Books of the Year in the *Daily Telegraph*, the *Financial Times*, the *Irish Times* and the *New Statesman*.

'As an inside account, *Fool's Gold* is hard to beat' David Smith, *Sunday Times*

'By far the most insightful of the first wave of books on the crisis' Donald MacKenzie, *London Review of Books*

'Her blow-by-blow story is an impressive piece of detective work. She pulls back the curtain on a closed, unaccountable world of finance' Will Hutton, *Guardian*

'A very readable, well-informed account of the way investment bankers invented, promoted and profited from the financial products that were at the heart of the banking collapse' Vince Cable, *Daily Telegraph*

'A compelling complementary analysis' Peter Riddell, *New Statesman*

'Absorbing . . . Tett sketches a system in the grip of a great error, emanating outwards from a cadre of elite traders who were able to repel any attempt to monitor, question or restrain them' Stephen Foley, *Independent*

Fool's Gold

How Unrestrained Greed Corrupted a Dream,
Shattered Global Markets and
Unleashed a Catastrophe

GILLIAN TETT

ABACUS

First published in Great Britain in 2009 by Little, Brown
This paperback edition published in 2010 by Abacus

A CIP catalogue record for this book
is available from the British Library.

ISBN 978-0-349-12189-5

Typeset in Bembo by M Rules
Printed and bound in Great Britain by
Clays Ltd, St Ives plc

Papers used by Abacus are natural, renewable and
recyclable products sourced from well-managed forests and certified
in accordance with the rules of the Forest Stewardship Council.

Mixed Sources
Product group from well-managed
forests and other controlled sources
www.fsc.org Cert no. SGS-COC-004081
© 1996 Forest Stewardship Council
FSC

Abacus
An imprint of
Little, Brown Book Group
100 Victoria Embankment
London EC4Y 0DY

An Hachette UK Company
www.hachette.co.uk

www.littlebrown.co.uk

For Analiese and Helen Marie

Contents

Preface to the Paperback Edition

Back in early 2007, before the credit bubble burst, I hit upon the idea of writing a book about credit derivatives and other forms of complex finance because I thought the public should understand more about the dangers they posed. Back then, the UK and most of the rest of the Western world was in the midst of a dizzy credit boom, and there wasn't much scrutiny in the press about complex finance. The area seemed too technical to be of much interest to non-bankers; indeed, the only group of people who seemed to care about the issue were those bankers in London and New York who were directly involved in it, eagerly finding ways to get rich.

No longer. The first edition of my book was published in the spring of 2009, as the financial world was still reeling from the bursting of the credit bubble. It would be quite wrong to claim that the credit derivatives sector – or, indeed, the world of financial innovation in general – was the *only* factor behind this terrible financial crisis, the worst seen for seventy years. Poor mortgage regulation, global savings imbalances, a failure of bank oversight, lax credit ratings, a crazy consumer debt binge, as well as excessively loose US monetary policy all played critical roles too, as I explain in this book. A key issue, however, one that exacerbated the credit bubble during the boom – and then vastly complicated the disaster when the bubble burst – was the presence of all those credit derivatives contracts.

When the insurance giant AIG teetered in the autumn of 2008, for example, it emerged that its London-based entity known as AIG Financial Products had cut so many credit derivatives contracts with other banks in America and Europe that any collapse of AIG threatened to spark a string of bank collapses. Indeed, this was a fundamental reason why the US government stepped in to prop up AIG, producing a bill for taxpayers that had risen to around $180 billion by the autumn of 2008. And a key factor behind that bill was the presence of those credit derivatives contracts written in London by AIG's division, which linked the group with banks in London, Paris, Edinburgh or Frankfurt – as well as Wall Street.

So, while the tale I tell in this book – a tale of how those derivatives were invented and became such a driver of the credit bubble – may not *entirely* explain *all* of the financial crisis, it does illuminate a crucial part. Moreover, this is a part that many policy makers, regulators and voters in London, Brussels, New York and elsewhere are still struggling to understand.

I first crashed into this world back in early 2005, when I happened to spot – almost by chance – a frenzy of activity occurring in the credit sector that was being under-reported by the mainstream press. Between 2005 and 2007, I tried to penetrate this world, writing a string of articles for the *Financial Times* (including, as it happens, the antics of the JPMorgan bankers who form the main narrative of this book). As I tried to piece together the tale of what the purveyors of derivatives were up to, I was startled by the scale of it. By 2005, the credit derivatives world, for example, was exploding, with more than $20 trillion contracts in the markets, most of which had been written in London or New York. The balance sheet of AIG alone was being stuffed with more than $400 billion worth of credit derivatives deals, which would later turn sour, producing that stupendous taxpayers' bailout bill.

Yet there was barely a whisper of this activity in public view. Men such as Gordon Brown, then UK Chancellor, for example, might sometimes have applauded the operations of the City of London – but they almost never discussed the workings of the derivatives sector at all, let alone referred to what the London subsidiary of AIG was doing. Nor did his American counterparts. Instead, when politicians, journalists or non-bankers discussed the financial world, it was almost always in terms of the stock market, or – on occasion – the type of mergers and acquisition work that banks were carrying out. Indeed, the difference was so stark that I sometimes likened the financial system to an iceberg: there was a small piece of activity, in particular the equity markets, poking above the surface, in plain sight, and then a vast chunk that was submerged from public view. Until, of course, late 2008.

As you read this book, one issue that I encourage you to reflect on is exactly *why* it took a crisis for those outside the credit derivatives sector to delve deeply into the way derivatives were structured and the risks they carried. Why had there been such a climate of silence? Why, for example, were so few people in the British parliament asking what was really driving the revenues of the City of London – barely two miles down the road. After all, if more people had asked hard questions at an earlier stage about what was happening in the credit derivatives world, and why credit was booming, there is every reason to think that the worst excesses might never have happened. Debate and scrutiny might have sparked concern and brought about more common sense, not just among the regulators but among the bankers too.

Of course, some journalists and politicians argue that the bankers were deliberately concealing the risks in credit derivatives. Personally, though, I suspect that the problem was more subtle than that – while at the same time more alarming, in terms of its implications for modern society, both inside and outside the financial world.

When I first started asking questions about credit derivatives back in 2005 and 2006, it was clear that some bankers were consciously obsuring aspects of the business – for example, as I portray in this book, bankers were usually reluctant to discuss *precisely* how their teams were creating their derivatives. They were also secretive about their profits, the risk models they were using to test the derivatives, and their internal systems for pricing them. Such information was considered to be 'proprietary', and thus kept secret not just from journalists but from other bankers too. I also found, however, that plenty of activity was not regarded as top secret and that the bankers would talk about it fairly readily.

When I asked specific questions about new credit derivatives ideas, they were usually willing to talk in some detail. I therefore believe that if any regulator, shareholder, politician or journalist had asked a few questions about AIG's credit derivatives activity back then – or even just popped into the AIG London offices – they could have gleaned a rough sense of what the insurance group was up to. It's also true that a fair amount of detail was published in AIG's own accounts. This is why I think we have to look to another reason for the silence.

Many years ago, before I became a journalist, I earned a PhD in social anthropology, and one of the writers I studied who made a big impact on me was Pierre Bourdieu, an anthropologist-cum-sociologist who was part of a wave of creative intellectual thought that emerged in France in the 1970s. In his seminal work *Outline of a Theory of Practice*, Bourdieu observed that the way that elites tend to control a society is not simply by controlling the physical means of production (money and other resources), but also by influencing the cultural discourse, the way the society talks about itself, or its cognitive map. Moreover, when it comes to influencing a cognitive map, what matters is not merely what is publicly discussed, but also what is *not* mentioned in public – either because it is deemed impolite, taboo, boring or simply because it is taken completely for granted. Areas of social silence, in other words, are crucial to supporting a story that a society is telling itself, such as that about the credit boom.

Sometimes such a silence is maintained through overt strategies devised by members of a social group. They can consciously choose to hide facts, as part of a plot. But on many occasions, Bourdieu observed, social silences arise less deliberately, as a result of patterns of social conformity or shared ideology and assumptions – for example about the ability of the market to regulate itself. And it is at this semi-conscious level that the most insidious types of social silence develops; insidious particularly when they serve the interest of one particular group. Or as Bourdieu wrote: 'The most successful ideological effects are those which have no need of words, and ask no more than a complicitous silence.' In many ways, the tale of the boom and bust of credit is exemplary.

Both inside and outside the banking world, a social silence developed about credit derivatives. This was in part because the topic was thought to be so technical, and therefore generally uninteresting to non-specialists, but it was also because the lack of scrutiny suited the banking industry so well. Opacity in the world of finance breeds fat margins. Another factor at play was the widely accepted presence of so-called silos – or self-contained realms of activity and knowledge that only the experts in those areas can truly understand. The banking system was producing fat profits as well as a stream of cheap credit for consumers. The boom had a strong allure.

The situation was almost akin to that of the European medieval church: although almost nobody in the congregation really understood the financial 'Latin' in which the service was being conducted, few rebelled because they were receiving blessings. The congregation was mystified, but it accepted that the priests were the keepers of the faith.

These days, of course, it has become self-evident that this lack of questioning – the excessive laziness-cum-trust on the part of those who should have been probing more trenchantly – was a crucial reason why the banking system was able to spin so badly out of control. The real tragedy of this story, in other words, was that most of the folly was *not* due to a plot; instead, it was hidden in plain sight.

Therein lies a larger lesson of the financial crisis. The modern world is littered with pockets of specialist knowledge, where technical experts work in mental and structural silos. Indeed, these silos are proliferating, for as the pace of innovation speeds up, and spreads further and further around the globe, our world is becoming more technologically complex by the day. Just think of the advances being made in genetic engineering, environmental science, telecommunications, and energy, to name but a few. In theory, as these innovations spread, we are all being connected more closely to one another. In practice, though, innovation is causing as much fragmentation as unity. After all, only a tiny pool of people today have the educational training or technological knowledge to truly understand the details of some of these silos; even fewer have the ability to hop between silos.

Alongside the need for technical experts, therefore, we also need generalists who can act as cultural watchdogs and translators. The world is critically short today of these cultural translators. Of course the media might appear to be charged with this role, but in practical terms, the media's resources are increasingly squeezed, limiting the time reporters have to do the kind of in-depth digging that is required. As for the politicians and regulators who are tasked with oversight, they are too often compromised by conflicts of interest and are at any rate spread dangerously thin.

The good news, in one sense, is that the damage to the financial world from this crisis has been so severe that this problem *is* now being rectified in some ways. In the period since the first edition of my book was published, regulators and politicians have – albeit belatedly – been scrutinising the innovations that bankers are producing. The new fashion among Western policy makers is so-called macro prudential supervision, or the idea of taking a much more encompassing approach to regulation, leaving no pockets left unexamined. The senior management of the major banks and insurance groups are also now frantically trying to devise new methods to enable them to keep tabs on their silos – and track the activity of their junior bankers. Politicians have been working on reform ideas as well.

How far these measures will go is a crucial question the public must be asking, and that is one reason this book is just as relevant today as when I first wrote it. As you read about how regulation failed and the activities of the bankers spun so desperately out of control, the nature of the reforms that are required will be clearly illuminated. I also address this issue expressly at the end of the book. But the relevance of this tragic story reaches further, to this issue of the many other silos developing in our world that are potentially dangerous. The story of the 2008 financial crisis is a story not only of hubris, greed, and regulatory failure, but one of these deeply troubling problems of social silence and technical silos. If we do not use the crisis as an occasion to seriously tackle these problems, then it is a crisis we may well be doomed to revisit, albeit in an innovative new form.

Gillian Tett
December 2009

Preface

Were the bankers mad? Blind? Evil? Or were they simply grotesquely greedy? To be sure, there have been plenty of booms and busts in history. Market crashes are almost as old as the invention of money itself. But the latest and ongoing crisis stands out due to its sheer size; economists estimate that total losses could end up being $2000 billion to $4000 billion, a sum that is not dissimilar to the value of British gross domestic product. More startling still, this disaster was self-inflicted. Unlike many banking crises, this one was not triggered by a war, a widespread recession or any external economic shock. The financial system collapsed in on itself, seemingly out of the blue, as far as many observers were concerned. As consumers, politicians, pundits, and not the least financiers, contemplate the wreckage, the question we must drill into is *Why*? Why did the bankers, regulators and ratings agencies collaborate to build and run a system that was doomed to self-destruct? Did they fail to see the flaws, or did they fail to care?

This book explores the answer to the central question of how the catastrophe happened by beginning with the tale of a small group of bankers formerly linked to J.P. Morgan, the iconic, century-old pillar of banking. In the 1990s they developed an innovative set of products with names such as 'credit default swaps' and 'synthetic collateralized debt obligations' (of which more later), which fall under the rubric of credit derivatives. The

Morgan team's concepts were diffused and mutated all around the global economy and collided with separate innovations in mortgage finance. That played a critical role in both the great credit bubble and its subsequent terrible bursting. The J.P. Morgan team were not the true inventors of credit derivatives. But the story of how the particular breed they perfected was taken into far riskier terrain by the wider banking world offers a sharp perspective on the crisis. Equally revealing is the little-known tale of what the J.P. Morgan bankers (and later JPMorgan Chase) did *not* do, when their ideas were corrupted into a wider market madness.

The story of the great credit boom and bust is not a saga that can be neatly blamed on a few greedy or evil individuals. It tells how an entire financial system went wrong, as a result of flawed incentives within banks and investment funds, as well as the ratings agencies; warped regulatory structures; and a lack of oversight. It is a tale best understood through the observation of human foibles, as much as through economic or financial analysis. And while plenty of greedy bankers play crucial parts in the drama – and perhaps a few mad, or evil, ones too – the real tragedy of this story is that so many of those swept up in the lunacy were not acting out of deliberately bad motives.

On the contrary, in the case of the J.P. Morgan team who form the backbone of this tale, the bitter irony is that they first developed their derivatives ideas in the hopes that they would be good for the financial system (as well, of course, as for their bank, and their bonuses). Even today, after all the devastation, some of the tools and innovations developed during the credit boom should be seen as potentially valuable for twenty-first-century finance. In order to understand how that could be, though, a deep understanding of how and precisely why they came to be so abused is vital. I offer this journey through the story as one attempt to begin to come to grips with the answers to that crucial question.

*

First, a brief note of explanation of why I chose to focus on
the J.P. Morgan team. My own path into this story started in the
spring of 2005, in a plush, darkened conference room in Nice.
A couple of weeks earlier, I had taken up the post of capital
markets editor of the *Financial Times*, and so I had flown down
to the French Riviera to take part in a conference to discuss the
credit derivatives world. Back then, in the gloriously naive days
of the financial boom, the issue of credit derivatives was something that most journalists (and their readers) considered rather
obscure and dull. Indeed, I had often viewed it that way myself.
Unlike most other newspapers, the *FT* had always strived to
cover the workings of the vast debt and derivatives market; however, these topics had traditionally commanded less attention and
status than the high-profile, glamorous issues such as corporate
finance, mainstream economics – or the stock market. Sectors
such as equities or corporate activity have traditionally been
easier for journalists to cover, since they are less opaque and
include visible characters.

However, in late 2004, when I was working on the Lex analysis column of the *FT*, I realized that something highly significant
was under way in the vast, murky debt world. Initially, I was
unsure quite what the story was; but I could sense that something was bubbling. So when a chance arrived to run the capital
markets team, I grabbed it, and headed to Nice to get an introduction to this newfangled world. (As I would later discover,
banking conferences tend to occur in places such as Boca Raton,
Barcelona, the French Riviera or other smart holiday resorts,
rather than cities like Hull or Detroit.)

Walking into that gathering for the first time was a disconcerting experience. The hall was full of young men and women,
decked out in the smart-casual wear that is the unofficial conference uniform for the City or Wall Street: chinos, shirts,
loafers, matched with chunky, expensive watches (for men) or
equally expensive, but discreet earrings (for women). References

to billions – or even trillions – of dollars were casually tossed into conversation. Yet much of the time, the bankers avoided direct references to any mention of what companies or consumers might do with the money, such as building factories or buying food; instead finance was presented as an abstract mathematical game that took place in cyberspace, and which could only be grasped by a tiny elite. Finance was not about grubby cash, but a string of mathematical equations, Greek letters or phrases such as 'Gaussian copula', 'standard deviation', 'attachment point', 'delta hedging' or 'first-to-default basket'.

I was utterly baffled. I had done plenty of maths at school, but nothing had equipped me for this. But, as I sat in the darkened conference room, I also had a sense of déjà vu. Over a decade earlier, before I had started working as a financial journalist, I had done a PhD in social anthropology, the branch of the social sciences devoted to studying human culture from a micro-level, holistic perspective, based on on-the-ground fieldwork. Back then, I had used my training to make sense of wedding rituals and ethnic conflict in Tajikistan, a mountainous central Asian region. However, as I looked around me in that Nice conference hall, in the spring of 2005, the same approach I had once used to decode Tajik weddings seemed useful in the credit derivatives tribe too. As a rank outsider I understood little of what was being discussed; however, conferences seemed to fill a similar structural function as wedding ceremonies. Both events allowed an otherwise disparate tribe of players to unite, mingle and forge all manner of fresh alliances on the margins of the main event. They restated, and thus reinforced, the dominant ideology – or cognitive map – that united the group, transferring it from generation to generation. The PowerPoints the bankers presented on topics such as the CDO waterfall, did not merely convey complex technical data; they also reinforced unspoken, shared assumptions about how finance worked, including the idea that it was perfectly valid to discuss money in abstract, mathematical, ultra-complex terms, without any reference to tangible human beings.

The participants in the Nice banking conference were barely aware of such 'functions', and they had little incentive to reflect on their activity, or explain it to outsiders. Business was booming. That validated their cognitive map. In any case, almost nobody outside their world had ever shown much interest in what they did. I was the first reporter from a mainstream newspaper that had bothered to attend that particular conference; to other mainstream reporters, even those in the business sphere, CDOs seemed far too geeky a topic to arouse interest.

Uneasily, I looked around the hall, trying to get a compass to help me navigate; who were they key players? How could I interpret this strange language? 'Who are those people up on the stage?' I whispered to a chino-wearing man sitting next to me in the dark hall. On the stage a panel of young financiers were earnestly debating the prescribed topic: 'Do investors truly understand CDO default risk?' (The answer, it appeared, was 'not always'.)

My neighbour looked nervous; he whispered that his bank banned employees from talking to journalists 'since you guys keep writing all that shit about derivatives blowing up the world'. But then he relented: 'They used to all work at J.P. Morgan.'

'J.P. Morgan?' I asked, surprised. In the early part of the twenty-first century, it was Goldman Sachs, and its powerful alumni network, that seemed to dominate the world of finance, inspiring envy from rivals. J.P. Morgan, by contrast, seemed rather dull by comparison; so why was it so present now?

'It's like this Morgan mafia thing. They sort of created the credit derivatives market,' my neighbour whispered, and then he shut up abruptly, as if he had given away some kind of state secret.

*

I never saw that particular financier again, thus never discovered
if he had a personal link to that Morgan mafia. Yet my curiosity
was piqued. In the months that followed, I set out on an intensive mission, to try to make sense of this strange, unfamiliar
credit world. Along the way, I also tried to untangle why J.P.
Morgan had played such a key role in this newfangled sphere.
When I first set out on this journey, I had absolutely no idea of
the momentous events which would eventually shatter this credit
world. By chance, I had seen a banking system implode once
before in my career, since I worked in Japan in the late 1990s.
However, when I wrote about that disaster I never imagined, for
a moment, I might see that pattern unfold again in Western
finance, far less in the CDO sphere. What drew me to the credit
world was just a journalist's hunch that a big story was bubbling
which seemed widely ignored.

Later, around 2006, I became seriously alarmed by what I saw,
and started to warn that a reckoning loomed. Then, later still,
when the financial system started to collapse, I realized that the
tale of the credit world in general, and the J.P. Morgan group in
particular, offers some good insights into what went wrong. That
is not, let me stress, because the J.P. Morgan group personally
engaged in the abuses that eventually destroyed some banks.
They did not. Nor were the Morgan mafia the only players that
created the market for complex financial products. Numerous
other bankers were involved in this process too. To write a book
which is comprehensible, I have been forced to streamline the
story. Yet the strange journey that the Morgan group have travelled over the last two decades does provide insights into why the
financial system spun out of control, and why a set of ideas
which once seemed 'good', turned so terribly 'bad'. It is a tragic,
salutary tale, not just for bankers but for all of us.

Fool's Gold

PART ONE

Innovation

CHAPTER ONE

The Derivatives Dream

On half a mile of immaculate private beach, along Florida's
fabled Gold Coast, sits the sugar-pink Boca Raton hotel,
designed in a gracious Mediterranean style by the Palm Beach
architect Addison Mizner. Since the hotel opened in 1926, it has
styled itself a temple to exclusivity, boasting Italianate statues and
manicured palm trees, a dazzling marina with slips for thirty-two
yachts, a professional tennis club, a state-of-the-art spa, a designer
golf course, and a strip of private beach. A glitzy roll call of
celebrities and the wealthy have flocked to this resort, billed as a
'private enclave of luxury', where they can relax well away from
prying eyes.

On one summer's weekend back in June 1994, a quite different clientele descended: several dozen young bankers from the
offices of J.P. Morgan in New York, London and Tokyo. They
were there for an off-site meeting, called to discuss how the bank
could grow its derivatives business in the next year. In the humid
summer heat, amid the palm trees and gracious arches, the group
embraced the idea of a new type of derivative that would trans-
form the wider world of twenty-first-century finance, and play

a decisive role in the worst economic crisis since the Great Depression. 'It was in Boca where we started talking seriously about credit derivatives,' recalls Peter Hancock, the British-born leader of the group. 'That was where the idea really took off, where we really had a vision of how big it could be.'

As with most intellectual breakthroughs, the exact origin of the concept of credit derivatives is hard to pinpoint. For Hancock, a highly cerebral man who likes to depict history as a tidy evolution of ideas, one step of the breakthrough occurred at the Boca Raton off-site. Some of his team, however, have only the haziest, alcohol-fuddled memories of that weekend. The young bankers had arrived in Florida determined to party as hard as they could, full of youthful exuberance and a sense of entitlement.

They worked for the 'swaps' department – a particular corner of the derivatives universe, which was one of the hottest, fastest-growing areas of finance. In the early 1980s, J.P. Morgan, along with several other venerable banks, had jumped into the new-fangled derivatives field, and activity in that arcane business had exploded. By 1994, the total notional value of derivatives contracts on J.P. Morgan's books was put at $1.7 trillion, and derivatives activity was generating half of the bank's trading revenue. In 1992 – one year when J.P. Morgan broke the number out for public consumption – the total was $512 million.

More startling than those numbers was the fact that most members of the banking and wider investing world had absolutely no idea how derivatives were producing such phenomenal sums, let alone what so-called 'swaps' groups actually did. Those who worked in the area tended to revel in its air of mystery.

At the time of the Boca meeting, most of the J.P. Morgan group were still under thirty years old. Some had just left college. But they were all convinced, with the heady arrogance of youth, that they held the secret to transforming the financial world, as well as dramatically enhancing J.P. Morgan's profit profile. Many arrived in Boca presuming that the weekend was a lavish thank you from the management.

On Friday afternoon they greeted each other in wild high spirits and headed for the bars. Many had flown down from New York; a few had come from Tokyo; a large contingent had flown over from London. Within minutes, drinking games were under way. As the night wore on, some of them commandeered a minivan to visit a local nightclub. Others hijacked golf carts and raced around the lawns. A gaggle assembled around the main Boca Raton swimming pool, threatening to throw each other in.

As the revelry around the pool intensified, Peter Voicke, a buttoned-up German who held the title of head of global markets, and, though only in his late forties, was the most senior official present, earnestly tried to calm them all down. Voicke had agreed to stage the off-site in the hope it would forge camaraderie. 'It is important to develop a healthy esprit de corps!' he liked to say in his flat Teutonic accent. But the camaraderie was getting out of hand. In no mood to heed his admonitions, several young colleagues pushed Voicke into the pool. 'My shoes, my shoes!' he shouted, as expensive loafers drifted off his feet.

The drunken crowd then turned on Bill Winters, a jovial American who, at thirty-one, was the second most senior official attending. Half-heartedly, he tried to dodge the crowd, but as he ducked his face slammed into an incoming elbow and a fountain of blood spurted out. 'You've broken my nose!' he shouted, as he too tumbled into the pool. For a moment, the drunken laughter stopped. Voicke was obviously furious. Now Winters was hurt. But then Winters let out a laugh and hauled himself out of the pool. He clicked his nose back into place and the games resumed.

At some banks, dousing the boss would have been a firing offence. But J.P. Morgan prided itself on a close-knit, almost fraternal culture. Those on the outside viewed the J.P. Morgan crowd as elitist and arrogant, overly enamoured of the bank's vaunted history as a dominant force in American and British finance. Insiders often referred to the bank as a family. The derivatives group was one of the most unruly but also most close-knit teams. 'We had *real* fun – there was a great spirit in the group back then,' Winters would later recall with a wistful grin. When he and the rest of that little band looked back on those wild times, many said they were the happiest days of their lives.

One reason for that was the man who ran the team, Peter Hancock. At the age of thirty-five he was only slightly older than many of the group, but he was their intellectual godfather. A large man, with thinning hair and clumsy, hairy hands, he exuded the genial air of a family doctor or university professor. Unlike many of those who came to dominate the complex finance world, Hancock sported no advanced degree in mathematics or science. Like most of the J.P. Morgan staff, he had joined the bank straight out of university, but notwithstanding the lack of a PhD, he was intensely cerebral, devoted to the theory and practice of finance in all its forms. He viewed almost every aspect of the world around him as a complex intellectual puzzle to be solved, and he especially loved developing elaborate theories about how to push money around the world in a more efficient manner. When it came to his staff, he ruminated obsessively on how to deploy the team for optimal performance. Most of all, though, he loved brainstorming ideas.

Sometimes he did that in formal meetings, like the Boca offsite. But he also spewed out ideas like a contrail in his wake as he strode around the bank's trading floor. The team called his outbursts of creativity 'Come to Planet Pluto' moments, because many of the notions he tossed out seemed better suited to science fiction than banking. But they loved his intensity, and they were passionately loyal to him, knowing that he was fiercely devoted to protecting, and handsomely rewarding, his tribe. They were also bonded by the spirit of being pioneers.

The J.P. Morgan derivatives team was engaged in the banking equivalent of space travel. Computing power and high-order mathematics were taking the business far from its traditional bounds, and this small group of brilliant minds was charting the outer reaches of cyberfinance. Like scientists cracking the DNA code or splitting the atom, the J.P. Morgan swaps team believed their experiments in what bankers refer to as 'innovation', meaning the invention of bold new ways to generate returns, were solving the most foundational riddles of their discipline. 'There was this sense that we had found this fantastic technology which we really believed in and we wanted to take to every part of the market we could,' Winters later recalled. 'There was a sense of mission.'

That stemmed in part from Hancock's intense focus on the science of people management. He was almost as fascinated by how to manage people for optimal performance as by financial flows. The moment he was appointed head of the derivatives group, Hancock had started experimenting with his staff. One of his first missions was to overhaul how his sales team and the traders interacted. Against all tradition, he decided to give the sales force the authority to quote prices for complex deals, instead of relying on the traders. He expected that doing so would more intensely motivate sales, and the change produced good results. He then started inventing new systems of remuneration designed to discourage taking excessive risks or hugging brilliant projects too close to the vest. He wanted to encourage collaboration and longer-term thinking, rather than self-interested pursuit of short-term gains. The teamwork ethos was already well entrenched, especially by comparison with most other Wall Street banks, but Hancock fervently believed that J.P. Morgan needed to go even further.

In later years, Hancock pushed his experimentation to unusual extremes. He hired a social anthropologist to study the corporate dynamics at the bank. He conducted firm-wide polls to ascertain

which employees interacted most effectively with those from
other departments, and he then used that data as a benchmark for
assessing employee compensation, plotting it on complex, colour-
coded computer models. He was convinced that departments
needed to interact closely with each other, so that they could
swap ideas and monitor each other's risks; silos (or fragmented
departments), he believed, were lethal. At one stage he half-
jokingly floated the idea of tracking employee emails, to measure
the level of cross-departmental interaction in a scientific manner.
The suggestion was blocked. 'The human resources department
thought I was barking mad!' he later recalled. 'But if you want to
create the conditions for innovation, people have to feel free to
share ideas. You cannot have that if everyone is always fighting!'

One of Hancock's boldest experiments focused on the core
group within the swaps team known as Investor Derivatives
Marketing. The bankers attached to this team sat around a long
desk under low ceilings on the third floor of the J.P. Morgan
headquarters, and the group's role was somewhat anomalous.
Though some marketing of products to clients was done, it acted
more like an incubator for ideas that had no other obvious
departmental home and handled a ragbag of products, including
structured finance schemes linked to the insurance world and
tax-minimizing products.

A few months before the meeting in Boca Raton, Hancock
had approached Bill Demchak, an ambitious young banker with
a good reputation around the bank, to run the IDM group.
Determined to drive innovation, Hancock told him: 'You will
have to make at least half your revenues each year from a product which did not exist before!' By Wall Street standards, that
was a startling mandate. Normally a group that hit on a brilliant
money-making idea would claim exclusive ownership and milk
it for as long as they could. Hancock wanted IDM to invent
products and almost immediately hand them over so that they
could move on to new inventions.

Demchak readily accepted the daunting mandate. He was amused by the challenge, and in many ways he appeared the perfect man to act as a foil for Hancock's creative ambitions. He came from an unassuming background, and hadn't forgotten his roots, having grown up in a middle-class family in Pittsburgh and studied business at Allegheny College in Pennsylvania. He earned an MBA from the University of Michigan and joined J.P. Morgan in the mid-1980s. Generally he had a jovial demeanour, but if he felt someone had crossed him or was being stupid, he could explode. He was hard-working, but also loved to party. 'If you met him, you wouldn't know he was from Wall Street!' one of his college buddies from Pittsburgh observed.

Demchak's razor-sharp mind dissected problems at lightning speed. A particular talent was lateral thought, pulling in ideas from other areas of banking. He was also a natural leader, and he instilled extreme loyalty among his staff. His colleagues often joked that if it was not for the practical Demchak, Hancock 'would have stayed on Pluto'. He was the perfect man to implement his boss's schemes.

Hancock installed another ambitious banker in the London office of the team. Bill Winters, who had taken the breaking of his nose with such good cheer, also came from a relatively modest background by comparison with the Ivy League pedigrees of so many of the banking elite. He had studied at Colgate University in New York State, and joined the bank in the mid-1980s. He was blessed with good looks – female colleagues thought Winters looked a little like the actor George Clooney – but he preferred to stay out of the limelight. And whereas Demchak was given to explosions when he faced resistance, Winters was more flexible and tended to dance around problems, getting what he wanted with finesse. He was intensely hard-working.

Hancock first noticed Winters in the late 1980s, when he was working in the area of commodities derivatives. 'We sent him down to Mexico and somehow – I still don't know how – he persuaded the government to hedge half of its oil production and interest rate exposure with us.' Hancock recalled. 'There was no drama, he just did it. That is his style.' Hancock appointed him to run the European side of the derivatives team with the expectation that the 'two Bills', as their colleagues dubbed them, would work well together in tossing innovative ideas back and forth across the Atlantic.

Central to the swaps team's quest now was to take the new-fangled breed of financial products called derivatives into new terrain.

When bankers talk about derivatives, they delight in swathing the concept in complex jargon. That complexity makes the world of derivatives opaque, which serves bankers' interests just fine. Opacity reduces scrutiny and confers power on the few with the ability to pierce the veil. But though derivatives have indeed become horribly complex, in fact they are as old as the idea of finance itself.

As the name implies, a derivative is, on the most basic level, nothing more than a contract whose value derives from some other asset – a bond, a stock, a quantity of gold. Key to derivatives is that those who buy and sell them are each making a bet on the future value of that asset. Derivatives provide a way for investors to either protect themselves, for example, against a possible negative future price swing, or to make high-stakes bets on price swings for what might be huge payoffs. At the heart of the business is a dance with *time*.

Say, on a particular day, the pound-to-dollar exchange rate is such that one British pound buys $1.50. Someone who will be making a trip from England to the US six months from now and thinks the exchange rate may become less favourable might decide to make a contract to ensure that he can still buy dollars at that rate just before his trip. He might enter into an agreement to exchange £1000 with a bank in six months' time, at $1.50, no matter what the actual exchange rate is by then. One way to arrange that deal would be to agree that the trade *must* happen, no matter what the actual rate of exchange is at the time, and that would be a *future*. A variation would be that the traveller agrees to pay a fee, say $25, to have the *option* to make the exchange at the $1.50 rate, which he would decide not to exercise if the rate actually became more favourable.

Versions of derivatives trading have existed for centuries. Rudimentary examples of futures and options contracts have been found on clay tablets from Mesopotamia dating from 1750 BC. In the twelfth and thirteenth centuries, English monasteries made futures deals with foreign merchants to sell wool up to twenty years in advance, and famously in seventeenth-century Holland, when tulip prices started to soar, merchants' frantic buying and selling of tulip futures led to a craze that ended in a spectacular crash.

The modern era of derivatives trading began when the Chicago Board of Trade was established in 1849, allowing for the buying and selling of futures and options on agricultural commodities. Wheat farmers might buy futures before harvest on the price their wheat would bring in, hoping to hedge against low prices in the event of a bumper crop. Speculators would take on the risk of the losses farmers feared in the hopes of big payoffs that all too often turned horribly sour.

In the late 1970s, a bold new era of derivatives innovation was inspired by a set of technological breakthroughs and increasing volatility in the financial markets. It brought derivatives from the world of commodities into the domain of finance. The post-Second World War Bretton Woods system of credit and exchange controls that had maintained relative stability in world markets broke down, and the values of foreign currency, which had been pegged to the dollar, became free-floating. That led to unpredictable swings in exchange rates. Oil-price shocks then sparked a pernicious blend of recession and inflation in the US, with inflation eventually peaking at 13.2 per cent in 1981. Shocked investors scurried to find ways to protect themselves from the devastating impact of the high interest rates – the prime rate rose to a high of 20 per cent in the US in June 1981 – and from relentless swings in exchange rates.

Historically the best way to insulate against such volatility was to buy a diversified pool of assets. If, for example, a company with business in both the US and Germany was concerned about swings in the dollar-to-Deutschmark rate, it could protect itself by holding equal quantities of both currencies. Whichever way the rate might swing, the losses would be offset by equal gains. But an innovative way to protect against swings was to buy derivatives offering clients the right to purchase currencies at specific exchange rates in the future. Interest rate futures and options burst on to the scene, allowing investors and bankers to gamble on the level of rates in the future.

Another hot area of the derivatives trade, which evolved shortly thereafter, was the highly creative business Peter Hancock's team specialized in, known as 'swaps'. In these deals, investment banks would find two parties with complementary needs in the financial markets and would broker an exchange between them to the benefit of both, earning the banks large fees.

Say, for example, two home owners have $500,000 ten-year mortgages, but one has a floating rate deal, while the other has a rate fixed at 8 per cent. If the owner with the fixed rate expects the rates to fall, while the other owner expects them to rise, then rather than each trying to get a new loan, they could agree that each quarter, during the life of their mortgages, they will 'swap' their payments. The actual mortgage loans do not change hands, they stay on the original banks' books, making the deal what bankers call 'synthetic'.

Salomon Brothers was one of the first banks to exploit the

potential of derivatives swaps, brokering a pioneering deal between IBM and the World Bank in 1981. In 1979 David Swensen, a PhD from Yale who had recently started working on the Salomon Brothers trading desk, spotted that IBM needed to raise a good deal of cash in dollars and was holding excess quantities of Swiss francs and German marks from having sold bonds to raise funds in those currencies. Normally IBM would have had to go to the currency market to buy dollars. Swensen realized, though, that IBM might instead be able to swap some of its francs and marks for dollars without actually having to sell them if some party could be found who could issue bonds in dollars to match IBM's bonds in francs and marks.

The World Bank was a likely candidate: it always needed cash in many currencies. As with the two home owners who write a contract to swap the terms of their mortgages, IBM and the World Bank could swap their bond earnings, and their obligations to the bond holders, without any bonds actually changing hands. In 1981, after two years of wrangling over the details, Salomon Brothers announced it had concluded the world's first currency swap between IBM and the World Bank, worth $210 million for ten years.

This new form of trade spread fast across Wall Street and the City of London, mutating into wildly complex deals that seemed to give bankers godlike powers. With derivatives they could dismember existing assets or contracts and write contracts that resurrected them in entirely new ways, earning huge fees.

Of course, making these deals still relied on bankers being able to find two parties who both believed they would benefit. In synthetic finance, just as in 'real' markets, trades can only occur if there is a buyer for every seller. But given the growing globalization of banking, and the number of players in the world economy who had complementary needs and different expectations about future market conditions, the bankers had a wealth of options. Some players needed Deutschmarks; others wanted dollars. Some wanted to protect against expected interest rate rises; others believed that rates were likely to fall.

Players also had different motives for wanting to place bets on future asset prices. Some investors liked derivatives because they wanted to *control* risk, like the wheat farmers who preferred to lock in at a profitable price. Others wanted to use them to make high-risk bets in the hope of windfall profits. The crucial point about derivatives was that they could do two things: help investors *reduce* risk or create a good deal *more* risk. Everything depended on how they were used, on the motives and skills of those who traded in them.

By the time the J.P. Morgan swaps team gathered in Boca Raton in June of 1994, the total volume of interest rate and currency derivatives in the world was reckoned at $12,000 billion – a sum larger than the American economy. 'The speed at which the market grew just took everyone by surprise. It was quite remarkable,' recalled Peter Hancock, who had been a vital participant in the boom.

In many ways, Hancock's career made him the perfect man to be at the centre of that extraordinary innovation storm. He was born in 1958, into an upper-middle-class British family based in Hong Kong. Like many children from that background and generation, he was dispatched half a world away to a British boarding school, where he excelled at rugby and decided that his ambition was to be a great inventor. Having spent many happy hours immersed in science books, he went to Oxford to study physics, but his plans were derailed when he was badly injured in a rugby game. Stuck in bed for some time, he couldn't get to the physics laboratory and decided to switch to philosophy, politics and economics, easier to study lying down. By the time he graduated, he became intrigued about banking and the principles of free markets. 'I decided that being an inventor would have to wait,' he recalled. He had decided he wanted a career that paid

better than those in science. It was a common decision for bright
students at the time. The City of London and Wall Street looked
increasingly alluring.

On graduation, he applied for jobs at a range of international
firms, hoping for a globe-trotting career. But when he was
offered a job in the London branch of Morgan Guaranty Trust
Company (or 'The Morgan Bank'), later rebranded J.P. Morgan,
he quickly accepted. It was an unusual choice for a British grad-
uate. The City of London was dominated by British-owned
banks, and though American groups had raised their presence in
the City during the 1970s, those Wall Street institutions over-
whelmingly recruited graduates from the US.

But J.P. Morgan had always had a transcultural identity. Well
known as one of the large Wall Street firms, its roots lay in the
City, where the American banker Junius Spencer Morgan took
charge of the English brokerage George Peabody & Co. in 1864
and renamed it J.S. Morgan & Co. His son, John Pierpont
Morgan, worked at the firm for some years and was then
dispatched to New York, where he formed a partnership with
the wealthy Drexel family, Drexel Morgan & Company, which
after Anthony Drexel's death was renamed J.P. Morgan. The
American bank quickly swelled into a powerhouse. J. Pierpont
Morgan personally brokered many major deals, audaciously
merging a number of steel companies he had bought to form US
Steel, and financing major concerns in railroads, shipping, coal
mining, and other key industries. By the late nineteenth century,
the group had become so dominant that it appeared to wield as
much power in the financial markets as the American government itself.

When crisis hit Wall Street in 1893, Morgan personally
orchestrated a syndicate to provide the US Treasury with $65
billion in gold, keeping it solvent. In the Panic of 1907, when
the New York Stock Exchange plunged to half of its value,
Morgan put up vast sums of his personal fortune and rallied

other leading bankers to do the same, shoring up the banking system.

In the years after the Second World War, the bank lost some of its pre-eminence. After the crash of 1929, a populist backlash against Wall Street led to the introduction of the Glass-Steagall Act, which forced banks to split off their capital markets operations – the trading of debt and equity securities – from their commercial banking businesses. The J.P. Morgan empire was required to fragment into separate entities, including Morgan Stanley, the US brokerage, Morgan Grenfell, a British brokerage, and J.P. Morgan, which was devoted to commercial banking. But the bank maintained an unusually close set of ties with both governments, and powerful blue-chip corporate clients, such as Coca-Cola and AT&T. The international heritage of the bank was also preserved, so much so that J.P. Morgan staff sometimes joked that joining was akin to entering the diplomatic or British colonial service – albeit a lot better paid.

When Peter Hancock joined the bank he was dispatched to New York to attend a year-long training course, together with around four dozen other recruits, only half of whom were American. 'It was an extraordinary experience. We had Chinese, Malaysians, French – you name it. And we were all housed together in one small building down on the Upper East Side of Manhattan,' Hancock recalled. The course itself, however, didn't have much to satisfy Hancock's penchant for invention.

The 'Commercial Bank Management Program', as it was called, was conducted in the bank's historic headquarters at 23 Wall Street, right across the street from the Stock Exchange in an imposing, column-fronted building where J. Pierpont Morgan himself had worked. The first half of the course was spent in a classroom, learning fundamental banking skills little different from the practices in J.P. Morgan's time: the nuts and bolts of assessing credit risk by reading a company's balance sheet and analysing its business. The goal was to drill into them how to measure the chance a company would default on a loan, the lifeblood of J.P. Morgan's style of banking. For the second half of the training, the recruits acted as the junior analysts in actual deals being done.

The trainees were required to spend a good deal of time crunching corporate numbers. Only a few years earlier, those calculations had to be done by hand. When they needed to look up bond prices, they consulted a massive book of tables. By the time Peter Hancock took the course, however, hand-held calculators programmed to use complex mathematics to assess corporate cash flows and measure risk were becoming the rage. A new technological elitism was taking hold and the trainees were in the vanguard of a bold new breed of banker.

For the Morgan Bank trainees, though, the mathematics was stressed to be only *part* of what banking was about; social factors, such as client relationships and reputation, were also heavily emphasized. Back in the 1930s, during the height of the populist backlash against Wall Street, the son of J. Pierpont Morgan – J. P. 'Jack' Morgan, Jr. – had been grilled by Congress about his ethos. He declared that the aim of his bank was to conduct 'first-class business, in a first-class way'. Fifty years later, that mantra of Jack Morgan struck much of the banking world as quaint. Years of bold innovation had made high-risk trading and aggressive deal-making the gold standard of the street, and a 'kill or be killed' ethic prevailed.

At 23 Wall Street, though, the senior bankers still talked about banking as a noble craft, where long-term relationships and loyalty mattered, both in dealing with clients and inside the bank. While at other banks the emphasis had turned to finding star players, offering them huge bonuses and encouraging them to compete for pre-eminence, at Morgan Bank the emphasis lay on teamwork, employee loyalty and long-term commitment to the bank.

Many of the staff had only ever worked at J.P. Morgan, and

while the bank paid less than most of its rivals, the trade-off was greater job security. The young trainees on the training programme were solemnly told that while the bank would tolerate 'errors of judgement', an 'error of principle' was a sacking offence. 'First-class banking' remained the mantra.

Hancock sailed through the course and was dispatched back to the London office, where he spent a couple of years analysing the creditworthiness of North Sea oil companies. That was considered a plum job, because the Norwegian and British oil industries were starting to boom. But Hancock was hungry for more. As he looked around the City, he could see the revolution in derivatives and swaps building, and he wanted in.

The Morgan Bank was considered too stodgy to be a pioneer in the fast-lane business. Aggressive Salomon Brothers and iconoclastic Bankers Trust were the real innovators. But shortly after Salomon announced its big IBM–World Bank swap, J.P. Morgan started looking for ways to do more such deals.

Initially, the epicentre of experimentation was not J.P. Morgan's headquarters, but the London branch of a corporate offshoot known as Morgan Guaranty Limited (MGL). While the Glass-Steagall regulations prohibited the main New York bank from playing in the capital markets, Glass–Steagall didn't apply overseas. London's regulatory authorities took a more laissez-faire attitude, generally permitting banks to engage in a wider range of services, and as a result, Morgan Guaranty had built up a good capital markets business. In the 1960s the talented trader Dennis Weatherstone led the development of a flourishing foreign exchange business, and in the seventies the office moved into the world of sovereign and corporate bond issuance. Business boomed in part because American companies realized they could pay less tax by raising finance in London rather than in New York.

That booming corporate bond business created the opening for Morgan Guaranty to move into the swaps world, and from the early 1980s the Morgan Bank started to offer its clients deals through its London branch that allowed them to take advantage of the swaps magic. 'This was an example of a fantastic innovation which really served a client need. It really solved problems in a useful way,' Jakob Stott, one of the young bankers who was on the swaps team, recalled.

To begin with, arranging these deals was an uphill performance. Before a contract could be struck, two parties with matching needs had to be found. That alone could take weeks. On one of the first of these deals, a swap between the Austrian government and Commerzbank, staff spent an entire afternoon tapping out the details on a telex machine, spelling out all the future cashflows to their clients. As the 1980s wore on, though, the pace of business picked up. So did the profits.

The young traders in the group were thrilled with the increasing power, and freedom, they enjoyed. Few at the bank outside the swaps team itself knew how their trades worked, and the leader of the team, Connie Volstadt, widely recognized as one of the most brilliant minds in the derivatives world, was given great autonomy. Volstadt showed outright disdain for the Morgan Bank senior management, and would reveal the scantiest details about the team's business. Indeed, the team members loved teasing those in the more hidebound departments. 'We had this sense of being special, of being detached from everyone else, a little team that was very tightly bound together,' recalled Stott.

From time to time, the senior management would try to clip the swaps team's wings. In 1986 Lewis Preston, then the chief executive of J.P. Morgan, flew to London and challenged the manner in which Volstadt was recording the value of deals. At the time, J.P. Morgan, along with every other bank, was unclear how to measure the worth of the swaps trades, as accounting guidelines were still being worked out. 'You say your group has made a $400 million profit,' Preston challenged Volstadt. 'But it looks to me as if you have a $400 million loss!' Furious, Volstadt assigned a team of junior analysts and interns to re-examine every single paper ticket recording the deals, and when he proved his case, Preston backed down. The episode was indicative of the way the upper management viewed the swaps traders: as a bunch of brilliant but stroppy teenagers.

As Hancock watched the high-octane business of the swaps group from his humdrum perch in J.P. Morgan's commercial banking team, he was fascinated and eager to join in. So in 1984 he joined the London bond group and in 1986 he wangled his way to New York, where the bank was expanding its derivatives operation. The J.P. Morgan managers had realized, to their utter delight, that there was no explicit provision in Glass–Steagall against trading in derivatives products.

Initially, Hancock's role on the team was rather humble. He managed a small treasury team that used swaps to manage the bank's on-balance-sheet assets and liabilities. But Hancock was articulate, and opportunistic, and soon found ways to make himself visible. After the 1987 stock market crash, interest rates fell and the bank suffered sizeable unexplained losses in its derivatives books. Hancock was asked to explain what had happened to the bank's senior management and ended up managing a small desk at headquarters that traded products known as 'floors' and 'caps'. Then, when the Bank rebranded itself as J.P. Morgan in 1988, Hancock, a keen sailor, organized a team that sailed round Manhattan with a vast J.P. Morgan logo on its sails. That garnered attention, particularly since Hancock's team narrowly beat Goldman Sachs's boat. He learned everything he could about how the derivatives world worked. He also impressed Dennis Weatherstone, CEO of the bank. Weatherstone was a legendary character. He had hailed from working-class British stock, and first joined the bank aged sixteen, as a messenger boy in London, but later became a brilliant foreign exchange trader and eventually rose to the very top.

In 1988 a shock occurred that created Hancock's opening.

Connie Volstadt defected to Merrill Lynch, taking half a dozen of his team. It bequeathed a conundrum.

At other banks, the obvious way to fill the huge revenue hole left by Volstadt's departure would have been to hire a new guru, and build a new team from rival banks. But J.P. Morgan rarely hired outsiders into senior positions. The vast majority of its senior staff had risen through the ranks, giving the bank its insular culture, for good and ill. So the senior management initially appointed some of Volstadt's junior team members to take over. Before long it was clear that they couldn't fill his shoes, and Hancock saw his chance.

In 1990, at thirty-two, he was considered too young to run a department. But he was good at navigating office politics and Hancock's name came into the frame. So, about a year after Volstadt left, Weatherstone announced that Hancock would lead the swaps team. 'Sometimes in life you just get a huge break, and you just have to grab it and run with it,' Hancock later recalled. The would-be inventor now had a chance to let his penchant for invention run.

Over the next four years, Hancock rode the crest of the derivatives wave. When swaps had taken off, J.P. Morgan wasn't at all viewed as an innovator. By 1994, its creative skills were as good as those of most rivals. Better still, the bank had advantages some rivals lacked. As a respected commercial lender, Morgan had access to a wide array of blue-chip companies and governments that were often eager to conduct derivatives deals. The bank was also one of the very few with a top-notch 'AAA' credit rating, which reassured clients that the bank could stand by its trades. By the end of the 1980s, derivatives groups were no longer only pairing with other parties to make derivative deals, they were using their *own* capital to make trades with clients on a huge scale. When clients cut deals with J.P. Morgan, the AAA rating assured them that the bank would always be around to fulfil its side of those deals.

As business boomed, the swaps department basked in the knowledge that it was producing an escalating share of the bank's profits. By the early 1990s it accounted for almost half the bank's trading revenues, and Hancock had been promoted to run not just the derivatives group, but the entire department it was part of, known as fixed income. He was considered a prime candidate for CEO.

A few months before the Boca off-site, a reporter from *Fortune* asked Hancock to explain how a complicated swap might work. His response reaffirmed for her that derivatives traders were 'like the spacecraft Galileo, heading for planet Jupiter'. 'It would be something,' Hancock apparently said, 'in which you get beyond binary risk and into a combination of risks, such as interest rates and currencies. Or take an oil company, which has risks of oil prices dropping and interest rates rising. To hedge, it could buy an oil price floor and an interest rate cap.' But maybe, said Hancock, the company would like something a little cheaper: 'In that case, we could do a contract that would pay out only if oil prices are low and interest rates are high at the same time.' The man who had dreamed of being an inventor was in his element.

Yet down in Boca, Hancock was not in celebratory mood. On the contrary, he knew that the derivatives sector was reaching a crucial point in its evolution and his team had to adjust. The essential problem was the phenomenon he described as the 'curse of the innovation cycle'. In manufacturing or pharmaceuticals, patent laws ensure that a brilliant new product or idea is protected; competitors cannot simply steal that innovation. In banking, patents haven't traditionally been an option. When financiers have a brilliant idea, no common statute stops competitors from copying it right away, and before long they are putting downward pressure on profit margins.

The swaps business typified this problem. As soon as Salomon Brothers cut its first deal, other banks such as J.P. Morgan had copied it, and the market mushroomed. The burst of activity had a vexing impact on profit margins. While the first wave of swaps deals had high margins, as copycats jumped in, competition brought fees down. For years the issue hadn't really worried Hancock, because the volume of deals was growing so robustly. But he could not know how long the trend might continue, and if he wanted to keep his department cranking, he had to find a *new* way before long to do deals. He was feeling tremendous pressure to find the next Big Idea.

So while his team viewed the weekend as a lavish party, Hancock had a serious agenda. By bringing his young group together from all over the world, and pushing them into close quarters for forty-eight hours, he hoped to spark the innovation flame.

On Saturday morning, the group assembled in a conference room, a few feet away from the sparkling blue sea, for one of a series of meetings. How, Hancock asked, could they unleash a new wave of innovation in derivatives? Could bankers apply the principles to new areas? What about the insurance world? Or loans and credit?

The team was in little mood for mental gymnastics. Some were jet-lagged and most were hung over. Bill Winters was nursing a badly swollen nose, and wondering how he would explain it to his wife back home. 'Frankly, I cannot remember much of our debate,' Bill Demchak, the team member who was Hancock's de facto deputy, would later say with a sheepish laugh. All he could remember, he added, was that when he checked out of his hotel, his bill included charges for a smashed jet-ski and a vast quantity of cheeseburgers. They had been charged to him as a joke, by the rest of his team.

But Hancock's intensity was impossible to resist. He strode around the room, firing off ideas with his Planet Pluto energy, and soon enough the debate heated up. One key idea began to emerge: using derivatives to trade the risk linked to corporate bonds and loans. Commodity derivatives, a voice pointed out, let wheat farmers trade the risk of loss on their crops. Why not create a derivative that enabled banks to place bets on whether a loan or bond might default in the future? Defaults were the biggest source of risk in commercial lending, so banks might well be interested in placing bets with derivatives that would allow them to cover for losses, providing a form of insurance against defaults.

In truth, that was not a new idea. Three years earlier the highly inventive Bankers Trust had conducted the first pioneering deals along those lines. So had Connie Volstadt's team at Merrill Lynch. But the notion hadn't taken because those trades didn't appear particularly profitable. As the debate swirled around the room in Boca, though, Hancock and the others became excited about the concept. After all, they reasoned, the world was full of institutions – and not just banks – that were exposed to the risk of loan defaults. J.P. Morgan itself had a mountain of loans on its books that was creating regulatory headaches. What would happen, they asked, if a derivative product of some kind could be crafted to protect against default risk, or deliberately to gamble on it? Would investors actually want to buy that product? Would regulators permit it to be sold? If so, what might it mean for the financial world if default risk, the risk most central to the traditional craft of banking, was turned into just another plaything for traders?

They had no idea that weekend how to answer those questions, but Hancock's team were not used to taking 'no' for an answer. They spent their days stretching their minds to the limit, and they could see that the concept was potentially revolutionary. If you could really insure banks and other lenders against default risk, that might well unleash a great wave of capital into the economy. 'I've known people who worked on the Manhattan Project – for those of us on that trip, there was the same kind of feeling of being present at the creation of something incredibly important,' Mark Brickell, one of the bankers on the J.P. Morgan swaps team later recalled.

Recalling the Boca meeting Hancock said: 'The idea that we gave most emphasis to was using derivatives to manage the risk attached to the loan book of banks.' It was not until many years later that the team grasped the full implications of their ideas known as credit derivatives. As with all derivatives, these tools were to offer a way of *controlling* risk, but they could also *amplify* it. It all depended on how they were used. The first of these results was what attracted Hancock and his team to the pursuit. It was the second that would come to dominate the business a decade later, eventually contributing to a worldwide financial catastrophe.

CHAPTER TWO

Dancing Around the Regulators

There was a critical juncture, around the time that Peter Hancock's team seized on the idea of credit derivatives, when financial innovation might have followed a subtly different path. In the few years leading up to Hancock's Boca off-site, regulators, and many prominent banking experts, grew concerned about the boom in derivatives and the proliferation of exotic new types, and fiercely debated whether regulations should be imposed.

Peter Hancock found himself at the heart of this debate. In 1991, three years before the Boca Raton meeting, he had received an unexpected summons from Morgan CEO Dennis Weatherstone. 'Corrigan wants to talk to us about derivatives,' Weatherstone said, ordering Hancock to attend the meeting 'since you can explain this stuff so well'. Hancock had distinctly mixed feelings about the invitation. E. Gerald Corrigan, then aged fifty, was the seventh president of the New York Federal Reserve, a position he had held since 1985. It was a powerful role, including the oversight of New York commercial banks, and Corrigan, a forceful, burly character with a gravelly voice, was not afraid to express his views bluntly.

By 1991 he had already worked at the Fed for a couple of decades, serving as special assistant for a period to the legendary Paul Volcker, and he had seen the financial system suffer through several business cycles and bouts of panic. He cut his teeth handling the Herstatt Bank crisis of 1974, when the failure of a small German group rocked the Euromarket, and had confronted the Latin American debt crisis, the collapse of Continental Illinois Bank and the failure of Drexel Burnham Lambert. 'I have seen it all before,' Corrigan was fond of growling. All that experience had left him uneasy about the tendency of bankers to sow havoc when left to their own devices.

The NY Fed's vast granite headquarters were a five-minute stroll from the J.P. Morgan offices. Even so, Hancock had never passed through those intimidating steel doors. Bankers who worked on the commercial lending side of J.P. Morgan often chatted with central bankers, but central bankers and swaps traders had no such regular back and forth. As a result, Corrigan's 'invitation' left Hancock uneasy: what was the New York Fed planning to do with his beloved derivatives?

Corrigan himself was unsure. He had summoned Weatherstone and Hancock primarily because he was worried that he knew too little about derivatives, and he wanted to get more facts before deciding about possibly regulating them. J.P. Morgan was an obvious place to start, given its long-standing links with the Fed. Indeed, only a couple of years before, J.P. Morgan had hired the former executive vice-president of the Fed, Steven Thieke, to act as its chief risk officer (one of the few cases where the bank hired from outside for a senior post).

For several hours, Corrigan grumpily peppered Weatherstone and Hancock with questions about the swaps world, and Hancock answered as best he could. He had the impression that Corrigan had only a modest knowledge of how derivatives worked. But, after all, why should that be a surprise? Almost nobody outside the teams of traders really understood the details.

He left with the impression that while Corrigan was not auto-
matically opposed to derivatives, he was not particularly thrilled
with all of the innovation going on. What, Hancock wondered,
would Corrigan do next?

Part of the problem with deciding what to do about derivatives
regulation was that there was so little specific data available about
the growth of the business. In the stock market, most trading
takes place on public exchanges, such as the New York Stock
Exchange or NASDAQ, which are tightly regulated to protect
investors. Most commodities derivatives contracts also trade on
regulated exchanges, such as the Chicago Mercantile Exchange,
and are regulated by the Commodities Futures Trading
Commission. Some interest rate and currency derivatives were
traded on exchanges too. Many others, though, were brokered
privately between banks and clients in what are called 'over-the-
counter' deals, because the parties negotiate directly. What's
more, few regulations had been crafted to monitor and set
guidelines for such OTC trades.

Since the dawn of modern finance, governments have been
beset by the question of how closely banking should be regulated. On the one hand, twentieth-century American and
European governments have generally accepted that the business
of finance should be exactly that, a *business*, run privately in a
profit-seeking manner. But finance is also not quite like other
areas of commerce. Money is the lifeblood of the economy, and
unless it circulates readily, the essential economic activities go
into the equivalent of cardiac arrest. Finance serves a public util-
ity function, and the question government regulators must
wrestle with is how far private financiers should be allowed to
seek a profit and to what degree they must be required to ensure
that money flows safely.

In practice, during the twentieth century both American and
European governments resolved the dilemma by keeping

banking private, but swaddling it in rules to ward against excesses. During the course of the century, those rules had expanded into what felt to bankers like a straitjacket of regulation. Some of the laws were national in scope, such as the Glass-Steagall Act in the US, which separated commercial banking from investment banking. The Federal Reserve also imposed rules specifically on American commercial banks – investment banks remained outside its purview – including the stipulation that the total size of their liabilities could not be higher than twenty times the size of their equity. If banks overexpended their assets, failing to keep adequate reserve capital to cover potential losses, they were at risk of collapse, as happened so spectacularly after the Crash of 1929. The regulations in London also imposed minimal reserve requirements.

On top of the national regulations, a set of international stipulations, known as the Basel Accord, has been agreed by the Group of Ten nations, plus Luxembourg and Spain. A first set of agreements were drawn up in 1988 in the Swiss mountain town under the management of the Basel Committee of Banking Supervision (BCBS), whose governing body is based at the Bank of International Settlements (BIS). The first set of rules, known as Basel I, imposed globally consistent standards for prudent banking, most notably by demanding that all banks maintain reserves equivalent to 8 per cent of the value of their assets, adjusted for risk. These rules were expanded and modified for some years, with a revised version referred to as Basel II issued in 2004 but not yet agreed to by all parties.

By the early 1990s, regulators were dogged by the fact that many of these rules had been drafted *before* the explosion of derivatives innovation. They could be extended into the derivatives world to some extent – aspects of the Basel Accord set out, for example, levels of reserves that banks must hold if they were engaging in derivatives activity. But the urgent issue now was that the business had expanded so much, and in such complex ways, that regulators couldn't get good estimates of the risks involved.

The issue didn't worry regulators too deeply at first. In the early 1980s, swaps deals accounted for so little of overall banking activity, and were being done by such a relatively small and elite group of players, that regulators regarded the sector as a sideshow. What traders did with their newfangled derivatives contracts seemed as peripheral to the 'real' economy as the gambling in Las Vegas. But, as the 1980s wore on, and the business began to take off, some regulators grew uneasy. They began to tweak the banking rules in a manner that forced banks to lay aside more capital against their derivatives business. That left bankers nervous. They feared that profits could drop if regulators became even more involved. In response to this, in 1985, a group of bankers working for Salomon Brothers, BNP Paribas, Goldman Sachs, J.P. Morgan and others held a meeting in a Palm Beach hotel with a view to agreeing on standards for swaps deals. The idea was to hash out common legal guidelines for the deals. Out of that, they decided to create an industry body to represent the swaps world, subsequently known as the International Swaps and Derivatives Association, and one of the first things ISDA did was to conduct a survey of the market. When the results were published they were startling. In 1987 ISDA reckoned the total volume of derivatives contracts was approximately $865 billion.

Shocked by that number, some Western government officials started to flex their muscles. The Bank of England had hitherto paid relatively little attention to what groups such as Morgan Guaranty were doing with their swaps business. The Bank carried the main responsibility for oversight of London markets but it tended to shy away from actively meddling in activities that took place away from regulated exchanges, preferring to rely on 'self-regulation' rather than draconian systems of control. However, in the mid-1980s the Bank began discreetly to urge banks to create more order by adopting common practices for swaps, and legal contracts, organized by industry groups. This approach had worked relatively well in relation to the Eurobond world, so the Bank hoped it would prove effective for swaps too.

Some of the American regulators, however, wanted to take a more forceful stance. In 1987 the Commodities Futures Trading Commission proposed to start regulating interest rate and currency swaps, in the same way it monitored the commodities derivatives world. That idea spread horror across the banking world. The derivatives traders feared the CFTC would do a clumsy, heavy-handed job. Not to mention that any existing derivatives contracts would be thrown into a legal limbo because the legislation the CFTC proposed stipulated that all deals not done on its exchange would be illegal.

ISDA leapt into action, sponsoring a lobbying campaign on Capitol Hill against the idea. Somewhat to their surprise they prevailed two years later when the CFTC backed down. That victory was just temporary, though. By the early 1990s government scrutiny of derivatives was intensifying again, as the business continued to boom and a range of exotic new offerings were introduced. In truth, most regulators and central bankers still didn't know in any detail how the swaps world worked. Its esoteric nature raised the troubling issue at the centre of the regulatory dilemma: how could they allow this booming business to keep flourishing but also ensure that it didn't end up jeopardizing the free flow of money around the 'real' economy? Regulators didn't want to stifle positive innovation, but they were growing leery. That was the impetus of Jerry Corrigan's investigation of the business in the autumn of 1991.

A few weeks after he had summoned Dennis Weatherstone and Peter Hancock to meet with him, in January 1992, Corrigan delivered a stern speech to the New York State Bankers Association. 'Given the sheer size of the [derivatives] market,' he said, 'I have to ask myself how it is possible that so many holders of fixed- or variable-rate obligations want to shift

those obligations from one form to the other.' Translated from
central bank jargon, this suggested that Corrigan was dubious
about the banks' motives for making these deals. 'Off-balance-
sheet activities have a role,' he continued, 'but they must be
managed and controlled carefully, and they must be understood
by top management, as well as by traders and rocket scientists. I
hope this sounds like a warning, because it is!'

Derivatives bankers were shocked. Corrigan seemed poised to
institute regulation. Sure enough, a few weeks later it emerged
that international regulators, led by Corrigan, were preparing to
define how the Basel rules should be applied to market trading
activities with more precision. Then, around the same time, a
member of Hancock's team, Mark Brickell, received a surprising
overture from a Washington-based organization, the Group of
Thirty. Brickell had joined J.P. Morgan straight out of Harvard
Business School around the same time as Hancock, and was a
true believer in the gospel of swaps. Hancock had selected him
to act as his key point-man in lobbying regulatory officials and
politicians, who had been asking so much of late about the
derivatives business. Brickell was ideally suited for the job. He
was an intense man, with passionate libertarian views, who had
entertained the idea of pursuing a career in politics. Unlike most
swaps traders, he therefore relished dealing with politicians.
Indeed, so enthusiastic was he about lobbying that by 1992 he
held the post of chairman of ISDA. He was Hancock's and the
industry's Rottweiler in fending off regulatory concerns.

The G30, it turned out, was planning to write a study of the
derivatives world, and the caller told Brickell the group wanted
J.P. Morgan to lead the process. It was clear that the report could
be crucial for setting government policy; the G30 was a highly
influential group of economists, academics and bankers, set up in
1978 with funding from the Rockefeller Foundation, with a
mission to promote better international financial cooperation.
Paul Volcker led the group.

J.P. Morgan officials debated what to do. Inside the swaps group, the young traders were wary of collaborating on the study. At best, they feared it might result in J.P. Morgan sharing proprietary secrets; at worst, it would lead to regulations that the bank would be seen as instrumental in instituting. 'The whole project was fraught with peril for the swaps world,' Brickell later said. 'There was a clear danger of having any recommendation codified as regulation.' Dennis Weatherstone nevertheless insisted that the bank cooperate. As CEO, he was highly mindful of its legacy of public duty, and he suspected that Corrigan, and therefore the weight of the New York Fed, was behind the initiative.

In any case, Weatherstone was concerned himself about the risks of the swaps business. If the industry kept growing without controls, he feared the chances were good that excesses would lead to an implosion that would not just hurt other banks but J.P. Morgan too. 'If you're driving along the motorway in a smart Maserati and see an old car belching fumes,' he sternly told Hancock and his other young turks, 'it's no good just driving on. If that old car crashes, it could wipe out the Maserati too.'

So Weatherstone agreed to chair the G30 report, and Hancock, Thieke, Brickell and other J.P. Morgan bankers set to work on it with a host of representatives from other banks. Patrick de Saint Aignan, a derivatives banker at Morgan Stanley, and David Brunner of Paribas co-headed the report; officials from HSBC, Swiss Bank and Chase Manhattan also took part. Peter Cooke, a former Bank of England regulator, offered advice; so did Merton Miller, the Nobel laureate and leading free-market economist from the University of Chicago. 'We knew that we were setting the foundation for the derivatives world,' Brickell recalled.

It was high time to do so. Between 1992 and 1993, the value of deals rose from $5.3 trillion to $8.5 trillion, according to ISDA data. What was more striking, however, was that deals were becoming more complex, and were being sold to a wider range of customers. The original customers for swaps had been large international corporations or banks, with sophisticated treasury departments and investment analysts – Coca-Cola, IBM, the World Bank. By 1992, small banks, mid-sized companies, pension funds and many other asset managers were joining the market. And more and more of them were turning to derivatives not to control future risks, but to make big gambles and realize big returns.

The rush into derivatives was partly driven by aggressive marketing efforts by the banks and regulatory changes in the asset management world. Another factor that fuelled the trend, though, was falling interest rates. After Paul Volcker had jacked up rates in 1979, inflation tumbled. By 1983 it was running at 3.2 per cent, down from 13.5 per cent in 1981. The Fed was then able to trim short-term interest rates, which stimulates economic growth. In 1987, Alan Greenspan replaced Volcker as Fed chairman and from 1989 onwards he steadily reduced rates to fight a mild recession. That was good news for borrowers, and it also boosted bank profits, because when rates are low, banks can borrow money cheaply and lend it out to customers at higher rates, making easy returns. But falling rates made it harder for investment managers to earn decent returns by purchasing relatively risk-free government or corporate bonds. Those pay less when rates fall. Thus, while the absolute level of rate was still relatively high (at least, compared to what would occur a decade later), the direction prompted some bond investors to look for new tactics.

Merrill Lynch, Bankers Trust, Salomon Brothers and J.P. Morgan itself suggested to their clients that they could use derivatives to boost their returns, and the banks invented a new wave of products to provide that service, with obscure names like 'LIBOR squared', 'time trade' and 'inverse floaters'. Some federal agencies also began offering investment products that included derivatives, such as Sallie Mae, the student loan provider. Most of these products produced high returns by employing two key features. They involved bets on the level to which interest rates would fall in the future, and with rates falling so dependably under Alan Greenspan's watch, those bets produced easy money with what seemed like very little risk.

Most of these deals also involved a concept that is central to the financial world known as 'leverage'. This essentially refers to the process of using investment techniques to magnify the force or direction of a market trend dramatically (just as a lever will increase the force of a machine). In practical terms, the word can be used in at least two ways in relation to derivatives. Sometimes investors employ large quantities of debt to increase their investment bets. For that reason, borrowing itself has often come to be called 'leverage' in recent years. However, the economic structure of derivatives deals can also sometimes leave investors very sensitive to price swings, even without using large quantities of debt. Confusingly, that second pattern is also referred to as 'leverage'. In practice, though, these two different types of leverage tend to be intermingled. And the most important issue is that both types of leverage expose investors to more risk. If the bet goes right, the returns are huge; if it goes wrong, the losses are big too. Using leverage in the derivatives world is the financial equivalent of a property developer who buys ten houses instead of five; owning more properties will leave that developer more exposed to losses and gains if house prices rise or fall, particularly if the properties are financed with debt.

In 1992 and 1993, though, many investors thought it was worth taking those risks, by buying products with high leverage. 'It was a type of crazy period,' recalls T.J. Lim, one of the early members of the J.P. Morgan swaps team, who worked with Connie Volstadt in the eighties and decamped with him to Merrill Lynch. 'The herd instinct was just amazing. Everyone was looking for yield. You could do almost anything you could dream of and people would buy it. Every single week somebody would think of a new product.'

Some prescient warnings were issued. Allan Taylor, the Bank of Canada chairman, said that derivatives were becoming like 'a time bomb that could explode just like the Latin-American Debt Crisis did', threatening the world financial system. Felix Rohatyn, a legendary Wall Street figure who worked at Lazard Frères in corporate finance, far removed from derivatives, called derivatives 'financial hydrogen bombs, built on personal computers by twenty-six-year-olds with MBAs'.

Those 'twenty-six-year-olds' disagreed. The innovation frenzy showed exactly why derivatives were so powerful, and why government control must be fought off. 'The surest way to stifle innovation is to take current best practices and covert them into rigid requirements,' Brickell liked to say, paraphrasing Friedrich von Hayek, the libertarian Austrian economist, and one of Brickell's intellectual heroes. Indeed, if there was one thing that united swaps traders, aside from a fascination with deconstructing financial instruments, it was the belief in the efficiency, and superiority, of free markets.

Brickell took the free-market faith to the extreme. His intellectual heroes, in addition to von Hayek, were the economists Eugene F. Fama and Merton H. Miller, who had developed the 'Efficient Markets Hypothesis' at Chicago University in the 1960s and 1970s, which asserted that market prices were always 'right'. They were the only true guide to what anything should be worth. 'I am a great believer in the self-healing power of markets,' Brickell often said, with an intense, evangelical glint in his blue eyes. 'Markets can correct excess far better than any government. Market discipline is the best form of discipline there is.'

Peter Hancock shared that view, though he rarely expressed it so forcefully in public. So did most other swaps traders. Of course, they knew perfectly well that financial markets were not truly free. On the contrary, the financial system was smothered in the government rules that had followed repeated crises. What made derivatives so thrilling for Brickell and other true believers was that they lay *outside* the purview of that legacy regulation. They allowed pioneering financiers to compete freely, unleashing their creativity, just as theory advocated.

This did not equate to a world with *no* rules, Brickell always liked to stress. On the contrary, the derivatives market could only function if the participants played according to a common law book. Indeed, crafting those legal guidelines had been a founding purpose of the ISDA. What made ISDA's approach so different was that it asserted that rules were best designed *by the industry itself*, and upheld by voluntary, mutual accord. Government bureaucrats should not be the sheriffs or high priests of this world; bankers and their lawyers were better informed, and they had strong incentives to comply. Like a hunter-gatherer tribe, all derivatives traders had an equal interest in upholding the norms. That was why any recommendation the G30 report might make about legislation to institute regulation was to be fought, argued Brickell, tooth and nail.

Another key factor that influenced how J.P. Morgan bankers, and others, viewed regulation was the development of an idea known as 'Value at Risk', or VaR. In previous decades, banks had taken an ad hoc attitude towards measuring risks. They extended loans to customers they liked, withheld them from those they did not, and tried to prevent their traders from engaging in any market activity that looked too risky, but without trying to quantify those dangers with precision. In the 1980s, though, Charles Sanford, a visionary financier at Bankers Trust, developed the industry's first fully fledged system for measuring the level of credit and market risk, known as RAROC. That eventually prompted others bankers to start trying to measure risk not according to vague hunches, but by using precise quantitative techniques.

Weatherstone, the Morgan CEO, played a crucial role in that wider industry trend. Having built his career on the volatile foreign exchange trading desks, not in the staid commercial arm of the bank, he was keenly aware of how risk could come back to bite you, if you did not prepare. The terrible stock market crash of 1987 hammered that point home again, when all the banks suffered losses. So, in 1989 – two years after that crash – Weatherstone introduced a near-revolutionary practice into J.P.Morgan, known as the '4–15' report. At 4.15 p.m. each day, after the markets closed, a report was sent to him that quantified the level of risk the bank was running in all areas of its business. Initially the report was crude, limited to painting an approximate picture of all the bank's trading businesses. Weatherstone decided he wanted more, and he asked a team of quantitative experts to develop a technique that could measure how much money the bank stood to lose each day if the markets turned sour. It was the first time that any bank had ever done that, with the notable exception of Bankers Trust.

For several months the so-called 'quants' played around with ideas until they coalesced around the concept known as Value at Risk, or VaR. They decided that the goal should be to work out how much money the bank could expect to lose, with a probability of 95 per cent, on any given day. The 95 per cent was an accommodation to the hard reality that there would always be some risk in the markets that the models wouldn't be able to account for. Weatherstone and his quants reckoned there was little point in trying to run a business in a manner that would obsessively worry about very worst case scenarios. If a bank worried about that every day it could barely afford to conduct business at all. What Weatherstone wanted to know was what levels of risk the bank was running in a bad-to-normal state of affairs, like a farmer who steels himself to expect periodic floods, snowstorms and droughts, but who doesn't worry about an asteroid impact that might bring on Armageddon. Hence the use of a 95 per cent confidence level.

The system essentially worked by taking data from the previous few years, and working out how much money the bank risked losing at any one time, if markets turned sour. The key simplifying assumption on which the models rested was that the future was likely to look like the recent past. Dennis Weatherstone was well aware that this assumption might not always be correct. He knew that it was only a rough approximation to reality. Models were *only* tools and could not be used without applying human intelligence, as he sternly lectured the J.P. Morgan staff. They were not the only way of measuring potential future losses. 'We were all taught to think that models are useful, but that they also have limits,' Peter Hancock later recalled. 'It is an obvious point, but it is also something people so often forget.'

Yet the beauty of VaR was that it allowed bankers to measure their risks with far more precision than ever before. A mind-boggling array of future dangers could be reduced to a single clear number, showing how much a bank stood to lose. The J.P. Morgan bankers assumed that would make it much easier for banks to control their risks, in relation to derivatives, or anything else. That had a bigger implication: with tools such as VaR at their fingertips, banks now had both the incentives and the ability to navigate wisely in the derivatives world, *without* the need for government interference. Or that, at least, was the argument that derivatives bankers liked to present.

On 21 July 1993 the long-awaited G30 report was finally unveiled. It was a hefty, three-volume tome. Right from the start, Dennis Weatherstone had insisted that the study be a serious, highly detailed guide. If the report could show that the industry already had a credible internal code of conduct, there should be less need for bureaucrats to impose rules. 'This should not be a study that gathers dust on a shelf,' Weatherstone declared. 'I want to produce a guide by practitioners that has so much useful, practical advice that it will be referred to for years to come.'

The G30 tome met that criterion in spades. The document started with some vague rhetoric that stressed the value of derivatives for the financial system as a whole. But it then laid out, in exhaustive detail, the best norms for running the business. One section urged all banks to adopt VaR tools. Another demanded that banks' senior managers learn in detail how derivatives products worked. Another section urged banks to use ISDA's legal documents for cutting deals. The report also demanded that banks record the value of their derivatives activity each day, according to real-time market prices, following the principles of what has become known as 'mark-to-market'. This would bring consistency in valuations where before banks had been accounting the values of the derivatives deals in a host of ways. It also underscored the assumption that market prices were the 'best' guide to value.

Equally important was what the G30 report did *not* say. The tome did not suggest that government should intervene in the market, in any way. Nor did it drop any hint that the derivatives world might benefit from a centralized clearing system, like that for commodities derivatives and the New York Stock Exchange, to settle its trades. These clearing systems not only recorded the volume of trades, providing a valuable barometer of activity that signalled signs of trouble, but also protected investors from the eventuality that the party on the other side of the trade – the counterparty – might fall through on a deal, leaving the trade in limbo. Without a clearing house, derivatives traders always faced this so-called 'counterparty' risk.

Brickell and the other members of ISDA were opposed to setting up a clearing system because they feared it would be the thin edge of a wedge of further regulations. They insisted that counterparty risk could be handled perfectly well by following the ISDA guidelines, posting some collateral against the risk of default, and just good smart trading. 'The swap [market] framework is a model of market discipline,' Brickell argued. 'Within it, every participant scrutinizes the reputation and credit quality of his counterparties, and adjusts the flow of his business accordingly.'

As regulators and central bankers digested the weighty G30 report, a few commentators expressed concern that the report simply did not go far enough. Brian Quinn, an executive director of the Bank of England, said that it 'struck me as somewhat complacent', in regard to the risks posed by the derivatives world. However, the Bank of England showed little inclination to start directly regulating the OTC derivatives sector. On the contrary, it continued to lean towards a policy of self-regulation in which the industry itself was urged to maintain discipline by upholding a set of common standards. The guidelines laid out in the G30 report were thus generally welcomed by British regulators, even if they felt the level of self-discipline could be tougher. And, just as Dennis Weatherstone had hoped, regulators generally appeared impressed by the detailed nature of the guidelines. 'If the market players continue forward in the spirit of the G30 study then regulators will have much less to do,' observed J. Carter Beese, a Securities and Exchange commissioner in November 1993. Hancock, Brickell and the rest of the swaps market heaved a sigh of relief.

Then disaster struck. By early 1994, Fed Chair Alan Greenspan was starting to fear that the US economy was overheating after several years of loose monetary policy. On 4 February 1994 he suddenly raised the Federal funds rates by 25 basis points from 3 to 3.25 per cent. The move, which came amid other unexpected economic data, stunned the markets, triggering a sharp fall in bond prices. It also caused carnage in the derivatives world. So many of the derivatives deals made in 1992 and 1993 were premised on rates continuing to fall, and with the sudden hike these deals produced enormous losses.

An early victim was Procter & Gamble. The company had made a deal with Bankers Trust, with a face value of $200 million, that promised to reduce its medium-term financing costs, but only if interest rates kept falling. With the rate increase, the company was forced instead to book a pre-tax $157 million loss. Then more shocks emerged. Gibson's Greetings, a medium-sized card company, announced a loss of $23 million, the Mead Corporation, another small American company, revealed similar losses, and Paine Webber, the asset management group, posted a loss of a whopping $268 million. A $600 million fund linked to Askin Capital management collapsed. Orange County, the Californian municipality, suffered the biggest loss of all. In the early 1990s Robert Citron, county treasurer, had decided to boost the municipality's investment returns by purchasing 'inverse floater' products from Merrill Lynch. Initially, the tactic was successful; in 1993 Citron's investment pool delivered returns of 8.5 per cent, against the state average of 4.7 per cent. Orange County, as so many other derivatives users had begun to do, had borrowed heavily to place these bets, greatly leveraging its core assets, and its losses totalled over $2 billion. The municipality was forced to file for bankruptcy.

These ruinous losses prompted investor and public fury. Procter & Gamble sued Bankers Trust and Orange County sued Merrill Lynch. Meanwhile the mainstream American and British media unleashed a torrent of criticism. *Adam Smith's Money World* declared that derivatives might be the financial equivalent of the next space shuttle disaster. *Fortune* published a cover with the word 'derivatives' on the jaws of a giant alligator. 'Financial derivatives are tightening their grip on the global economy,' the article ominously warned. 'And nobody knows how to control them.'

The sense of outrage was not confined to the US. During the early 1990s the UK and the rest of Europe had not followed the same rollercoaster path of interest rates and thus did not suffer the same spate of derivatives scandals in 1994. However, some British institutions were exposed to loss-producing American derivatives contracts, and a few years before the Orange County debacle the UK had been rocked by its own derivatives scandal in relation to Hammersmith and Fulham Borough Council. The Orange County debacle thus left indignant British commentators fuming – once again – about the risks of mis-selling in the derivatives world.

As the indignation on both sides of the Atlantic grew, America's General Accounting Office issued a highly critical 196-page study on the state of the derivatives world, with conclusions diametrically opposed to those of the G30 report. Derivatives trading, it declared, was marked by 'significant gaps and weaknesses' in risk management, that created a wider systemic risk. Indeed, so high were the dangers, it argued, that derivatives might even end up producing a debacle as bad as the Savings and Loans shock. There was an 'immediate need' for Congress to step in, urged Charles Bowsher, head of the GAO.

Democrats and Republicans swiftly responded, and by the summer of 1994, no fewer than four bills proposing regulations had been submitted to Congress. These went dramatically further than anything submitted before in the US, or in London. 'The GAO and I see eye to eye on the need for increased disclosure, for improved supervision and for stronger international coordination of derivatives regulation,' declared Texas Democrat Henry Gonzalez, who was chairing the banking panel and backing one bill. Edward Markey, a Massachusetts Democrat, who was chairing a Congressional panel overseeing the securities markets, warned: 'The question now is no longer whether regulatory or legislative changes will be made . . . but what form such changes should take.'

Derivatives traders were horrified. J.P. Morgan itself weathered the scandals moderately well. The losses at Procter & Gamble badly damaged the standing of Bankers Trust.

Merrill Lynch's image was badly wounded by the Orange
County scandal.

While some of J.P. Morgan's clients also suffered losses, they
were less visible than those of other groups. That partly reflected
luck. The team had also shied away from some dangerous
schemes.

Before Orange County had cut its disastrous deal with Merrill
Lynch, for example, the municipality had approached J.P. Morgan
asking to cut a similar trade. Bill Demchak, then one of the young
salesmen on the derivatives desk, flew out to meet the treasurer of
the municipality and quickly concluded that the Orange County
officials had no idea how derivatives really worked. 'Under no circumstances should we deal with this client!' he declared.

At the time, such caution had cost Hancock's team sizeable
fees, reinforcing the take among its rivals that the bank was
stodgy. 'The reality was that we just did not chase the last dollar –
we were less commercial in that respect,' Hancock later said. By
the summer of 1994, the bank was relieved to have dodged the
Orange County scandal. As rivals writhed, J.P. Morgan swooped.
'We got a lot of business after those scandals, restructuring deals
that had gone wrong, because we were one of the banks that
clients still trusted,' Demchak recalled.

Hancock knew that it would be essentially meaningless for J.P.
Morgan to grab a bigger slice of the derivatives pie, however, if
the business was going to be strangled by regulations. So, behind
the scenes, Brickell and other ISDA officials leapt furiously into
lobbying action, determined to block the bills before Congress.
Brickell paid frenetic visits to Republican and Democratic
Congressmen. He also relentlessly called journalists, trying to persuade them to stop writing about derivatives in such a negative
light. He then met with regulators around the world, preaching
the gospel that the industry was perfectly capable of cleaning up
its act on its own, using the G30 report as its template.

History was not on their side: on almost every occasion

during the previous hundred-odd years, lawmakers had responded to financial scandal by producing a new set of government rules. Yet Brickell was a zealot. In his eyes, the battle in Washington was not about mere business, it was an ideological fight of the highest order.

The sheer intensity of his lobbying mission irritated many. Christopher Whalen, a director at Whalen Co., a Washington lobbying firm, observed at the time: 'ISDA came to Washington telling everyone they're stupid. Their message was that everything is okay [in derivatives] – a blanket statement, boom. That strategy has convinced everybody in Washington that they have something to hide.' Or as an aide to Edward Markey said: 'There is a disconnect in terms of a lack of understanding between many market participants of how the policy-making process works . . . The combination of arrogance and defensiveness is never one that works very well in Congress . . . [their attitude] was basically: "How dare anybody question the functioning of this market! How presumptuous!"'

But Brickell was relentless, and as the weeks passed, against expectations, his campaign turned the tide. One reason was that the Clinton administration was receptive. Before Clinton entered the White House, in 1992, he had taken an anti-Wall Street stance. Once ensconced, faced with the formidable lobbying power of Wall Street, the Clinton camp shifted view. 'Derivatives are perfectly legitimate tools to manage risk,' Treasury Secretary Lloyd Bentsen said in a May 1994 speech to securities dealers. 'Derivatives are not a dirty word. We need to be careful about interfering in markets in too heavy-handed a way. Right now our principal emphasis is on making sure existing regulatory authority is fully reviewed and implemented.'

Or as the historian Kevin Philips noted in a book at that time:

even before the man from Arkansas was inaugurated, it was clear that strategists from the financial sector, more than most

other Washington lobbyists, had managed the Bush-to-
Clinton transition without missing a stroke. Well-connected
Democratic financiers stepped easily into the alligator loafers
of departing Republicans. The accusatory rhetoric of the
campaign dried up. The head of Clinton's new National
Economic Council, Robert Rubin, turned out to have spent
the 1980s as an arbitrageur for Goldman Sachs.

The tenacious campaign that ISDA waged also chimed with
the views of Alan Greenspan. A staunch free-market believer, he
cautioned against the bills proposed. 'Legislation directed at
derivatives is no substitute for broader reform, and, absent
broader reform, could actually increase risks in the US financial
system by creating a regulatory regime that is itself ineffective
and that diminishes the effectiveness of market discipline,' he
admonished Congress in the early summer of 1994.

Even Jerry Corrigan appeared to have accepted ISDA's stance.
Corrigan had left the New York Fed in 1993 and moved to
Goldman Sachs as an adviser, and from that vantage point, he also
had reservations about introducing government rules. 'Derivatives
are like NFL quarterbacks: they get too much of the credit and
too much of the blame,' he said in a Congressional hearing.
'When I say I don't think legislation is needed, I'm not saying
that I'm satisfied with the status quo. But the things that need to
be done can be done under existing legislative authority.'

By end of 1994, the ISDA campaign had been so brilliantly
effective that all four of the anti-derivatives bills in Congress
were shelved. Henry Gonzalez, the sponsor of one of them,
commented in his Texan style about the effort: 'It has been like
a coyote out in the brush country baying to the moon at mid-
night, and only the poor ranchers waking up at night would
know that was the coyote as far as being heard.' It was an
extraordinary victory for ISDA: one of the most startling tri-
umphs for a Wall Street lobbying campaign in the twentieth

century. Moreover, as Brickell himself noted, 'to a great extent the stateside debate informed the thinking of policymakers outside the US too'. In previous years the British authorities had always seemed more inclined than their American counterparts to rely on the principles of self-discipline or self-regulation rather than formulaic regulations imposed by the state. With US politicians backing away from their regulation demands, there was now even less incentive for their British counterparts to jump in.

This battle set the terms for the derivatives innovation frenzy that followed over the next dozen years. Self-policing had won the day, and that was to make all the difference. Peter Hancock's team was about to conceive a way to make the idea of credit derivatives work, and in the absence of regulatory oversight the eventual innovation frenzy would later fuel a boom beyond all bounds of rational constraint – or self-discipline.

CHAPTER THREE

The Dream Team

In the weeks following the swaps team's Boca Raton off-site, stories of that weekend's escapades ripped around the bank. To the team members themselves, the tales were a source of pride, and an arcane bond. The stories added lustre to the aura around them, and the swaps desk was now considered as edgy as would ever be possible at staid J.P. Morgan.

Immediately upon returning, the team threw itself into crafting ways to make the idea of credit derivatives work. As Hancock perceived it, this was an innovation battle that he needed to wage on two fronts. He needed to produce some brilliant ideas that would take finance to a new frontier; and he needed to devise a social organization that would liberate his team's innovative juices.

Hancock had shrewdly selected Bill Winters and Bill Demchak to lead the effort, and they set to work building their teams. One of Winters's smart hires was Tim Frost, an ambitious young derivatives trader who hailed from Nottingham and had never quite lost the flat vowels. Another important addition was Tony Best, a smooth, skilled salesman with a cut-glass accent who had worked in swaps since the 1980s. Over in New York, Demchak hired a laconic, red-headed banker from New Orleans named Charles Pardue, who quickly proved his talents. Another key hire was Andrew Feldstein, an earnest American lawyer, introverted but exceedingly bright, who also had a penchant for lateral thought. 'Andrew and I have the same kind of mind,' Demchak liked to say. 'He is someone I can sit around for hours with, tossing around problems, picking things apart and then trying to reassemble them.'

In keeping with J.P. Morgan's international tradition, Demchak also recruited a clutch of non-Americans to his cause, some of whom were officially placed in the IDM team, while others were merely affiliated. One of those was Krishna Varikooty, a diligent young Indian, who was a talented mathematical modeller. Demchak would come to respect Varikooty deeply, impressed not only by his quantitative skills but by his ethics and stubborn stance when fighting for something he believed to be right. 'Krishna is like my conscience!' Demchak liked to joke.

A particularly notable hire was Blythe Masters, a young British woman. She was a pretty blonde with a slim frame and porcelain face. She had grown up in Kent, where she studied at a prestigious private school and developed an abiding passion for riding. From an early age, she displayed a stubborn, driven streak, which helped her to win a place to read economics at Cambridge.

Before going to university, Masters did an internship at J P Morgan, and the experience changed the course of her life. By chance, she was placed on the bank's derivatives team in London during the summer of 1987, when Connie Volstadt's team was re-examining its books to resolve the accounting dispute about the $400 million loss it had been accused of. Masters was drafted to help track down old trades and became fascinated with derivatives. 'I think these products appealed to me because I had a quantitative background,' she later explained, 'but they are also so creative.'

While her contemporaries spent their summer holidays during college cavorting on the beaches of Thailand or Inter-Railing around Europe, Masters returned each year to work at J.P. Morgan's London office. 'When she was at university she wasn't weird, or anything – she was up for a laugh,' one of her college friends recalled. 'But you always knew she was ambitious.' Immediately after graduation, in 1991, Masters joined J.P. Morgan's commodities desk, first in London and later in New York. But then her life took an unorthodox twist.

She started dating a fellow banker, became pregnant at twenty-three, and married. Some colleagues expected her to leave the bank, but she insisted she was committed to her career. Years later, when she had become a prominent spokesperson for the J.P. Morgan derivatives group, interviewed regularly by journalists, she was reluctant to discuss the events. 'Nobody ever asks *men* about their families, or their decision to have children!' she would point out to colleagues. 'Why should anyone care about mine?'

She knew only too well, though, that she would need to demonstrate conspicuous devotion to her job if she was to be taken seriously. When she went into hospital to have her baby, she slipped a tiny device to track market prices into her handbag, though she ended up barely using it. 'Funnily enough,' she told a reporter wryly, 'it turned out that being a mother was some-what more time-consuming than I thought.'

In other areas of banking, or at other banks, her career might have been hobbled before she had really started. But derivatives was such a new field that it was easier to break the mould, and Peter Hancock was a staunch believer in meritocracy. He didn't care what his team looked like, or much about their personal lives, as long as they were bright and collegiate. Above all, they had to share his intellectual curiosity. 'I suppose we created a place where people such as Masters could flourish,' he later commented. 'I don't think that would have happened at many other banks.'

Masters was by no means the only woman in Hancock's empire. Terri Duhon, a young maths whizz from a poor family in rural Louisiana, subsequently joined the IDM team. So did Betsy Gile, a cheery, no-nonsense woman who had previously worked in the lending business of J.P. Morgan. Another recruit, Romita Shetty, was an Indian-born credit expert who had started her career as an analyst at Standard and Poor's rating agency. When Demchak first offered her a job in IDM, he gave her no actual job description. The team, he explained, was free-floating: members would work on different projects and with different colleagues as needed. She jumped at the chance. 'What they were doing looked so exciting,' she later recalled.

Just as Hancock had hoped, his collection of bright young bankers quickly started fermenting creative ideas in a range of types of derivatives business. Masters was part of a group told to pursue the credit derivatives idea, and she threw herself into the assignment. She could see it had revolutionary implications.

From time immemorial, the worlds of business and finance have been beset with the problem of default risk, the danger that a borrower will not repay a loan or bond. Banks had long tried to minimize that problem in several ways. The most basic was to ensure that they only made wise lending decisions; hence J.P. Morgan's strong emphasis on its training programme. Diversifying a bank's customer base was another technique, akin to diversifying a stock portfolio. Banks also sometimes clubbed together to make joint loans, thereby spreading the pain of defaults, and they imposed absolute limits on the amount of money that could be loaned to given sectors – only so much in housing, another amount in consumer credit, and so on. A rule might stipulate, for example, that each department could have no more than $10 million of loans to homebuilders. Nonetheless, history is littered with examples of banks that collapsed because they misjudged default risk, or had too much exposure to a single sector or lender. The Savings and Loans debacle in the late 1980s and early 1990s was one case in point.

Masters and the rest of the IDM team knew that in the world of swaps, techniques had been found to separate out, as a derivative product, parts of the risk attached to bonds – say the risk that interest rates would rise and lead a bond's value to fall. Derivatives traders had been able to sell that risk as a product to investors who were willing to bet that interest rates would not actually rise. The bond holder, with the bank acting as broker, was able in effect to sell the risk of the bond to another, less risk-averse investor. So what would happen, Masters asked herself, if the same principle was applied to the default risk associated with a loan?

Such a development would overturn one of the fundamental rules of banking, that default risk is an inevitable liability of the business. If a technique could be developed to package default risk so that it could be traded, that would be an enormous boost for banking in general. For the first time in history, banks would be able to make loans without carrying all, or perhaps even any, of the risk involved themselves. That would, in turn, free up banks to make *more* loans, as they wouldn't need to take losses if those loans defaulted. The derivatives buyers who had gambled on that risk would take the hit.

Such derivatives could be especially useful for J.P. Morgan. By the early 1990s the bank was facing a particularly pernicious set of financial headaches. The Basel I accord of 1988 stipulated that all banks needed to hold capital reserves equivalent to 8 per cent of the corporate loans on their books: $8 of spare funds for every $100 lent out. The rule applied to all corporate loans for all banks, which were deemed to be investment grade by ratings agencies, irrespective of the precise risk attached to them, and

J.P. Morgan considered that extremely unfair. The bank concentrated on loans to high-quality corporate clients and foreign governments, and the default rate on those loans tended to be so low that keeping $8 of reserves for every $100 lent out seemed a complete waste of resources. Those loans were also not very profitable, because the riskier a loan, the more a bank can charge the client for it. This had seriously curbed the extent to which J.P. Morgan could grow its business.

To make matters worse, those at the bank trying to boost profits faced a related internal headache, separate from the Basel rules. To combat the danger of default, the bank imposed rigorous internal credit limits on each department, keeping a tight rein on the exposure to risk. By 1994, Hancock's derivatives group had expanded so fast that the net exposure it had incurred via swaps amounted to approximately $30 billion, and it was bumping up against its limit, finding itself hemmed in.

If the bank could find a way to shift that credit risk off its books, both the 'credit limit' headache and the Basel problem might disappear. That was a tantalizing prospect. 'If we could make this idea work, this thing could be huge!' Demchak told his team.

But *could* it be made to work? Over at Merrill Lynch, Connie Volstadt's team had already been playing around with similar ideas for a year. And at Bankers Trust two innovative traders called Peter Freund and John Crystal had actually cut a couple of deals using these concepts as early as 1991. That made Freund and Crystal the true 'inventors', or pioneers, of credit derivatives However, perhaps ironically, Bankers Trust itself never tried to turn its brainchild into a large-scale business. The bank was beset with management upheaval at the time. Moreover, the credit derivatives concept did not seem sufficiently profitable, relative to other business lines, to tempt Bankers Trust traders to devote enough time and energy to create a mass-market credit derivatives business.

Hancock's group, though, operated with different incentives. While at J.P. Morgan generally pay was also tied to profits personally accounted for, Hancock had impressed on the IDM bankers that they were supposed to chase ideas with long-term value, even at the expense of the quick buck. Moreover, the team knew that if they 'cracked' the credit derivatives puzzle they would solve a big problem for the bank, which would win them huge acclaim and would boost their careers. 'They say necessity is the mother of invention,' Feldstein later laughed. 'In the case of credit derivatives, we all knew there was a real need, a problem that had to be solved. So we all looked for ways to do that.'

Blythe Masters cast about for a way to make credit derivatives work, and eventually she spotted an opportunity at Exxon Oil. In 1993, after Exxon was threatened with a $5 billion fine as a result of the *Exxon Valdez* tanker spill, the company had taken out a $4.8 billion credit line from J.P. Morgan and Barclays. When Exxon first asked for the credit line – which is a commitment to provide a loan, if needed – J.P. Morgan was reluctant to say no because Exxon was a long-standing client. The loan epitomized the twin problem of capital requirements and internal credit limits. Like so many of J.P. Morgan's corporate loans, it would produce little, if any profit, and yet would gobble up credit, pushing the limits, and would require a large amount of capital reserve. In theory, the bank could have dealt with that headache by selling the loan to a third party, since a market for selling such loans did exist. But that would have violated its commitment to client loyalty.

Masters thought she could see a solution. In the autumn of 1994 she contacted officials at the European Bank for Reconstruction and Development (EBRD) in London to see if she could find a way to offload the credit risk of the Exxon deal, but *without* selling the loan. The EBRD might be interested, she figured, because it had complementary needs: it had

a large amount of credit available for extending to companies
with high credit ratings. The bank was also eager to find ways
to earn more money on its investments, as it was rigorously
restrained from high-risk activity, so generally earned low
returns.

Masters proposed that J.P. Morgan pay the EBRD a fee each
year in exchange for the EBRD assuming the risk of the Exxon
credit line, effectively insuring J.P. Morgan for the risk of the
loan. If Exxon defaulted, the EBRD would be on the hook to
compensate J.P. Morgan for the loss; but if Exxon did not
default, then the EBRD would be making a good profit in fees.
The EBRD might well be interested, Masters figured, because
the chances that Exxon would default were so slim. True to the
derivatives formula, the loan would not actually move from J.P.
Morgan's books to EBRD, so Morgan would be respecting its
client relationship, but wouldn't be eating up its internal credit
lines.

Andrew Donaldson, the EBRD's director, liked the idea. He
agreed that it was highly unlikely Exxon would default, and he
was impressed by the steady stream of income from the fees. It
was much higher than anything else he could earn on a highly
rated bond or loan. 'It seemed like a win-win situation,'
Donaldson later recalled. Just as Salomon Brothers' early interest
rate swaps deal between IBM and the World Bank had met two
sets of needs, the Exxon deal was brilliantly transferring risk in
a way that suited both parties.

For several weeks, Masters made endless phone calls to
London from New York as she and Donaldson – together with
a phalanx of lawyers – worked out legal terms for the deal. In
most sectors of finance, well-established rules governed deals.
The credit derivative concept was so new that they had to be
crafted on the fly; Masters was making history as she went.
Nobody quite knew what the fees paid to the EBRD should be,
or even quite what to call this 'product'. Eventually though, the

deal was done, and it was dubbed a 'credit default swap', which, as the business spread, was shortened to CDS.

Hancock and the team were jubilant. The Exxon deal showed that a substantial credit derivatives contract could be made to work. And it was not the only one. As Masters was cutting her deal with the EBRD, Robert Reoch, a British banker who worked in Winters's team in London, cut a deal with Citibank asset management that transferred the risk attached to Belgian, Italian and Swedish government bonds. However, it was one thing for a bank to arrange a few isolated deals; it was quite another to turn those deals into a full-blown business as lucrative as Hancock was aiming for. So as 1995 got under way, the group went into overdrive to attack the key obstacles to making the concept fly on a large scale.

One of those was convincing their internal commercial lending team, as well as regulators, that the concept was sound, which would open up a wide pool of loans on the bank's books to use for making swaps. They also had to figure out a way to 'industrialize' CDS deals, so that they could do many more of them much faster. One other key thing the team wanted to investigate was whether, by removing the risk of its loans in this way, the bank would be allowed to reduce its capital reserves. That was one of the most important potential payoffs, as a good deal of reserve cash would then be freed up for use in making profits. That was the dream: credit derivatives would allow J.P. Morgan – and in due course all other banks too – to fine-tune risk burdens, releasing banks from age-old constraints and freeing up vast amounts of capital, turbocharging not only banking but the whole economy.

Behind the scenes, Masters and Demchak started to visit US regulators. Two main institutions held responsibility for monitoring this activity: the US Federal Reserve, in New York and Washington, and the Office of the Comptroller of the Currency (OCC), in Washington. Neither had spent much time studying the idea of credit derivatives. After all, the concept had not even been invented when the Basel Accord, or any American financial rules, had been written. But that didn't mean they wouldn't weigh in with strict views if J.P. Morgan started doing lots of deals. Masters and Demchak posed the crucial question: if banks used credit derivatives to shift their default risk, would the regulators let them cut their capital reserves?

The omens looked promising. At the start of the decade, regulators had grappled with the Savings and Loans disaster, and had learned first-hand the dangers of banks concentrating loan risk, one of the big mistakes that S&L had made. Many regulators were consequently thrilled to learn that tools could be developed to *disperse* risk. Indeed, one senior American regulator was so knocked out by the idea that when he heard about what Masters was doing, he telephoned her to learn more. 'When I read the details, it seemed to me this was one of the best innovations I had ever seen. It was just a wonderful idea!' he later said.

Sure enough, in August 1996, the Fed issued a statement suggesting that banks would be allowed to reduce capital reserves by using credit derivatives. Masters, Demchak and Hancock were thrilled.

Even as that battle was being waged, Demchak and others on the team threw themselves into an internal lobbying campaign to sell the concept to their colleagues, particularly the loan officers. In some respects, that proved harder than dealing with the regulators. During the late 1980s and early 1990s, the wild antics of the swaps team had provoked unease among the older members of the bank's commercial lending arm. Those more traditional bankers now reacted with even more horror when Demchak declared he wanted to overhaul the way that commercial lending was done.

To bolster his case, Demchak unveiled a flood of supportive data. This was drawn from a crucial new twist on the original VaR idea that Weatherstone had developed. During the early

1990s, the quantitative experts inside J.P. Morgan had refined their quantitative tools. The first version of VaR was primarily concerned with measuring market risk. However, by the mid-1990s, J.P. Morgan analysts then used similar ideas to analyse the risk of untraded loans too, and then compared those numbers to the risks attached to bonds and other assets. The basic idea was look at all the assets that a bank held on its books, and work out which parts of the bank were producing good returns, relative to the risks – and which were not. The implications of this analysis looked alarming. By 1995, it seemed four-fifths of the bank's capital was tied up in activities that typically earned less than 10 basis points of return for the bank each year, meaning just 0.1 cent for each dollar used. Areas of the business which generated much higher profits, such as derivatives, were often short of capital. The bank's money simply wasn't being used as profitably as it should be, let alone in a manner that would enable the bank to hit a self-imposed target of a 20 per cent return on equity, each year. 'We have to change the way we do business!' Hancock declared, over and over again, convinced that if the bank didn't make this change, it faced a slow death.

The harder Demchak and Hancock pressed the case for reform, though, the more recalcitrant some of the commercial loan officers became. They had spent their careers evaluating loan risks, and they still set store by relying on relationships with firms, and reputations, in addition to the maths Demchak was relying on to produce his data. Demchak's zeal didn't help. Though he was most often easy-going, he found it hard to suffer fools. The more they resisted his arguments, the more biting Demchak's comments became. 'These guys are *dinosaurs!*' he wailed to his team, in fury. The loan officers retaliated by dubbing Demchak the 'Prince of Darkness', so intent did he seem on launching otherworldly schemes. Hancock was considered the king of these dark plans.

For months, the impasse lingered. Finally, in July 1997, an

unexpected twist broke the deadlock. In the middle of that year a financial crisis erupted in Asia and the commercial lending group suffered painful losses on loans across the region. That raised the pressure on the bank's new CEO, Douglas 'Sandy' Warner, who had replaced Weatherstone in 1995, to take some decisive action to improve the bank's profits. It was becoming increasingly clear – just as Hancock and Demchak had long complained – that the bank's level of profitability was lagging behind its rivals, and these losses were a body blow. Warner decided to throw his weight behind the value of the credit derivatives business.

He gave Hancock responsibility for managing not just the fixed-income business, but the commercial lending department too. That was a radical move for staid J.P. Morgan, since almost no other Western bank had ever tried to combine lending, bonds and derivatives into a single group before. Then Hancock handed responsibility for managing the loan book to Demchak. The Prince of Darkness was in charge, and able to remould the bank's credit risk in line with all his dreams.

But one more obstacle still stood in the path of the revolution, and it was a daunting one. They still had to find a way to process a high volume of deals rapidly; to *industrialize* the CDS trade, transforming it from a cottage industry into a mass-production business.

The crucial, last piece of the puzzle that fell into place went by the strange name of 'Bistro' (although bankers would later give the idea an even stranger tag of 'synthetic collateralized debt obligations'.) This brainchild emerged from months of heated debate and experimentation. By the mid-1990s, Hancock's group had two views on how to make credit derivatives work large-scale. In London, Bill Winters was inclined to try to create what bankers call a 'liquid market' in credit derivatives. That would entail finding a way to make credit derivatives as easy for clients and investors to buy and sell as stocks, and might also require setting up an exchange. 'Pile 'em high and sell 'em cheap – that has always been my mantra!' Tim Frost, one of the young traders in Winters's group, sometimes quipped. He was utterly convinced that a mass-market approach could be found for derivatives. He also had the 'can do' spirit to drive that dream.

Demchak's team in New York, however, preferred to focus on a different idea for turbocharging the market. That was, essentially, to bundle lots of deals together, pooling all of their risk, and then to create derivatives carved out of that whole pool, rather than swapping one loan at a time.

The key question for the team was, how could you bundle a whole host of loans together, extended to lots of different companies with different credit histories and business prospects, in such a way that investors could feel confident about the level of risk they were taking on in buying a slice of the total? If investors couldn't analyse the specific risk of default for all loans in the pool, one by one, as the EBRD could do in insuring Exxon's default risk, how could they be assured? Their solution to that puzzle came by linking derivatives technology to a technique known as 'securitization'. Experiments along those lines had already been bubbling for a couple of years at Swiss Bank Corporation, NatWest and Chase Manhattan. The Bistro plan essentially looked at some of those ideas – but packaged them with such crucial new twists that it transformed the field.

The securitization concept which lay at the heart of this breakthrough was even older than the 'swaps' idea. It had first cropped up in a significant manner back in the 1960s and 1970s, when some banks started selling off mortgage loans they were carrying to outside investors in an effort to diversify their port-folios. Those who bought them could make a good profit in the mortgage business without needing all the infrastructure required to originate loans. It was a win-win deal.

Making these sales took time, however, as investors wanted to scrutinize the details of the loans, to guard against the risk of default. So bankers came up with the idea of bundling up large quantities of loans in packages. That would spread the risk of any problematic loans over the whole bundle, so that if any borrowers with mortgages in the bundle did default, that loss would be covered by the profits made on the rest of the loans.

Over time, bankers realized that they could use the cash flow from the mortgage payments being made on that bundle of loans to make a tidy extra profit. If they issued securities, such as bonds, they could 'back' those securities with the cash flow from the mortgage payments – for example, making the regular payments to bond holders from that cash – and overall, they would make money from both the mortgage payments and the sales of the securities. These became known as mortgage-backed securities – hence the term securitization – and the business boomed.

Then, those trading in these securities got the crucial idea that Demchak's team now jumped at. They realized that they could divide the securities they sold into several 'tranches', each with a different level of risk, and of return, for the investor. The highest risk and highest return were called 'junior', the middle level 'mezzanine', and the lowest-risk and lowest return were called 'senior'. The idea was that if defaults on any mortgages in the bundle did occur, those losses would be charged against the junior-level securities first. If losses were so high that they weren't covered by the junior securities, then the mezzanine-level investors would take the additional hit.

Those who invested in the senior-level securities would almost surely never suffer losses, because the chances of so many defaults happening at the same time were extremely slim. Just as in a flooding house, where the water floods the cellar first while the roof stays safe, losses from defaults would flood the junior and mezzanine levels – drowning those bond holders' expected earnings – and the senior bonds would always be safe, except, that is, in the event of a truly major cataclysm. Due to their

higher risk of loss, the junior and mezzanine notes paid propor-
tionately higher returns, while, due to their extremely low risk,
the senior notes paid quite low returns.

The key attraction of this bundling, multi-tiered approach was
that investors could choose the level of risk they wanted. And
since investors were usually willing to pay a little more for the
sheer convenience of having someone else tailor their level of
risk, banks could often sell the complete set of notes for more
than the total value of the mortgage loans. The concept was akin
to a pizzeria that takes an eight-dollar pizza, cuts it into eight
pieces, and sells each piece for $1.25. Customers will sometimes
pay more to buy just the amount and flavour they want, whether
of pizza or of risk.

In the 1980s, bankers took the idea that had been used to
'slice and dice' mortgages and applied it to corporate bonds and
loans. Demchak and his team, though, then took this a step further and applied it to credit derivatives. The idea was that instead
of grabbing a portfolio of different mortgages, and then selling
investors a stake in that, a bundle of credit derivatives contracts
that insured somebody else against the risk of default would be
used instead. In financial terms, it was equivalent to taking thirty
different home insurance contracts, bundling them together, and
persuading a bigger consortium of outside investors to underwrite the risk that losses might affect those thirty homes.

As with the early mortgage bond deals, though, the investors
who were underwriting that 'insurance' – or that pool of CDS
contracts – could choose the level of risk they took. If an
investor wanted to roll the dice, they could agree to pay out the
first wave of claims that might hit if, say, a few contracts went
bad. Investors that wanted more safety might underwrite the
'mezzanine' – or in-between – level of risk. That was similar to
paying up on a collective insurance scheme when losses got
bigger than $5000, say, but not higher than $100,000. The
'safest' part of the scheme was the senior tier, where investors

would only be forced to pay the cost of defaults after the claims – or losses – had become so widespread that all the other investors had been wiped out. There were different tranches of risk.

To complete its scheme, the team also decided to borrow another trick from the domain of mortgage securitization. One widespread practice banks had engaged in was to create shell companies specifically for buying bundles of mortgages and selling the securities made from them. These companies were generally referred to as special purpose vehicles (SPVs), and they were usually located in offshore jurisdictions such as the Cayman Islands and Bermuda to ensure they did not incur US tax. Demchak's team decided to set up such an SPV to play the role the EBRD had filled in the Exxon swap. The shell company would 'insure' J.P. Morgan for the risk of the entire bundle of loans, with Morgan paying a stream of fees to the SPV and the SPV agreeing to pay Morgan for any losses from defaults. Meanwhile the SPV would turn around and sell smaller chunks of that risk to investors, in synthetically sliced-out junior, mezzanine and senior notes.

The really beautiful part of the scheme was that Demchak's team calculated that the SPV would need to sell only a relatively small number of notes to outside investors in order to raise the money to insure all of that risk. Normally the SPV would be expected to be 'fully funded', meaning that it would have to sell notes totalling the complete amount of risk that it was insuring. But the J.P. Morgan team reckoned that full funding just wasn't necessary; the number of defaults would be so low that so much capital just wouldn't ever be needed for covering losses.

Demchak's team worked stealthily on putting that theory into practice. Right from the start, they decided to shoot for the stars. 'Let's do ten billion dollars!' Demchak declared – he liked big, round numbers. The team identified 307 companies for which J.P. Morgan was carrying risk on its books that amounted to a total of $9.7 billion. Then they set up a shell company, and they calculated that the company would only need to sell $700 million of notes to cover any payouts to J.P. Morgan it might need to make – around 8 per cent of all the risk insured. This was akin to an insurance company offering insurance on a home worth $1 million, when it holds just $75,000 in its kitty. Just to be safe, though, Demchak decided that the SPV would invest that $700 million pot in AAA-rated Treasury bonds, so that if it ever were needed there would be no doubt the money would be there. That ultra-safe investment plan would also help assure investors that the scheme was sound.

The team then approached officials at Moody's credit-ratings agency to get its stamp of approval, which would be needed to convince investors. For several months, Demchak's team held intensive debate with the ratings agencies, just as bankers at NatWest, Swiss Bank Corporation and Chase had previously done over their own earlier, securitization schemes. Some ratings officials worried that $700 million was not enough to insure the entire pot of $10 billion-odd loans, and suggested ways of potentially tweaking the scheme. The J.P. Morgan officials, though, pointed out that the ratings agencies' own data indicated that the chance of any widespread default was laughably small. In essence, all that J.P. Morgan had done was to use the default models created by Moody's – and take it to the logical extreme.

So, finally, after much back and forth, they decided to accept J.P. Morgan's arguments. Out of the pool of $700 million notes, two-thirds were given the vital AAA tag. The rest were stamped 'Ba2'.

In December 1997, just as most of the New York financial world was packing up for the Christmas holidays, Demchak's team finally unveiled its creation. They had given it the ugly name 'broad index secured trust offering', shortened to Bistro. With great hopes the group set out to sell the notes. Some investors were dumbfounded. 'It looks like a science experiment, with all those arrows!' one baffled fund manager quipped.

Masters, however, was formidably good at marketing. Over and over again, she explained to potential investors how the scheme worked, with a near-evangelical passion. She got results. Within a matter of days, the team had sold all the $700 million notes. Indeed, the appetite was so strong that Masters concluded there was scope to conduct plenty more such deals.

The team was jubilant. They felt they had stumbled on a financial Holy Grail. At a stroke, they had managed to remove credit risk from the bank's books on an enormous scale. That would immediately enable J.P. Morgan to relieve some of the pressure on internal credit limits. The team also hoped that once regulators had a chance to examine the scheme, they would agree to let the bank reduce its capital reserves. But there were wider economic implications too, not just for J.P. Morgan but for the financial system as a whole.

If it was now so easy to shift large volumes of credit risk off the bank's books, banks would be able to truly fine-tune their loan portfolios. 'Five years hence, commentators will look back to the birth of the credit derivatives market as a watershed development,' Masters ambitiously declared, '. . . credit derivatives will fundamentally change the way banks price, manage, transact, originate, distribute and account for risk.' She, like her colleagues, took it as self-evident that these 'efficiency gains' from shifting risk in this way could only lead to a *better* financial world, and they pleaded their case with an almost religious zeal.

'When you heard these guys speak, you realized that they really believed this stuff,' Paula Froelich, a journalist from Dow-Jones who had extensive contact with the Bistro team during that period, recalled. 'They thought they were the smartest guys on the planet. They had found this brilliant way to get around the [Basel] rules, to play around with all this risk. And they were just so proud of what they had done.'

CHAPTER FOUR

The Cuffs Come Off

Bistro-style CDS trades took off fast. In early 1998, the J.P. Morgan swaps team conducted a second $10 billion deal, 'insuring' another huge chunk of the bank's loans and bonds. That success led the team to start marketing the service to others.

Japanese banks were among the first to bite. By 1998, Japan was in the throes of a full-blown banking crisis, which had left the largest banks desperate to find a way to reduce their risk. In the summer the team cut a series of billion-dollar deals with lending institutions including Fuji, IKB, Daiwa and Sanwa. Soon afterwards, Masters arranged a Bistro structure for the Pittsburgh-based bank PNC. Demchak already knew that group well, since PNC was his home-town bank, and he had helped to restructure some troubled interest rate derivatives deals that PNC had made in the early 1990s. A flock of other American regional banks and European banks expressed interest. The European banks were usually reluctant to reveal the names of the companies whose loans were included in CDS deals; they feared they would lose customers if companies found out that their bank was buying insurance against its loan-book risk. Undaunted, Demchak's team tweaked the scheme again. In the early deals they printed the names of the bonds and loans being covered. They later stopped printing the names of the companies whose loans were included in deals and marketed the tool as a way to maintain 'client confidentiality' even while reshaping a bank's balance sheet.

Other banks did the same. In early 1998, Credit Suisse unveiled its own Bistro-style CDS structure. So did BNP Paribas. More US and European banks quickly followed suit, triggering an explosion in credit derivatives activity. By December 1997, American banks had reported around $100 billion of such deals on their books. By the end of March 1998 that had grown to $148 billion in the US and was estimated to be about $300 billion globally. J.P. Morgan alone accounted for $51 billion of that. The market for credit derivatives had grown overnight from a cottage industry into a bazaar where tens of *billions* of dollars of risk was changing hands.

Demchak's team was both stunned and thrilled. When they had first dreamed up the scheme, they hadn't expected it to be a goldmine of profits. Their intent was to fine-tune the bank's exposure to risk in order to free up credit-limit constraints and reserve capital. But as the idea spread, the team started to hope that these deals might generate quite substantial revenues from clients through hefty fees. The status and reputation of those associated with creating Bistro soared, both inside and outside the bank. Masters was promoted to be the head of credit derivatives marketing. Feldstein was put in charge of high-yield loans. Demchak was handed responsibility for the entire credit division. Hancock rose too: he was named both Chief Financial Officer and Chief Risk Officer for the entire bank, a post that put him in running for CEO when Sandy Warner retired.

"The business opportunities created by credit derivatives, their relevance to clients, the size of the credit markets globally and the gross inefficiencies in pricing and liquidity that exist are frankly staggering,' Masters said in a press interview in the summer of 1998. 'The pace of change in the way banks manage credit risk has accelerated to a point where we can confidently predict credit risk management will be completely different in two years than it was even two years ago.'

Demchak had decided at an early stage that Masters would be the perfect 'face' to sell the idea to the outside world. Some of her colleagues resented that, pointing out that the true flashes of inspiration had come from Feldstein, Demchak or Varikooty. Masters herself sometimes worried about the risks of being in the spotlight. But nobody could deny that she was a highly effective promoter. 'Blythe Masters still looks more like a J.P. Morgan intern (which she was 10 years ago) than the head of the credit derivatives marketing team,' one article said, 'but it takes about a minute of conversation to learn that she possesses the knowledge and experience to lead the bank's team . . . in overseeing the marketing of a $51 billion business.'

At other banks, such success would have led to huge bonuses and pay packages, whereas J.P. Morgan paid the team relatively modestly. In 1998 they were handed a set of bonuses that were high by the standards of the rest of the bank, but low by comparison with rivals. Most took home at least $500,000 of pay that year, and many received more than $1 million. Headhunters swarmed, though, offering to double, triple or quadruple that compensation if they would move. 'There would be all these cars with headhunters just hanging outside the door,' Demchak later remembered. 'Some even turned up with contracts from other banks, ready to sign.'

Almost nobody left; the team spirit was just too strong. By the summer of 1998, activity was so frenetic that the team was spending almost all its waking hours together, either hunched over desks arranging deals, or letting off steam at bars after long work hours. In other departments of the bank, there was a long-standing tradition that brokers would take traders out in the evenings to party. The credit derivatives group was so new that there was no such tradition, so the Bistro group took themselves out, heading to Harry's Bar or the Bull and Bear, or Wall Street bars, or sometimes to Atlantic City for a wild night of gambling. On warm summer weekends they would head out to Long Island, where Masters and Demchak had each spent some of their swelling pay on beach-front houses. They were always *together*. 'We just hung out 24/7. It was incredibly intense,' Terri Duhon later recalled. For a few, the intensity took its toll on their family lives, prompting divorces.

Inside the office, the team increasingly developed its own sub-culture. When they had a moment from arranging deals, they would stage contests on the trading floor to see who could throw a Frisbee or baseball furthest before a computer screen was hit. Once, Masters declared she wanted to celebrate 'bow-tie' day, so the team arrived wearing cheap, colourful ties, to the astonishment of the rest of the bank.

Pranks proliferated. One trader took to stripping down to his underwear 'to let the air in' after all-night sessions arranging deals. A salesman started nicknaming all his clients after famous soccer players in the bank's internal sales reports. When the regulators suddenly visited one day and demanded to see the books, Demchak had to explain why 'David Beckham' was buying Bistro notes on a massive scale.

Other divisions sometimes complained that the antics were getting out of hand; that Demchak was becoming 'boorish' and the team was behaving like a frat house. Demchak brushed the complaints aside as sniping due to jealousy. He wasn't worried; he knew his team was slavishly devoted to him, and to Hancock, and, most importantly, to the mission of proving the revolutionary implications of credit derivatives. 'Yes, it was a bit like a frat culture at times,' Demchak would later recall with a wistful smile. 'But we had an amazing team spirit, it was just an amazing time. And, of course, we assumed it would last for ever.'

*

The first sign that there might be a structural weakness in the architecture of the Bistro idea emerged in the second half of 1998. During the early months of the year, Masters and Demchak repeatedly pestered regulators, trying to get a clear answer about how far the bank would be able to cut its capital reserves by using the Bistro scheme. They had conducted the first couple of deals without knowing for sure. After all, the bank had other more fundamental reasons for wanting to reshape its credit risk, irrespective of any capital 'win'. But when Demchak's group started performing deals for other banks, the question of reserve capital became more important. The others wanted to do these deals primarily to cut their reserve requirements.

In 1996, the Federal Reserve wrote its first formal letter to the banking community about credit derivatives, in that it warned that regulators would only allow the banks to cut capital reserves if they had *truly* removed the risk of loans from their books. Demchak and Masters decided to push the Fed and OCC about exactly what guidelines they would approve of for lowering capital reserves for bundle or credit derivatives, not just in respect to J.P. Morgan, but to all the other banks too.

The regulators were still unsure. When officials at the OCC and Fed had first heard about credit derivatives, they had warmed to the idea that banks were trying to manage their risk. But they were also uneasy because the newfangled derivatives didn't fit neatly under any existing regulations. They were particularly uncertain about what to make of the low level of funding available for covering losses on J.P. Morgan's creation. The original £10 billion Bistro deal stipulated that if financial Armageddon ever did hit and wiped out all of the $700 million funding cushion, J.P. Morgan itself would absorb the additional losses. In the eyes of Masters and Demchak, that still meant that the bank had removed all the pieces of credit risk that actually mattered; the chances that losses would ever eat through $700 million were vanishingly slim. Effectively, there was no real risk, and no real liability. In any case, Hancock liked to argue, it was ridiculous to worry about the eventuality of massive defaults. If the corporate sector ever suffered a tidal wave of defaults large enough to eat through the $700 million funding cushion, then the disaster probably would have already wiped out half the banking system anyway. There was no point, he argued, in running a bank on the assumption that the financial equivalent of an asteroid strike would devastate Wall Street.

That argument didn't wash with European regulators. Officials at the Fed were uneasy too. Christine Cumming, a senior Fed official, indicated to Masters and Demchak that the J.P. Morgan team should look for a way to remove or insure the amount of risk that was unfunded in the Bistro scheme if they wished to get capital relief.

So Masters and the rest of the team set out to find a solution. They started by giving that bundle of risk a name. They had never referred to that portion of the risk pool in any standard way. Masters liked to refer to it as 'more than triple A', since it was deemed even safer than triple A-rated notes. But that was too clumsy to market. So they came up with the name 'super-senior'. The next step was to explore who, if anyone, would want to either buy or insure it.

The task did not look easy. As Masters said later, 'There were just not that many natural buyers,' because the pay-off for taking it on would be relatively low. As far as the bank was concerned, this risk was not really at all risky, so there was absolutely no point in paying anything other than a token amount to get it insured. On top of that, whoever stepped up to acquire or insure the super-senior risk had to be brave enough to step into an unfamiliar world.

Masters eventually spotted one solution to the super-senior headache. In previous decades, one of J.P. Morgan's long-standing blue-chip clients had been the mighty insurance company

American International Group. Like J.P. Morgan itself, AIG was a pillar of the American financial establishment. The insurer had risen to prominence by building a formidable franchise in the Asian markets during the early twentieth century. That business was later extended in the US, making the company a powerful force in the American economy after the Second World War. AIG was considered a weighty and utterly reliable market player, and like J.P. Morgan, it basked in the sun of a triple-A credit rating.

But within AIG, an upstart entrepreneurial subsidiary was booming. In the late 1980s the company hired a group of traders who had previously worked for Drexel Burnham Lambert, which had infamously developed the junk bond business under the leadership of Michael Milken in the mid-1980s, before it blew up. They had been tasked by AIG with developing a capital markets business, known as AIG Financial Products, which was based in London, where the regulatory regime was less restrictive. This was run by Joseph Cassano, a tough-talking trader from Brooklyn.

Cassano was creative, bold and highly ambitious. More important, AIG, as an insurance company, was not subject to the same burdensome capital reserve requirements as banks. That meant AIG would barely need to post capital reserves if it insured the super-senior risk. Nor was the insurer even likely to face hard questions from its own regulators, because, though AIG's insurance arms were regulated by state-level insurance groups, AIGFP had largely fallen through the cracks of oversight. It was regulated by the Office for Thrift Supervision, but OTS officials had only limited expertise in the field of cutting-edge financial products.

Masters pitched to Cassano that AIG take over J.P. Morgan's super-senior risk, either in the form of a purchase of securities, or by simply signing credit derivatives contracts that would insure Morgan against any loss. Cassano happily agreed. It was a 'watershed' event, Cassano later observed. 'J.P. Morgan came to us, who were somebody we worked with a great deal, and asked us to participate in some of what they called Bistro trades [which] were the precursors to what [became] the CDO market.' It seemed good business for AIG.

AIG would earn a relatively paltry fee for providing this service, of just 0.02 cents on the dollar each year. But, that said, if 0.02 cents are multiplied a few billion times, it adds up to an appreciable income stream, particularly if almost no reserves are required to cover the risk. Once again, the magic of derivatives had produced a 'win–win' solution. Only many years later did it become clear that Cassano's trade set AIG on the path to near-ruin.

With the AIG deal in hand, the team returned to the regulators and pointed out that a way had been found to remove the rest of the credit risk from their Bistro deals. Then the group started plotting other sales of its super-senior risk to other insurance and reinsurance companies. The insurance companies snapped it up, not just from J.P. Morgan but from other banks too.

Then, ironically, just as this business was taking off, the regulators weighed in again. Officials at the OCC and Fed indicated to J.P. Morgan that after due reflection they thought that banks did *not* need to remove super-senior risk from their books after all. The lobbying by Masters and others had seemingly paid off. The regulators were not willing to let the banks get off scot-free. If they held the super-senior risk on their books, they would need to post reserves worth 20 per cent of the usual capital reserves (or 20 per cent of 8 per cent, meaning $1.60 for every $100 that lay on the books).

There were also some conditions. Capital reserves could only be cut if banks could prove that default risk on the super senior portion of the deal was truly negligible, and if the notes being issued by a Bistro-style structure carried an AAA stamp from a 'nationally recognized credit-ratings agency'. Those were strict terms, but J.P. Morgan was meeting them. The implications were huge.

Banks had typically been forced to hold $800 million reserves for every $10 billion corporate loans on their books. Now that sum could be just $160 million. The CDS concept had pulled off a dance around the Basel rules. The feat was so clever that some bankers started to joke that 'Bistro' really stood for 'BIS Total Rip Off', referring to the Bank for International Settlements (BIS), which had overseen the Basel Accord.

For a while, Demchak's team stopped transferring super-senior risk from J.P. Morgan's books. But then Bill Demchak got uneasy. The super-senior was ballooning to a staggering figure, because when the bank arranged CDS transactions for clients, it typically put the super-senior risk in the deal on its own balance sheet. In theory, there was no reason to worry about that. After all, Hancock, Demchak and Masters had repeatedly told the regulators that the super-senior risk was safe. But by 1999, the total pipeline of super-senior risk had swelled towards $100 billion. Something about that mountain of risk started to offend Demchak's common sense. 'If you have got $60 billion, $100 billion or however many billions of something on your balance sheet, that is a *very* big number,' he remarked to his team. 'I don't think you should ignore a big number, no matter what it is.'

Time and again, Demchak had battled with the 'dinosaurs' in the commercial lending department, brandishing the risk-assessment models as proof that the bank was mismanaging its risk. Yet, even as he had evangelized about these models, he had never been tempted to think for a moment that models were anything more than a *guide*. They were exceedingly useful, if not essential, for navigating in the world of modern finance. But they were not infallible, no matter how well crafted they were. Models were only as good as the data that was fed into them and the assumptions that underpinned their mathematics.

Demchak was acutely aware that the modelling of risks involved in Bistro-style deals had its limits. One of the trickiest problems revolved around the issue of 'correlation,' or the degree to which defaults in any given basket of loans might be inter-connected. Trying to predict correlation is a little like working out how many apples in a bag might go rotten. If you watch what happens to hundreds of different disconnected apples over several weeks, you might guess the chance that one apple might go rotten – or not. But what if they are sitting in a bag together? If one apple goes mouldy will that make the others rot too? If so, how many, and how fast? Similar doubts dogged the corporate world. J.P. Morgan statisticians knew that company defaults are connected. If a car company goes into default, say, its suppliers may go bust too. Conversely, if a big retailer collapses, other retail groups may actually benefit. Correlations could go both ways, and working out how they might develop among any basket of companies is fiendishly complex. So what the statisticians did, essentially, was to study the past correlations in corporate default and equity prices and program the models to assume the same pattern in the present.

This assumption wasn't deemed particularly risky, as corporate defaults were rare, at least in the pool of companies that J.P. Morgan was dealing with. When Moody's had done its own modelling of the basket of companies in the first Bistro deal, for example, it had predicted that just 0.82 per cent of the companies would default each year. If those defaults were uncorrelated, or just slightly correlated, then the chance of defaults occurring on 10 per cent of the pool – the amount that would have been required to eat up the $700 million of capital raised to cover losses – was tiny. That was why J.P. Morgan could declare super-senior risk so safe, and why Moody's had rated so many of the Bistro notes triple A.

The fact was, though, that the assumption about correlation levels was just that: human guesswork. And Demchak and his colleagues knew perfectly well that if the correlation rate ever turned out to be appreciably higher than the statisticians had presumed, serious losses might result. What if, for example, a situation transpired in which when a few companies did default, numerous others would too? The number of defaults that might set off such a chain reaction was a vexing unknown; maybe no chain reaction would result from a few defaults, but if ten happened, say among big economic players – the rot might spread, destroying the entire portfolio.

Demchak had never seen that happen, and the odds seemed extremely long, but even if there was just a minute chance of such a scenario, he didn't want to find himself sitting on a pile of assets as big as $100 billion that could conceivably go bust. It just did not feel prudent. So he decided to play it safe, and told his team they needed to look for ways to cut their super-senior liabilities again, irrespective of what the regulators were requiring.

Taking that stance cost the bank a fair amount of money, because it had to pay AIG and others fees to insure the risk, and those fees steadily rose as the decade wore on. In the first such deals that J.P. Morgan had cut with AIG, the fee had been just 0.02 cents for every dollar of risk insured each year, or in banking terms 2 basis points. By 1999 the price was nearer 11 basis points. But Demchak was determined that the team must be prudent.

Around the same time the team stumbled on a second, potentially more worrisome, problem with the Bistro concept. As the innovation cycle turned and earnings from CDS deals declined, Bill Demchak asked his team to explore new ideas for the Bistro concept, either by somehow modifying the structure or by putting new kinds of loans or other assets into the mix. Mortgage loans were one type they decided to experiment with.

Terri Duhon took charge of the endeavour. In 1998, Demchak had asked her to run the so-called 'exotics' book, which

handled a large volume of CDS transactions. Only ten years earlier, Duhon had been a high school student in Louisiana. When
she told her relatives she was going to work in a bank, they had
assumed she was going to be a teller. Now she was managing
tens of *billions* of dollars. She was trained as a mathematician, and
she thrived on adrenaline – in her spare time, she rode Harley
Davidsons – yet even so she found the thought of being in
charge of all those zeros awe-inspiring, if not a little scary. 'It was
just an extraordinary, intense experience,' she would later recall.

A year after Duhon took on the post, she got the word that
Bayerische Landesbank, a large German bank, wanted to use the
Bistro structure to remove the risk from $14 billion of US mort-
gage loans it had extended. She debated with her team whether
to accept the assignment, because working with home loans
wasn't a natural move for J.P. Morgan. The bank had never done
serious business in offering mortgages, and on the few occasions
when it had tried trading mortgage-backed bonds, its efforts had
backfired. In the early 1990s, for example, it had taken the rare
step of hiring an outside team to trade mortgage bonds, and the
team had suffered such huge losses that it had ultimately been
shut down. The senior J.P. Morgan management considered the
experience as a salutary lesson on how difficult it was to judge
mortgage risk. Duhon knew, though, that some of the bank's
rivals were starting to conduct CDS deals with mortgage risk. So
the team decided to accept the assignment.

As soon as Duhon talked with some quantitative analysts,
she encountered a problem. When J.P. Morgan had offered the
first Bistro notes in late 1997, the bank had access to extensive
data about all the loans that it was repackaging. So did the
investors, as the bank had deliberately named all of the 307
companies whose loans were included in the deal. In addition,
many of these companies had been in business for decades, so
extensive data was available on how they had performed over
many business cycles. That gave J.P. Morgan's statisticians, and

investors, great confidence about predicting the likelihood of defaults.

The mortgage world was significantly different. For one thing, mortgages were generally dumped into pools of debt that were entirely *anonymous*, since when banks sold bundles of mortgage loans to outside investors, they almost never revealed the names and credit histories of the borrowers. Investors had to rely on data from the lender itself about the default risks of the borrowers. Worse, when Duhon went looking for data to track mortgage defaults over several business cycles, she discovered it was in short supply.

In the later twentieth century, while America's corporate world had suffered several booms and recessions, the housing market had followed a steady path of growth. Some specific *regions* had suffered downturns. Prices in the Texas property market, for example, fell during the Savings and Loans debacle of the late 1980s. Yet, in the period since the Second World War, there had never been a nationwide house price slump. The last time housing prices had fallen en masse, in fact, was way back in the 1930s, during the Great Depression.

The lack of data made Duhon nervous. When bankers assembled models to predict defaults, they wanted data on what normally happened in both booms *and* busts. Without that, it was impossible to know whether defaults tended to be correlated or not, and in what circumstances they were isolated to particular urban centres or regions, and when they might go national. Duhon could see no way to get such information for mortgages. That meant she would either have to rely on data from just one region and extrapolate it across America, or make even more assumptions than normal about how defaults were correlated. She discussed what to do with the mathematically gifted Krishna Varikooty and the other quantitative experts.

Varikooty was renowned on the team for taking a sober

approach towards risk. He was a stickler for detail, who loved to get things right, and that scrupulousness sometimes infuriated colleagues who were itching to make deals. But Demchak always defended Varikooty. 'Once, people shouted at Krishna and made him upset, and Demchak just went ballistic,' one of his team-mates later recalled. Varikooty's judgement on the mortgage debt was clear: he could not see a way to track the potential correlation of defaults with any degree of confidence. Without that, he declared, no precise estimate of the risks of default in a bundle overall could be made. If defaults on mortgages were *un*correlated, then the Bistro structure should be safe for mortgage risk, but if they were highly correlated, it might be catastrophically dangerous. Nobody could know.

Duhon and her colleagues were reluctant simply to turn down Bayerische Landesbank's request. Their client was intensely keen to go ahead, even after the uncertainty in the modelling was explained, and so Duhon came up with the best estimates she could to structure the deal. She used the Savings and Loans data from Texas as a proxy to imagine what might happen if a disaster ever struck the US mortgage market as a whole, and to cope with the uncertainties the team stipulated that a bigger-than-normal funding cushion be raised, which made the deal less lucrative for J.P. Morgan. The bank also hedged its risk. That was the only prudent thing to do, and Duhon couldn't see it doing many more, if any, such deals. Mortgage risk was just too uncharted. 'We just could not get comfortable,' Masters later said.

In subsequent months, Duhon heard on the grapevine that other banks *were* starting to do CDS deals with mortgage debt, and she wondered how the other banks had coped with the data uncertainties that so worried her and Varikooty. Had they found a better way to track the correlation issue? Did they have more experience with dealing with mortgages? She had no way of finding out. Because the CDS market was unregulated, the details of deals weren't available, and she had no good intelligence

sources at the other banks. Like most of those working on Demchak's team, she had spent her whole career at J.P. Morgan.

The team did only one more Bistro deal with mortgage debt,
a few months later, worth $10 billion. Then it dropped that line
of development altogether. Years later, Duhon was stunned
when she learned of the staggering volume of mortgage-based
CDS deals the rest of the banking world went on to do.

Five years after the Boca Raton event, the J.P. Morgan derivatives team hosted a conference for its clients, at Wall Street's
Cipriani ballroom. The venue was one of the most prestigious
and elegant in the financial district, a cavernous room with a
classical domed ceiling, glittering chandeliers and a marble floor
the size of several tennis courts. Before the event, some of the
team had worried whether they could attract enough clients to
fill the grand space. Blythe Masters was determined, however, to
bring in a good crowd. Soon after joining Demchak's team, she
had persuaded the group to start pooling details about all their
potential customers and she created a list jokingly referred to as
'MOAD' – as in the 'Mother Of All Databases' – which she and
her colleagues now tirelessly worked. So many clients responded
that the event was standing room only.

By October 1999, the official volume of credit derivatives
deals in the market was estimated at $229 billion, six times the
level just two years earlier. J.P. Morgan alone accounted for
almost half of the total. The bank had not just kick-started the
business; it virtually was the market. The J.P. Morgan clients,
investors and rivals packed into the Cipriani ballroom that day
were eager to find out what the young derivatives turks were
planning next.

As the audience filed into the Cipriani, they were given a
hefty seventy-three-page tome decorated with a blurred picture
of orange and white squares on a black background, not unlike
a piece of artwork by Mark Rothko. Next to that was the title

The J.P. Morgan Guide to Credit Derivatives, and inside the book, which Demchak's team sometimes referred to, with only a faint sense of irony, as 'the bible', pages of dense text set out in exhaustive detail exactly how credit derivatives worked, and the rationale behind their creation. 'Until recently, credit remained the major component of business risk for which no tailored risk-management products existed,' the book solemnly declared. But now there was banking salvation: 'By separating specific aspects of credit risk from other risks, credit derivatives allow even the most illiquid credit exposures to be transferred to the most efficient holders of that risk.'

In later sections, the book explained at length how the risk attached to credit derivatives could be calculated, and the approach that regulators and lawyers typically adopted when evaluating these instruments. It also described how J.P. Morgan's VaR and credit risk assessment models worked. By the end of 1999, the bank had handed out fifteen thousand copies of those models to clients, for free. From some perspectives, distributing research tools in this manner did not make much business sense. Rivals laughed that once again it was a sign of just how uncommercial J.P. Morgan could sometimes be. But Hancock and his colleagues reckoned there was a bigger game to be played. If they could convert everyone else to adopt the same quantitative creed, they might adopt the derivatives gospel too – or so the hope went.

There were two issues the bible notably did *not* discuss in any detail. One was the headaches posed by super-senior risk. The only reference to that came towards the back of the book, in a turgid paragraph that essentially stated that super-senior was so exceedingly safe that it could be held on a bank's balance sheet with just a sliver of reserves. Of course, J.P. Morgan itself had decided to offload its own mountain of super-senior risk to insurers such as AIG. But the team left that out of the bible. No mention was made, either, of the team's unease about making Bistro deals out of mortgage debt.

On that glorious, triumphant day in the Cipriani, the team saw no reason to trumpet caution. As far as they were concerned, Bistro-style CDS was a wonderful invention, which had not just turbocharged their careers, but was *liberating* the banking system from age-old constraints. Only many years later did they come to realize that the Bistro creation would evolve to produce some very perverted offspring.

CHAPTER FIVE

Merger Mania

By late 1999, the J.P. Morgan derivatives team was hardly alone in believing that credit derivatives were key to building a brave new banking world, but the role they would play was eclipsed for many years by other forces. As the advent of the twenty-first-century loomed, the wider financial and corporate world was in a state of ferment. The technological revolution inaugurated by the internet was producing transformations in business and the global economy as profound as the discovery of electricity or the building of the railroads. At a stroke, investors and businesses all over the world could find new trading partners and tap into once-remote pools of capital, and competition became ever more intense. At the same time free-market ideology was winning minds over more and more of the globe. Innovation, competition, efficiency and deregulation were the rage, not just in finance but in other spheres too. Pundits, politicians, bankers and bureaucrats alike argued that globalization was inevitable and to be embraced: the product of the increasingly unfettered forces of a new and improved capitalism.

The dot-com bubble blew up to staggering proportions as it

became fashionable to believe that the internet was rewriting the fundamentals of business and a mantra of 'growth over profits' took hold. Start-ups spent astonishing amounts of venture capital in the quest to 'get large or get lost'.

In the mid-1990s, the tech-heavy NASDAQ index was trading around 800. On 10 March 2000 it hit a peak of 5,048.62. That same month Cisco, the manufacturer of so much internet-related technology, briefly became the most valuable company in the world, with a $500 billion market capitalization. Such technology-driven euphoria had not been seen since the railroad boom of the 1840s or the automobile boom of the 1920s.

Accompanying the globalization boom was regulatory change. The walls erected to separate spheres of banking started to crumble. J.P. Morgan's Dennis Weatherstone had been a leading advocate of the loosening. In 1989, he had persuaded the US government to let J.P. Morgan enter bond underwriting, one of the mainstays of investment banking, and one year later the bank was allowed to begin underwriting equities too. Pressure built for other banks to break through these barriers, and a wave of consolidation in the banking world was unleashed both in the US and Europe. The freewheeling financier Sandy Weill embarked on a bold plan to merge Citibank with financial services powerhouse Travelers Group, which had previously bought the hard-charging brokerage Salomon Brothers, to create a financial behemoth called Citigroup. The brokerage Morgan Stanley acquired Dean Witter, creating a merged retail and institutional securities giant. By the late 1990s, the last remaining pieces of the Glass-Steagall Act looked like quaint relics, and Wall Street successfully lobbied for their final demise. On 12 November 1999, President Bill Clinton signed a bill repealing the last of the Depression-era rules.

The repeal of Glass-Steagall legitimized the concept of combining commercial and investment banking to construct 'one-stop shopping' empires, and many more mergers quickly followed. Not just across different sectors of finance but across national borders too. The formerly stodgy German commercial lender Deutsche Bank announced that it was purchasing the freewheeling Bankers Trust. Deutsche Bank also hired a large chunk of Merrill Lynch's former trading group, tasking them with creating a derivatives business. Credit Suisse, the once-dull Swiss group, grabbed DLJ, another American broker. The industry was rapidly adjusting to a new reality that banks needed to be big, and offer a full range of services, in order to compete at all.

As institutions merged, financial activity broke through long-standing barriers. The art of trading corporate bonds had always been siloed off from the business of extending loans and under-writing equities. Now investors began hopping across asset classes, not to mention national borders, with abandon. Aggressive and high-risk hedge funds exploded on to the scene, some growing so large that they were competing in earnest with the new banking behemoths. The financial world was becoming 'flat', morphing into one seething, interlinked arena for increasingly free and fierce competition.

Those playing in this twenty-first-century domain of unfet-tered cyberfinance knew these changes carried risks. The fate of the hedge fund maverick Long Term Capital Management was a deeply troubling cautionary tale. LTCM, which had been created in 1994, epitomized the new era of finance. It was run by a group of academics and traders who ardently believed in libertarian eco-nomics, and who were dedicated to the cause of using computing power and mathematical skills to hunt for trading opportunities all over the world. Robert Merton, a Nobel laureate and one of the partners in LTCM, was a friend of Peter Hancock, and he – like the J.P. Morgan team – passionately believed in the liberating power of derivatives. LTCM grew to a staggering size and earned astonishing returns by using computing power to make big-ticket bets on spreads in the pricing of assets in all corners of the global markets. But the fund spectacularly imploded when the global markets experienced an intense panic following a financial crisis in Russia in 1998. Ironically, a key reason for this panic was that computer models had made markets and investors so closely integrated that they were behaving in a manner not factored into the hedge fund's models. The saga was a stark reminder that innovation can swing both ways.

But as spectacular as LCTM's collapse was, it put no brakes on the push for innovation. In 1999, the year after LTCM imploded, Gerald Corrigan, the former New York Fed governor, organized a group of senior Wall Street and European bankers to write a report on the lessons from the debacle. They concluded that banks needed to overhaul their dealings with hedge funds, keep much better control of their financial risks, report any large or concentrated exposure to clients and pay more attention to the dangers posed by excessive leverage and debt. The study did not, however, suggest that the *government* should step in to curb or control the flurry of innovation and competition. Sentiment was still moving in entirely the opposite direction.

Fed Chairman Alan Greenspan had long been a champion of free-market principles, and by 1999 he was a leading voice against regulation of the credit derivatives world. 'By far the most significant event in finance during the past decade has been the extraordinary development and expansion of financial derivatives,' Greenspan declared in a speech in March 1999. He was speaking at a banking conference held at Boca Raton, ironically – and perhaps appropriately – the same hotel where the J.P. Morgan bankers had concocted the idea of making credit derivatives a viable business. 'The fact that the OTC markets function quite effectively without the benefits of [CFTC regulation] provides a strong argument for development of a less burdensome regime for exchange-traded financial derivatives [than exists under the CFTC],' Greenspan continued.

These new financial instruments . . . enhance the ability to differentiate risk and allocate it to those investors most able and willing to take it. This unbundling improves the ability of the market to engender a set of product and asset prices far more calibrated to the value preferences of consumers . . . and enable entrepreneurs to finely allocate real capital facilities to produce those goods and services most valued by consumers, a process that has undoubtedly improved national productivity growth and standards of living.

What that piece of central banking jargon essentially meant was that Greenspan believed derivatives were making markets more efficient.

In the late 1990s officials at the Commodities Futures Trading Commission once again suggested that it might be a good idea for that body to exert its authority over the credit derivatives world. The idea was again quashed. In 2000, Washington lawmakers approved the Commodities Futures Modernization Act, which specifically stressed that 'swaps' were *not* futures or securities, and thus could not be controlled by the CFTC or SEC, or any other single regulator. 'Congress nailed the door shut in 2000 [on unified regulation], with the passage of the Commodities Futures Modernization Act,' observed ISDA lobbyist Mark Brickell. The derivatives sector was jubilant.

Those were heady days in the banking world at large, but at J.P. Morgan, business had started lagging. The swaps group was booming, but other parts of the bank had failed to keep up with the ever more muscular competition. In the spring of 2000 the bank staged a meeting for all its managing directors in the Sheraton Hotel, just off New York's Times Square. The meeting was billed as a chance for the senior and middle management to discuss the bank's strategy for the future. Holding forums to ventilate issues was another tradition the bank prided itself on. At

the start of the meeting the crowd was asked to vote anony-
mously, using hand-held electronic devices – a nod to the
computing revolution – on whether the bank was heading in the
right direction. The results from the cyber poll were grim: the
vast majority were *not* happy with how the bank was doing, and
were unclear about what the future strategy was.

As the pace of change had heated up in the recent past in the
financial system generally, the senior managers at J.P. Morgan
had found themselves dogged by a terrible, and bitter, irony. In
some respects, the bank's managers were thrilled by the wider
revolution afoot in the financial world. Hancock and his acolytes
had harnessed the power of computing to create their derivatives
innovations. The bank had also lobbied for years to repeal the
hated Glass-Steagall Act. But now J.P. Morgan was becoming as
much a victim as a beneficiary of these changes. During the late
1990s the internet boom delivered a stunning stream of revenues
for Merrill Lynch, Morgan Stanley, Citigroup, Chase Manhattan
and other banks able to arrange initial public offerings for dot-
com start-ups, or to trade shares. J.P. Morgan, though, had
missed out on much of that bonanza. It was weak in the area of
equity market underwriting, and it had not thrown itself into
financing risky start-ups, sticking with its tradition of providing
funding to established blue-chip groups. In 1998, in a token
effort to show it too was 'cool' and could play the IT game, the
management established a project dubbed 'lab Morgan', overseen by Nick Rohatyn, a rising J.P. Morgan banker (and the son
of Felix Rohatyn, a prominent Wall Street financier). Housed in
a loft-like office at the group's headquarters on 60 Wall Street,
with exposed brick walls and pipework, it was the bank's attempt
to show it could be hip and play in the world of cyberfinance.
Investors were unimpressed.

J.P. Morgan had also become dangerously small, beside the
new breed of behemoths. By late 1999, Citigroup wielded $716
billion of assets. J.P. Morgan, with $260 billion, was a third of the

size. Douglas 'Sandy' Warner, the new CEO, airily brushed aside comparisons. 'I don't think bigness is a strategy [for Morgan]. There needs to be a certain scale. Beyond that, the advantages are less compelling and can even be diminishing,' he had declared at the bank's annual meeting the year Weill announced his Citigroup merger plans. Instead of aiming for size, J.P. Morgan management stated, it would focus on profitable, 'smart', niches. That strategy had its own rewards. During the 1980s and early 1990s, Dennis Weatherstone had battled to reshape the bank's business away from commercial lending to investment banking, and by 1999 that had been implemented to an impressive degree. The so-called 'non-interest income' part of the bank's business, meaning activities outside lending, produced four-fifths of its revenues, considerably more than at any other large American commercial bank. More striking still, the bank was starting to feature in industry league tables tracking the investment banking world. It tended to rank around number six in terms of merger and acquisitions business; in American bond underwriting, it was in the top three, and in derivatives, usually at or near the top.

However, J.P. Morgan's problem was that the world around it was moving faster. As the *Wall Street Journal* had observed in 1998, 'From a standing start in 1980, Morgan is now on the cusp of the "bulge bracket" of the world's six top investment banks . . . increasingly, however, the biggest profits aren't going to a bulge bracket of six banks but to a "superbulge" of three firms – Merrill Lynch, Morgan Stanley Dean Witter and Goldman Sachs.' Worse, the type of investment banking business that J.P. Morgan was focusing on, with its heavy emphasis on derivatives, wasn't yielding the staggering profits being made from the internet boom.

Between 1997 and 1999, the level of return on equity at J.P. Morgan rose from 13 to 17 per cent, which should have been impressive. But that looked feeble compared to most of its peers. In 1999, the median ROE for the top 100 banks was 18 per cent, and Bank of New York had an ROE of 34 per cent, while Chase Manhattan, Merrill Lynch and Goldman Sachs all produced figures well over 20 per cent. Investors took note. Between the start of 1997 and early 2000, the share price of Merrill Lynch and Citigroup roughly trebled. J.P. Morgan's share price didn't even double. 'There just isn't any sense that the management knows what it is doing any more,' one managing director reflected, as she sat in the Sheraton conference room.

After the results of the poll were displayed, Peter Hancock leapt on to the stage. As CFO, it was his job to explain the management strategy, and with his trademark intensity, he attempted to reassure the audience. Outside the halls of J.P. Morgan speculation was rife that the bank would soon be forced into a merger, as so many of its rivals had been. The J.P. Morgan management was strongly resisting, and Hancock sketched out its alternative vision for revitalizing the bank, maintaining its hallowed role as an independent player. Morgan would continue to harness the power of financial innovation, such as derivatives, to make itself into a sharp, focused investment bank that could continually serve its clients with new products.

His listeners were unmoved. At the end of the meeting, another electronic vote was conducted, and the proportion in the crowd who believed in the bank's strategy had not risen at all. Most of the staff – the junior staff at least – shared Hancock's belief in the power of financial innovation. But they also knew that the rest of Wall Street was making much higher returns from the internet and financial merger boom than J.P. Morgan was producing with derivatives, and the senior managers came across as increasingly out of touch.

Privately, Hancock shared the frustration. By 2000, he had concluded that the only way the bank could really keep up with the competition was to take truly radical action. He thought that its strategy should be to focus extremely aggressively on a few, dedicated niches, such as derivatives, rather than conducting mergers in order to compete in the 'one-stop shopping' game. The future for J.P. Morgan, he believed, lay in being a boutique. But his was a minority view and it led him into conflict with others in the core management team, affectionately known within the bank as the 'House Arrest Group', so called because CEO Sandy Warner was ardent about mandatory attendance at the group's monthly gatherings.

All through 1999 and 2000, the 'HAG', as it was known, heatedly debated what course the bank should take. Members were split between sitting tight or pursuing a merger. By early summer, discussions were so intense that gossip was swirling around the bank that Warner had fallen out with Hancock. Some rumours even suggested that Hancock was about to launch a palace coup, but Hancock denied that.

Then abruptly, in the summer of 2000, Hancock resigned. The details of his leaving were murky. What was crystal-clear, though, was that he was bitterly disappointed by the management's indecision. And, after devoting the two decades of his career to the derivatives dream and the cause of J.P. Morgan, he was heartbroken by the bank's relative decline.

The bank tried to keep his departure secret, hoping to quell mounting speculation about J.P. Morgan's fate. For a while, Hancock simply disappeared from view, working out his notice largely from home. Meanwhile, behind the scenes, Sandy Warner opened merger discussions with Goldman Sachs. The bank had already held highly secretive talks with Goldman a few years earlier, as well as informal discussions with Citibank, Deutsche Bank, Chase Manhattan, Morgan Stanley and others. None of those prior overtures had come to anything because of the senior management's reluctance to lose their independence. After floating a merger deal by Warner, Sandy Weill of Citibank joked that the discussions made him 'think of yogurt' because the J.P. Morgan officials were so obsessed with their 'culture'. The 2000 talks with Goldman Sachs were no more fruitful;

Goldman was beset by its own internal disputes about strategy. Officials were also appalled by the price J.P. Morgan claimed it was worth. 'There was still this incredible arrogance and elitism at Morgan,' one of the parties later recalled.

The HAG committee slumped back into indecision. Then, in mid-August, when Warner was on vacation with his family in northern Michigan, he received a call from William Harrison, CEO of Chase Manhattan. Chase Manhattan was large, and had a long history on the American financial scene. On paper, the two institutions had complementary strengths. J.P. Morgan had a blue-chip client list and derivatives expertise; Chase Manhattan had a mass-market customer base and was highly skilled at cutting deals. Chase was also formidable in some derivatives spheres. Combining those strengths would create an investment banking giant. Based on their 1999 results, the combined balance sheets had $660 billion assets and more than $36 billion stockholder equity. In asset terms, that was playing near the same ballpark as the behemoth Citigroup.

The two banks, however, were very different animals. Chase Manhattan had emerged from a motley collection of banks bashed together in a series of mergers. The oldest piece of this contraption was the Bank of Manhattan Company, established in 1799, which began life as a water-carrier serving New York, and later branched into finance. In 1955, Bank of Manhattan purchased Chase, to form Chase Manhattan, and that entity emerged as a prestigious player in the 1970s and 1980s, under the leadership of David Rockefeller, scion of the banking family. But after it was weakened by real estate losses it was purchased by Chemical Bank in 1996. The combined entity then bought Hambrecht & Quist in 1999, a San Francisco-based specialist in high-tech finance. That turbulent corporate history left the bank without a strong identity or cohesive culture. To compensate, the bank was run along highly bureaucratic lines, but intense infighting had created a dog-eat-dog environment. That was the antithesis of J.P. Morgan, where most of its staff had spent their entire careers immersed in the inward-looking Morgan culture. As Clayton Rose, one of the senior J.P. Morgan bankers, observed in the late 1990s, 'When I joined this firm, you could shoot a gun and not hit a single mid-career hire.'

The cultural differences had led to widely divergent strategic imperatives. J.P. Morgan had been emphasizing the shedding of risk, using derivatives to remove a massive volume of it from the bank's books, diversifying its exposures, and freeing up capital resources. Doing so had taken years and cost the bank a fair share of profits, since J.P. Morgan sometimes had to pay more in fees to those who assumed that risk than it made back from the savings in capital requirements. Meanwhile Chase had spent the 1990s moving in precisely the *opposite* direction, taking on more and more concentrated risk to boost its profits. Most notably, from the mid-1990s onwards the company had rushed to offer funding to a host of dot-com companies, as well as to established groups that were perceived to be 'innovative'. WorldCom was a key client. So was Enron.

Chase had made a merger overture to the J.P. Morgan leadership three years earlier, but had been rebuffed. By the summer of 2000, though, the tables had turned. Chase's earnings from its internet investments and financing of a swathe of fast-growing companies in the telecommunications and energy spheres had generated such a stream of profits that its share price had surged, even as J.P. Morgan had underperformed. Harrison, the CEO of Chase, was a courtly Southerner and former commercial lender, who had no pretensions to being a brilliant Wall Street intellect, but he was tenacious. At six foot four, he was a former basketball star, who had played for the University of North Carolina Tar Heels, where he had earned a reputation for dogged determination. By 2000, Harrison had conducted multiple bank mergers, and he knew he was in the driver's seat.

On 13 September Chase Manhattan announced plans to purchase J.P. Morgan for an amount in shares that was worth slightly more than $30 billion, one of the largest deals ever recorded in the financial world. At a bound, J.P. Morgan had joined the great consolidation game.

The deal was presented to the outside world as a 'merger', for tax reasons as much as from any desire to preserve J.P. Morgan's dignity. In deference to the 'merger' label, Harrison and Warner were named co-heads of the bank, and representatives from each side were appointed as joint leaders of almost every department. It was dubbed the 'Noah's ark' strategy inside the bank, because leadership was going to be 'two by two'. It became clear at once that the label was a fiction: in every sense, Harrison – and Chase – had the upper hand. Or as *The Economist* observed:

> HOW are the mighty fallen! J.P. Morgan, once the dominant financial power in America, and arguably the world, swallowed up by Chase Manhattan, a big, old – but not terribly distinguished – rival. Even five years ago, that J.P. Morgan's blue-blooded bank should taint its aristocratic culture by merging with any other institution would have seemed inconceivable. But such has been the pace of change in global finance that nothing seems unthinkable anymore.

The branding of the new bank was humiliating to the J.P. Morgan staff. The bank had taken enormous pride in sporting the name of its founder, J. Pierpont Morgan, and insisted on using periods to separate the 'j' and 'p', to signify that the name referred to a legendary man. The new bank, though, was called 'JPMorgan Chase' (but the investment bank division was later named J.P. Morgan). The bank adopted the Chase logo, an octagon that harked back to the wooden planks nailed to together to create water pipes by the old Manhattan water group. The

J.P. Morgan team considered that logo – and its associations with
the lowly water business – unbearably tacky.

As they reeled in shock, Hancock's former acolytes tried to work
out what the merger meant for their derivatives dreams. On
paper, most of them seemed well placed to flourish. Mindful of
the need to hang on to J.P. Morgan's derivatives skills, Harrison
had agreed to put the innovation stars into seemingly plum positions. Demchak was named a co-head of credit; Masters was a
co-head of asset-backed securities; Feldstein head of the global
credit portfolio. In London, Bill Winters was named co-head of
fixed income and Tim Frost was appointed co-head of European
credit. Technically, that gave them all positions as good as in the
old J.P. Morgan bank, but now in a firm that was a true powerhouse.

These developments might have been appealing. Chase
Manhattan had always had a formidable sales force, covering
numerous corners of the financial world that J.P. Morgan had
never managed to reach. It also had its own pool of creative financiers, including some in the CDO world. And, of course, the
combined bank now had the advantage of vast size. The combined banks were estimated to control about half of the market
for interest-rate swaps, a potentially formidable platform. Indeed,
in early 2001, a few months after the merger was completed, the
bank was named 'Derivatives House of the Year.'

Yet, as the J.P. Morgan swaps crew tried to adjust to the Chase
influence, it was impossible to recapture the thrill of their early
achievements. The fraternal spirit had dissipated, as had the fun,
in the new dog-eat-dog atmosphere. Chase also had a different
approach altogether to managing risk. The senior managers at
Chase had always been wary of derivatives risk, but they had
never tried to shed credit risk on any large scale, or worried
about excessive concentrations of credit risk. On the contrary, to
boost its profits the bank had heavily weighted its loan book to

fast-growing sectors, such as the internet, with few controls.

From his perch as the new co-head of global credit, Demchak tried to convince the Chase side of the value of shedding risk, as his team had so successfully managed for J.P. Morgan. So did Feldstein. When they got a look at the Chase Manhattan portfolio, they became adamant. They were shocked by the concentrations of risk and he asked for the power to radically remodel the loan portfolio. The former Chase officials dragged their feet. Those concentrated credit risks had earned the bank extremely fat profits in the internet boom, and the bank's share price had soared, enabling it to purchase J.P. Morgan. The Chase officials saw no reason to copy a strategy J.P. Morgan had ridden with such a notable lack of commercial success.

To Demchak the business of remodelling the loan book was not just a good idea, it was an article of faith. He found the stance of the Chase bankers utterly infuriating, and he didn't bother to conceal his disdain. 'I can't believe they're running the bank like this!' he would wail to his colleagues, as his battle grew more and more intense. His mission seemed hopeless until a dramatic turn of events intervened.

On 2 December 2001, the American energy group Enron filed for bankruptcy. The news stunned the markets and the corporate world. Enron had been a poster child for innovation and free-market competition. It employed 22,000, reported revenues of $101 billion in 2000, and had been named as 'America's most innovative company' by *Fortune* magazine for six years in a row. However, in the autumn of 2001 it emerged that those stunning profits had been a mirage: the company had used creative accounting tricks to inflate its results, seemingly with the knowledge of its banks and accountants. When those schemes came to light, confidence in Enron collapsed, and the company filed for what was then the largest bankruptcy in American corporate history.

The news delivered a shocking blow to JPMorgan Chase. During the 1990s, Chase had developed a tight relationship with Enron. It had lent the company vast sums, underwritten its bonds and created a series of structured financial products and schemes in collaboration with the company, including some of those with which Enron had inflated its results. Just two months before Enron's implosion, co-CEO Harrison went out of his way to tell bankers and journalists in the City of London just how 'proud' he felt that Enron was a key client. Now Harrison found himself vehemently denying that the bank had engaged in any wrongdoing. 'I believe we handled everything with integrity, but we had too much exposure,' he told employees in a speech broadcast over the company's internal voicemail system in early 2002.

The bank's losses from Enron's failure were put at first at $900 million, but that number doubled as the scale of the damage emerged.

Irrespective of Harrison's denials, it swiftly became clear that former Chase employees had not only created some of the controversial Enron schemes, but had done so knowing that they were distorting the energy giant's balance sheet. A structure known as 'Mahonia' was a case in point. In 1995 Chase created an off-balance-sheet vehicle bearing that name as a tool to channel funds to Enron, and the bank subsequently used it to conceal up to $8.5 billion of debt in its accounts. Technically, the Mahonia structure was legal. 'We did it according to accounting conventions and rules. It was transparent. It was on our balance sheet, and to our best knowledge, it was on Enron's balance sheet,' Harrison explained. However, US lawmakers dubbed Mahonia one of a collection of 'shame trades', and railed against both Enron and its two main banks, JPMorgan Chase and Citigroup. When it emerged that these two banks had earned around $200 million in fees creating such structures, the anger flared.

Then even worse carnage struck. In the second half of 2000, the internet bubble started to burst. After reaching 5000 in March 2000, the NASDAQ quickly plummeted to 3000, and a vast swathe of dot-coms went bust. In January 2001, the fibre-optics network operator Global Crossing, a client of Chase Manhattan, filed for bankruptcy protection, with debts of $12.4 billion. In July 2002 the telecom giant WorldCom imploded under $32 billion of debt. JPMorgan Chase had underwritten bonds for WorldCom and took another big hit. What was worse, by mid-2002 lawsuits in relation to WorldCom, Enron and Global Crossing were flooding into the bank. Unsurprisingly, its share price slumped to less than half the level when the merger was struck. 'It's unnerving how the bad news keeps piling up at J.P. Morgan,' observed *Business Week*. Or as the *Evening Standard* tartly declared: 'Name a scandal-plagued US company in the headlines and one bank keeps showing up behind the scenes: JPMorgan Chase.'

Demchak, Feldstein and the other so-called 'Heritage Morgan' bankers – as they had come to be called – were furious at the scale of mismanagement. Time and again, Demchak had warned of the need to diversify the risk from Chase loans, and that advice had been roundly rejected. He could take scant comfort now in knowing he had been proven right.

Demchak and his former J.P. Morgan colleagues mused about the bitter irony of it all. If they had just managed to stay independent for a few more months the share price would have crashed. Events would have turned out quite differently. They felt as if the fates were laughing at them. But even as they reeled from the carnage, the innovation cycle was about to heat up again. With the wonders of dot-coms soundly repudiated, attention would turn anew to the marvellous potential of credit derivatives and other forms of financial innovation.

*

On 3 January 2001, the US Federal Reserve suddenly announced a 50 basis point cut in interest rates, reducing them to 6 per cent. That news stunned the markets almost as much as the internet collapse. In the preceding eight years, Alan Greenspan had made a virtue out of running monetary policy in a calm, controlled manner, lowering rates steadily but slowly at just 25 basis points a shot. This gradualist approach was said to mitigate volatility.

Greenspan was convinced, though, that the collapse of the internet bubble required a forceful response. Back in late 1989 and 1990, when the US economy had suffered a similar downturn, he had stuck to measured, slow rate cuts, and they had turned out to be too little, too late. The economy had sunk into a recession. He intended to avoid that mistake this time around.

A few weeks after that first dramatic rate cut, Greenspan reduced rates again, and in the following months he kept steadily cutting. When the attack on the World Trade Center sent the markets into a tailspin, he cut rates even further. By 2003, the prime rate was just 1 per cent, its lowest for many decades.

The policy worked, and worries of a recession abated. Though the crash had wiped out $5 trillion in the market value of technology companies between March 2000 and October 2002, by 2003 the mainstream economy was rebounding. In stark contrast to the bursting of the Savings and Loans bubble, no European or American institution actually collapsed from its losses. Greenspan and other policymakers partly attributed that to the fact that so many banks were using credit derivatives to spread their risk around. Unsurprisingly, the J.P. Morgan bankers agreed. 'Credit derivatives are a mechanism for transferring risk efficiently around the system,' Tim Frost cheerfully told journalists, noting that defaulted loans that would have knocked a hole in a bank's balance sheet ten years ago were 'now hits that we have spread around the system, and represent tiny blips on the balance sheets of hundreds of financial institutions'.

Indeed, as bankers and investors processed the lessons from the internet crash, credit derivatives began to look more and more appealing. So, just as bankers in the early 1990s had responded to falling interest rates by producing more complex and leveraged derivatives products, they now began searching for a new round of more complex credit ideas.

Investor attention was also drawn to another sector. The real estate world – unlike the corporate sector – was relatively unscathed by the internet bust. On the contrary, the low interest rates Greenspan had instituted had given the housing market quite a boost, as mortgages became less and less expensive. Unbeknown to the J.P. Morgan bankers, and against their better judgement, these two booming businesses of mortgages and derivatives were about to become fatefully intertwined.

PART TWO

Perversion

CHAPTER SIX

Innovation Unleashed

The onset of the new decade unleashed a new era of credit. Alan Greenspan's lowering of interest rates prompted an explosion of borrowing, by both businesses and consumers. The boom was particularly pronounced in the housing market, as mortgages became ever more affordable. Even as the stock market tumbled, the credit market had kicked into overdrive, and it was becoming clear that the new action in investing was on the credit side of the business, *not* in equities.

In the early years of the decade, many banks threw themselves more aggressively into the credit derivatives business, which translated into greatly increased competition for the JPMorgan Chase team. It also opened up tantalizing opportunities for other employment even as the frustrations of the merger grew more dispiriting. The bank remained plagued by its Noah's ark bureaucracy and vicious internal fights. Moreover, so many bad loans made to internet companies were plaguing the bank's balance sheet that Demchak and his group could clearly see the bank was heading for a grim few years in which profits would be squeezed as political scandals mounted. 'This is just no fun any more,' Demchak remarked regularly to his colleagues.

Despite all the larger bank's setbacks, though, and the growing frustrations, the team continued to rack up strong profits. In the middle of 2001, Demchak was told that he would be promoted. In addition to running global credit, he was told he would be given responsibility for derivatives and the commodities section, making him one of the most senior investment bankers in New York. But to the shock of his team, the very day after he was offered his new job, he tendered his resignation. 'I just cannot do this any more!' he declared. When the team heard the news, some of them cried, not only because Demchak was leaving, but because they knew his departure also spelled the end of their remarkable run together. The team would never be the same without him.

Demchak was immediately approached by rival banks who were building their derivatives groups. Goldman Sachs was particularly persistent. But Demchak felt too exhausted and disenchanted to move right away to another bank. He also had no burning *need* to work; the value of stock held by managers of the J.P. Morgan side of the bank had surged with the merger. So for a while Demchak dreamed of dropping out of finance to fulfil a long-standing desire to train as a boat builder. He travelled to the coast of Maine, finding it therapeutic to work with wood and traditional tools, and to hang out with craftsmen who knew nothing about credit derivatives and cared less. In time, he persuaded some of them to decamp from Maine to the Hamptons, where Demchak had a house.

In due course, Demchak toyed with the idea of joining a hedge fund or a private equity group, but he decided he simply didn't want to spend so much of his time staring at a computer screen again. Eventually, in 2002, he accepted an offer from PNC, the Pittsburgh-based lender, becoming vice chairman. Far from the glamour of Wall Street and the esoteric world of high finance, PNC afforded Demchak the chance to return to his Pittsburgh roots.

The offer was also alluring because the bank was badly in need of Demchak's particular skills in managing risk. When the internet bubble burst, PNC had almost imploded from losses, and it desperately needed to remodel its balance sheet and credit portfolio to reduce its risk burden. That was music to Demchak's ears. PNC's balance sheet was tiny compared to J.P. Morgan's, but it was large enough to offer plenty of challenge, and Demchak was being given the chance to apply all his theories about credit management just as he saw fit, with no internal bureaucratic fighting required. Managers at the Pittsburgh bank were hungry for his ideas on loan portfolio management, and Demchak was keen to get it right, third time round. The bruising fights from earlier years had taught him some painful lessons. By 2002 he was wiser when dealing with critics, and less ideological in propounding his views. The former Prince of Darkness had matured. Better still, he was able to take a number of his beloved team with him. Krishna Varikooty, for one, was keen to follow him. Back at JPMorgan Chase, once Demchak had decamped, the rest of his team quickly followed suit. Like pollen seeds, the former team scattered across the financial world, implanting their ideas into dozens of firms. Terri Duhon was lured away to ABN AMRO; while Betsy Gile, the credit manager, joined Deutsche Bank, where she helped to remodel the German bank's credit portfolio. Romita Shetty, the Indian banker, went first to Royal Bank of Scotland and then to Lehman Brothers.

A number of the team either started or joined investment funds. Andrew Feldstein left to launch a hedge fund. Over in London, Tim Frost became a partner in the investment fund Cairn Capital. Jonathan Laredo, a credit analyst in London, joined another fund, called Solent, and Charles Pardue created Prytania, a consultancy and fund.

Hedge funds hadn't played much in the credit sphere before, but the credit derivatives explosion was creating a host of new trading opportunities that they began to find attractive. 'The good thing about the credit markets at the moment is that they are liquid enough to trade, but not so evolved that there are no [price] inefficiencies,' Feldstein observed after setting up his fund. Hedge funds thrive on exploiting such discrepancies in the market's pricing of assets.

A subtle geographic shift was under way as well. Back in the 1980s, when the swaps business had first boomed, London had played a central role in that market. Subsequently, though, the New York markets had risen in visibility, not just in relation to the credit derivatives team at J.P. Morgan, but more widely too. But around the turn of the century, London's derivatives market started to gain in prominence again in a whole realm of sectors, including credit derivatives.

That partly reflected the fact that London offered a very welcoming regulatory environment. When the Labour government of Tony Blair came into power in the late 1990s it made clear that it endorsed a so-called light-touch regulatory regime, which aimed to boost the standing of the City. That encouraged innovation, in derivatives, hedge funds and much else. The launch of the euro also spurred creative thought. During the 1970s and 1980s Europe lagged well behind America in terms of the size and sophistication of its overall capital markets, because European companies had traditionally relied on bank loans, not corporate bonds, to raise funds. However, by the late 1990s the launch of the single currency prompted European companies and investors to rethink the way that finance was done. As they embraced capital markets ideas, many investors and issuers moved straight to using derivatives, rather than cash-based instruments such as bonds. It was a 'leap-frogging' pattern, comparable to what happens when developing nations discover telephones and move straight to using mobile phones rather than messing around with landlines. Moreover, many European investors also liked derivatives because they were flexible enough to be adapted to multiple different legal and tax regimes. 'There was a greater need for the derivatives market in London [by the late 1990s].' Frost explained to a British reporter a couple of years after leaving J.P. Morgan. 'London needed the development of derivatives to develop a tradable debt securities market . . . It's a great British success story. London is the centre of innovation. Some of the most talented people in the world wash up here and add value to this new fast-growing market.'

During his time at J.P. Morgan, Frost himself had paid a key role in bringing that about, by tirelessly championing the market with his formidable skills as a salesman. By the time he moved to Cairn in 2004, though, Frost believed that some of the creative energy was seeping away from the banks. 'The torch of innovation is being passed from the banks to the funds,' he told an ISDA conference. Mayfair, Knightsbridge and St James's were full of new funds, many of which were trying to dance in the new credit arena. And while funds were also springing up in New York and Connecticut, it was London where the evolution – and mutation – appeared to be most densely concentrated. 'The legal and shareholder framework in the major banks is now less conducive to innovation and risk-taking. That kind of environment is conducive to setting up your own firm and then taking risks,' Frost observed. 'It's conducive to risk-taking being done in St James's and Mayfair and Knightsbridge rather than in the City or Canary Wharf [where banks are based].'

Those members of the old team who stayed at the bank maintained a brave face. One of the loyalists was Blythe Masters, who was given control of credit policy after Demchak left. Another was Bill Winters, who continued quietly to run his trading empire in London. Tony Best and Jakob Stott, two former swaps traders who were allies of Winters, also stayed on. They tried to shrug off the exodus, denying that the bank was losing steam.

'We can promote outstanding people quickly here. That is what supports the business when people decide to leave – these very smart young people coming through,' Best observed. But there was no denying that as the brain drain accelerated, morale sagged. Making matters worse, competition had turned so fierce that J.P. Morgan was no longer the undisputed king of the credit derivatives market.

Innovation was on fire around the financial world. 'While JPMorgan has [been dealing] with these departures, the wider structured credit market has positively thrived as a result,' specialist financial magazine *Euroweek* reported. 'It is unlikely that the sector would have grown at such a pace had it not been for the sheer number of ex-Morgan market participants that are now employed elsewhere.'

Goldman Sachs was quick out of the gate in developing a formidable credit derivatives business, and other leading brokerages, such as Morgan Stanley and Lehman Brothers, also joined the game with gusto. Most startling of all, jumping into the credit game was Deutsche Bank, which burst on to the scene from a standing start.

Traditionally, Deutsche was a large, stodgy commercial bank. But in the mid-1990s it formulated ambitious plans for becoming a major player in the international investment banking world. It hired teams of derivatives and bond traders from Merrill Lynch, acquired the operations of Bankers Trust, which had been at the forefront of derivatives innovation in the 1980s and early 1990s, and set out to build a pre-eminent platform in financial engineering in both New York and London. Derivatives were a prime focus. While the American bond and equity markets were so dominated by giant Wall Street banks that Deutsche would have had trouble breaking into that turf, the derivatives business was so new that it offered plenty of opportunity for outsiders. Deutsche's derivatives team hired many smart traders from other banks, including several from the

J.P. Morgan team. Marcus Schüler, a highly visible salesman who had worked with Tim Frost in London, and Demchak acolyte Betsy Gile, both moved to Deutsche. The bank then invested impressive resources to grab a big position in the commoditized business of CDS trading. It paid off quickly.

In 2003, *Risk* magazine designated Deutsche Bank the 'Derivatives House of the Year,' knocking J.P. Morgan from that perch. Some Morgan staff started referring to Deutsche Bank as 'enemy number one.'

Lehman Brothers, Citigroup, Bear Stearns, Credit Suisse, UBS and Royal Bank of Scotland all also fiercely ratcheted up their derivatives operations. Not only was the competition demanding that they become more aggressive, but low yields on the more traditional credit investments were fuelling the drive for higher returns. Yields on ten-year government bonds had dropped from 6 per cent at the start of the decade to under 4 per cent by 2002. Thirty years earlier, American pension funds generally made easy money by investing in those bonds, which had paid yields of around 9 per cent a year, while the funds were expected to deliver returns of only around 4 to 5 per cent. Pension funds were now targeting higher returns even as the yield on bonds had fallen. Fund managers, and investors generally, were frantically looking for ways to boost profits, and that forced yet another turn of the innovation cycle. Banks devised a host of new tricks for offering investors better returns, which invariably revolved around creating products that employed more leverage, as well as more complexity and risk. The freewheeling experimentation centred on repackaging various credit into investment offerings, using either derivatives or bonds, or a combination of the two.

By early 2001, the first generation of Bistro deals had evolved into a class of standardized products widely referred to as 'synthetic collateralized debt obligations.' A particularly popular variation on the Bistro theme was known as 'single-tranche

CDOs'. These were essentially bundles of debt that were sold to a shell company, as with the Bistro scheme, but then the company offered only *one* class of notes as opposed to junior, mezzanine and senior. This meant that more of the risk of the loan bundles was retained on the shell company's books; not just the super-senior risk.

In 2002 and 2003, single-tranche CDOs became all the rage. But insatiable investors quickly began demanding even better ways to juice up returns, so the banks produced a new twist on the CDO idea called a 'CDO squared.' This was essentially a CDO of CDOs. In this scheme, rather than the shell company purchasing a bundle of loans, it would purchase pieces of debt issued by other CDOs and then issue new CDO notes. Typically, they would purchase only the riskiest notes from the *other* CDOs, because doing so allowed them to offer higher returns. Those investments were more dangerous for investors, but no matter, 'CDO squared' offerings became wildly popular. 'The product development now is incredibly fast,' observed Katrien van Acoleyen, an analyst from Standard and Poor's. 'People are trying to put all different types of underlying assets into these structures – asset-backed securities, emerging-market debt or mortgages . . . now there are even people talking about creating a CDO cubed (or a CDO of CDOs of CDOs).' The crucial goal of all this complexity was to create more leverage, and thus more potential return.

Around the turn of the century, Robert Reoch, one of the former J.P. Morgan derivatives bankers from Winter's team in London, was standing in the canteen at Bank of America, when he noticed a striking thing. A couple of years earlier, Reoch had joined Bank of America which, like many others, was eager to expand into the credit derivatives world. As Reoch stood in the lunch queue one day, while visiting the Chicago branch of the bank, he bumped into some bankers from the mortgage department. Until then, the two groups had had only limited contact at BoA or anywhere else. Derivatives traders viewed themselves as a different breed of financial animal to financiers working in the mortgage world, and vice versa. When Reoch exchanged pleasantries with his mortgage colleagues in the Bank of America canteen, though, he spotted that they were holding diagrams that looked akin to those he also used in relation to corporate credit derivatives. A 'bingo moment' took place, as he later observed. Both teams suddenly realized it made sense to collaborate with each other, since they were playing around with closely related concepts.

Similar intellectual collisions were quietly occurring all over the American financial world. Ever since the 1970s, bankers had used mortgages to create bonds or bundles of debt, later known as CDOs. By the dawn of the new decade, though, this activity became dramatically more intense, and mingled with other fields of finance, including credit derivatives.

The American housing market had benefited hugely from the low interest rates Alan Greenspan was holding to, and the rapidly mounting piles of mortgage loans were fertile fodder for the CDO machine. This was especially true because so many of the new mortgages were relatively high risk, which allowed the banks to offer extremely attractive returns.

During the 1990s, CDOs had been constructed only out of 'conforming' mortgages, meaning those that conformed to the high credit standards imposed by federal-backed housing giants Fannie Mae and Freddie Mac. That was in part because only a few lenders had been willing to extend mortgage loans to households that didn't comply with the Fannie and Freddie standards. In the late 1990s, though, a swathe of new mortgage lenders and brokers entered the mortgage field who specialized in offering 'non-conforming' mortgages, more commonly called 'subprime'. Loans were increasingly extended to borrowers with bad credit history. As more and more brokers jumped in, a free-for-all developed with the new players extending vast quantities of

loans, on whatever terms they wished, without much government oversight, let alone control. In 2000, the amount of
non-conforming mortgage bonds that were sold was tiny, running at a mere $80 billion, or less than a tenth of all mortgage
bonds. By 2005, sales of non-conforming mortgage bonds hit
$800 billion. Remarkably, that meant that almost half of all
mortgage-linked bonds in America that year were based on subprime loans.

Precisely because subprime loans were risky, the homeowners who took out such debt typically paid a higher rate of
interest than prime borrowers did, and that meant that the 'raw
material' of subprime loans produced higher-returning CDOs
than those built out of 'prime' mortgages. For returns-hungry
investors, subprime mortgage-based CDOs were gold dust.

The only real constraint on the business was the need for
lenders to find the cash to extend loans. In reality, though, that
had become hardly a constraint at all. Brokers and banks alike no
longer kept most of the mortgage loans they extended on their
books any longer than a few days, or even hours. Mortgage
lending had become an assembly-line affair in which loans were
made and then quickly reassembled into bonds immediately sold
to investors. A bank or brokerage's ability to extend a loan no
longer depended on how much capital that institution held; the
deciding factor was whether the loans could be sold on as bonds,
and the demand for those was rapacious. In this way, the lending
of the mortgages began to be driven by the demand of end-
investors, in what would prove to be a vicious cycle.

A fundamental danger of the mortgage CDO business was
that there was no good information on what might happen to
subprime mortgage defaults in a severe house price slump. As
Terri Duhon and Krishna Varikooty had discovered when they
tested the idea of bundling up mortgage loans to put into a
Bistro product, because the US hadn't experienced a nationwide
housing crash for seventy years, data on default patterns was

extremely scarce. Worse, it was virtually non-existent for the riskier subprime sector, because subprime mortgages represented such a small portion of the mortgage market before the turn of the century. While that information gap had worried the J.P. Morgan team enough back in 1999 to lead them to forgo Bistro deals with mortgage debt, by the middle of the new decade most bankers were willing to ignore the risks and sell these investments on a massive scale.

Banks repackaged mortgage-based bonds in ever more creative ways. The best known product was a CDO of asset-backed securities, or CDO of ABS. This was usually (but not always) filled with mortgage-linked bonds. In a sense, then, CDO of ABS were like CDOs *of* CDOs. They had an added layer of complexity to add more leverage. Within that field, another popular product was known as a 'mezzanine CDO of ABS,' which took pools of subprime mortgage loans and used them as the basis for issuing bonds carrying different degrees of risk. The bankers would then take just the risky bonds, say those rated BBB, *not* A or AAA, and create a new CDO composed entirely from those BBB bonds. That CDO would then issue more notes which were also ranked according to different levels of risk. The scheme looked fiendishly complex on paper, but it essentially involved bankers repeatedly skimming off the riskiest portions of bundles, mixing them with yet more risk, and then skimming it yet again – all in the hope of high returns.

The schemes became more creative still when banks started creating these products not out of actual bundles of mortgage loans, but out of derivatives made of mortgage loans. The idea was borrowed from the world of credit defaults swaps, and as with corporate-loan-based CDOs, these derivatives versions of CDOs enabled investors to place bets on whether mortgage bonds would default or not. These clever products were referred to as 'synthetic CDO of ABS.' They would lead to a frenzy of speculation, all based upon the fundamental premise that the default risk of bundles of mortgages had been virtually erased by the process of bundling and then slicing them into tranches. If banks chose to hold more and more of the risk in these tranches on their own books, selling only the more popular tranches of notes, such as mezzanine, that was no worry because the risk had been so effectively dispersed that the chance the banks would ever take a hit from it seemed so remote as to be unfathomable.

The banks also began to turn to inventive devices for moving those deals off their books. One of these was a type of quasi-shell company, known as a structured investment vehicle (SIV), for purchasing the loans and selling the bonds sliced and diced from them. This species had actually first emerged two decades earlier, when two bankers at Citibank, Stephen Partridge-Hicks and Nicholas Sossidis, hit on the idea as a way of getting around the Basel rules for capital requirements. SIVs were tied to banks, not completely separate as with the shell companies known as SPVs. The banks provided some of their funding, as opposed to all of that being raised by the shell company itself, through selling notes. But SIVs did partially fund themselves independently and they sat off the balance sheets of banks. They were thus a bit like the garage of a house: a useful place for banks to park assets they did not want inside their home banks. Another structure that fulfilled a similar function was a so-called bank conduit. This was similar to an SIV, but more closely linked to a bank.

The 'hybrid' status allowed the banks to evade the Basel rules which limited the amount of assets they could hold on their balance sheets, thereby freeing them to leverage their capital a good deal more. The key reason the banks were allowed to do so concerned the way in which SIVs raised the portion of their funding that didn't come from the banks, and this particular exploitation of Basel loopholes was to lead to terrible consequences once the credit bubble began to burst. The loophole was this: the Basel Accord stated that banks didn't need to hold capital resources for any credit lines that were less than a year in duration. So banks typically extended credit lines to SIVs and conduits that were 364 days or less. The banks did not reckon, though, that the SIVs and conduits would ever need to draw on these credit lines. In normal circumstances, they raised their funding in the short-term commercial paper market. In this market, the SIVs and conduits would sell notes that paid off in only a few months, somewhat like a credit derivative. Those buying the notes were, therefore, extending credit for many fewer days than a year. The cash they raised was used to purchase safe, long-term debt instruments, such as mortgage bonds. They made a tidy profit because their short-term borrowing costs were lower than the returns they made on the long-term bonds they bought. They were thus playing what's referred to as a 'carry trade', and while the profit margins on this bit of alchemy were small, the SIVs leveraged themselves so much – making substantial purchases of bonds vis-à-vis the amount of capital they had raised – that all in all they made quite a reasonable income. The strategy carried a key risk. Leverage not only magnifies gains, it also magnifies losses, and with such a constant need to replenish short-term funding, the SIVs and conduits were vulnerable to finding themselves cash poor. The danger was that if buyers of commercial paper – such as pension fund managers – ever stopped buying such notes, the SIVs and conduits would see their normal funding dry up. And the SIVs were usually required continuously to report the value of their assets at market prices – to mark-to-market. If those values ever dropped precipitously, commercial paper buyers might well decide to stay away. But the SIVs stuck to buying top-quality assets, only those carrying the triple-A tag from credit-ratings agencies, so the chances of that turn of events seemed vanishingly slim. Or so they assumed.

One of the truly staggering things about this boom in newfangled credit investment products was that very few non-bankers had any idea that institutions such as SIVs and CDOs even existed. Even regulators seemed only vaguely aware of what the banks were really doing. Yet SIVs were proliferating like mushrooms after a rainstorm. Some of that frenzy was occurring in New York and Connecticut. The main concentration of SIVs and other related vehicles, though, was found in London. In part, that was because a body of legal and financial expertise had grown up in the City to service these financial beasts and all the mutations they had spawned. The legal and regulatory framework was also very favourable since – in keeping with the 'light-touch' mantra that drove British regulatory policy – the UK government saw little reason to monitor what these entities were doing. They were rarely mentioned in any official reports produced by the Bank of England or Financial Services Authority, the entity that had inherited the main regulatory mantle. Nor were SIVs mentioned in the mainstream British press. The financiers had created a vast 'shadow banking' system that was out of the sight of almost everybody outside the specialist credit world.

Notwithstanding that lack of attention, the shadow banking world was frenetically active. In the 1980s and 1990s Europe had lagged well behind America in terms of its securitization sector. By the early years of the new decade, however, SIVs were exploding in size and European investors were gobbling up repackaged subprime mortgage debt at a voracious rate. Indeed, some American banks privately guessed that at least half of all subprime-linked CDOs were being sold not to Americans, but into Europe. Most of these sales were conducted via London trading desks. The investment culture in continental Europe left its asset managers predisposed to buy fixed-income assets. European banks also had an incentive to hold plenty of highly rated assets on their books since they were adopting the Basel II regulatory regime, which gave favourable treatment to highly rated assets, particularly those linked to mortgages. The Germans, and the other continental Europeans, 'were like the Japanese a decade earlier – the joke [on the trading desks] was that you could stuff them almost anything,' one American banker later recalled.

The frenzy was not limited to American debt: bankers were becoming increasingly creative about repackaging European debt too. Much of that activity revolved around British mortgages, where bankers essentially used the same techniques that they had developed for the subprime world and transposed them to the UK. Northern Rock was particularly active in terms of repackaging its mortgages. Spanish mortgages were also a hot favourite for CDOs. In addition, there was a voracious appetite for repackaged risky European corporate debt. Back in the 1990s almost all of Europe's leveraged loans (or those to companies with sub-investment-grade ratings) were held by banks; by the middle of the new decade half of these were being bought by funds, including CDOs, SIVs and a host of other shadowy entities.

As the pace of innovation heated up, credit products were spinning off into a multi-layered cyberworld that eventually even the financiers struggled to understand. These complex products could not be analyzed with just a pen and a piece of paper, or even a hand-held computer or two. The debt was being sliced and diced so many times that the risk could only be calculated with complex computer models. But most investors had no idea how the banks were crafting their models and didn't have the mathematical expertise to evaluate them anyway. Each player had its own twist on modelling, after all, and as Terri Duhon observed, 'Many different investment banks will provide significantly different prices on the same CDO tranche because they are using different models of correlation.'

Investors generally relied on the ratings agencies to guide them through this strange new land, which seemed a rational, easy solution to contending with the complexity. The ratings scale was so simple: if something was triple A it was supposed to default almost never; if it was triple B or triple C it had far more risk. In a world where so much else was baffling, those clear-cut designations were wonderfully comforting. Better still, they were backed up by massive research, which was a key element in the ratings agencies' sales pitch.

Like priests in the medieval church, ratings agency representatives spoke the equivalent of financial Latin, which few in their investor congregation actually understood. Nevertheless, the congregation was comforted by the fact that the priests appeared able to confer guidance and blessings. Such blessings, after all, made the whole system work: the AAA anointment enabled SIVs to raise funds, banks to extend loans, and investors to purchase complex instruments that paid great returns, all without anyone worrying too much.

Some bankers warned about the seduction. 'People who are focused on ratings alone are prime fodder for the investment banks to stuff [sell] things to,' argued Charles Pardue, a key player in the team that created Bistro. 'I don't think we should kid ourselves that everything being sold is fair value. I have been to dealer events where bankers are selling this stuff and the simplicity of the explanation about how it works scares me . . . there are people investing in stuff they don't understand, who really seem to believe the models, and when models change it will be a very scary thing.'

The ratings agencies, unsurprisingly, were adamant that such concerns were unfounded. Moody's, Standard & Poor's and Fitch had each invested heavily to develop cutting-edge systems for modelling the risks of the full range of new products. To allay fears that their calculations might be faulty, they had also tried to show investors exactly how these systems worked. 'We are very transparent in everything we do,' Paul Mazataud, a senior official in the structured finance team of Moody's, explained in an interview. Moody's even voluntarily posted details of its own model, called CDOROM, on the internet in 2004. 'Our model has become a bit like a template in the market,' Mazataud observed. 'Most CDOs are rated with this model and it is used by management in most synthetic transactions,' he continued, bursting with pride.

Yet such assurances failed to allay the unease of Pardue and others. Precisely because the agencies had diligently posted the details about how their models worked on the net, bankers found it easy to comb through the models looking for loopholes to exploit. And by 2005, they were doing quite a bit of that. Whenever a banker had an idea for a new innovation, it would be run through the agency models to see what rating the product was likely to earn. If it looked too low, or high, the design would be tweaked. The aim was to get as high a rating as possible, with the highest level of risk – so that the product could produce all-important higher investor returns. In banking circles, the game was known as 'ratings arbitrage'.

Officials at the ratings agencies knew perfectly well that this game was going on. But they felt in little position to fight back. Banks had far more resources than the agencies, so they could build better models and hire the smartest structured finance experts. The banks also held the whip hand in a commercial sense. While in the corporate bond world, the agencies rated the bonds of thousands of companies and were not dependent on any one company for fees, these credit products were being produced by a much smaller circle of banks. Those banks constantly threatened to boycott the agencies if they failed to produce the wished-for ratings, jeopardizing the sizeable fees the agencies earned from the banks for their services. From time to time, the ratings agencies took a stand, to show they couldn't always be pushed around, but they were careful not to offend the banks too deeply. When an agency gave a rating to a CDO, it sometimes commanded a fee of $100,000 per shot, or even several times that level. Moreover, the business was growing fast. So fast, in fact, that by 2005 Moody's was drawing almost half of its revenues from the structured finance sector; two decades before, that proportion had been modest.

The ratings that the agencies were issuing were subject to another pernicious problem. In trying to judge the risk of these products, the agencies faced the same vexing issue that had dogged the old J.P. Morgan Bistro team when it considered going into mortgage-based Bistro deals. How could default patterns be modelled? There was so little good data to work with. Was it safe to assume that defaults would play out in the future as they had in the past? Even if so, the historical data was so limited. The trickiest issue of all was working out the level of 'correlation' – figuring out how likely it was that one default would trigger others. Different modellers had alternative ways of dealing with the problem, partly because they often selected different pools of data to work from. 'The purest information to use is data on [historic] defaults but the sample is just too small,' Gareth Levington, a London-based managing director at Moody's explained. 'So we look at correlations on ratings movements. But there are other ways you can do it, with equity prices, say.'

Almost all of these slightly different techniques did, however, use the same fundamental mathematical approach – or 'statistical engine', as Moody's officials called it – which tried to plot the probability of future defaults based on historical data, using a 'bell-curve' type of chart which assumed that losses would occur in a relatively steady manner.

In March 2000, David Li, a researcher at J.P. Morgan published a ground-breaking paper presenting a method he had devised for estimating the degree of correlation based on a well-established statistical technique known by the formidable name of the Gaussian copula model. This was essentially a way of estimating the degree of dependencies of different kinds among a group of variables. He applied it to CDOs of corporate debt and his concept quickly spread until almost every bank, ratings agency and investment group adopted it for their own models. Indeed, some bankers liked to joke that the Gaussian copula was like the combustion engine of the CDO world: enabling them all to craft more and more CDOs faster and faster.

In many ways, Li's work was a boon for the industry. As the *Wall Street Journal* pithily pointed out, the launch of Li's Gaussian copula model meant that bankers not only had a method to weigh a 'bag of apples' (i.e. companies), but also to predict the likelihood they would all rot. That gave bankers the ability to trade different pieces of CDO risk with much more confidence. So much so, in fact, that a new business developed called 'correlation trading', which made investment bets based on how the correlation inside a CDO or between CDOs might move. But the model also introduced new risks. The more that banks all relied on Li's Gaussian copula approach, the more they were creating a *new* form of correlation risk. Because everyone was using the same statistical method of devising their CDOs to contain risk, in the event of economic conditions that defied that modelling, huge numbers of CDOs would suffer losses all at once. As Alex Veroude, the manager of a CDO for Gulf International Bank explained, 'The problem is that all the structures now are designed the same way, with the same triggers. That means that if there is a storm all the boats in the water will capsize.'

Worse still, the fundamental philosophy behind the Gaussian statistical technique did not appear to be well suited to cope with a situation where the boats might all capsize, en masse. Like any model, it was only as good as the data that was fed into the 'engine', and that data was usually based on what had happened in the past. If something completely unexpected ever occurred – an event that was *not* in the data set – the model would not work. Good statisticians tried to avoid that problem by working with as much data as they could. However, the credit world was so new that there was not always that much data available. How could the trajectory of a CDO squared be judged from past data when that 'past' was just two years old? Or, for that matter, a subprime-linked derivative that had never been widely traded? How could the models forecast what might happen if a true investor panic got under way, creating a selling chain reaction that had never been seen before? As David Li himself said about the model he had fashioned, 'The most dangerous part is when people believe everything coming out of it.'

But even if some observers of the boom were highly sceptical about just how well the risks had really been measured, few had any motive to stop it. No one could argue with the returns. The revenues of the largest investment banks grew 14 per cent between 2003 and 2004, to hit \$184 billion, producing \$61 billion profit. Citigroup, Goldman Sachs, Morgan Stanley and Deutsche Bank all reported particularly good numbers, with Goldman leading the pack with revenues of more than \$16 billion. Some of that was due to the banks' traditional businesses of equity market underwriting, share trading and merger advice recovering from the internet crash, but a key component of the growth was the credit boom. Between 2003 and 2004, the total market capitalization of major global banks rose by \$900 billion to \$5.4 trillion, a record high.

Amid this heady bonanza, however, one bank was notably *not* celebrating: JPMorgan Chase. By 2004, the bank that had kick-started the credit investment boom was, ironically, lagging badly behind the new pack of players, in large part because the J.P. Morgan management had opted out of the mortgage-based CDO and CDS business. Analysts were unimpressed with the bank's results, and the stock price was languishing. An injection of new energy was urgently needed, and the bank was about to get quite a shock to the system.

CHAPTER SEVEN

Mr Dimon Takes Charge

In January 2004, JPMorgan Chase was swept again into the global banking merger mania. This time the partner was Chicago-based Bank One. On 14 January, William Harrison, the CEO of JPMorgan Chase, announced a deal to purchase the bank for $58 billion, one of the biggest deals ever in the financial sector.

The rationale behind the purchase – at least as presented by Harrison – was that JPMorgan Chase wanted to expand its retail footprint across the whole of America. Bank One was the sixth-largest retail bank in the country, and had a formidable network in the Midwest, as well as being the largest single issuer of Visa cards. With 2300 branches in seventeen states, the JPMorgan Chase–Bank One merged entity would be almost as big as the Citigroup giant. The only other close competitor was Bank of America, which was in the process of merging with FleetBoston, to create yet another superbank.

Savvy as the deal might be, some analysts suspected that Harrison was trying to dig himself out of a hole. As the losses from Enron, WorldCom and other clients of JPMorgan Chase had piled up and the bank's stock price tumbled, he had come under mounting pressure, and Harrison was not a man to go quietly. He needed a way to deflect the criticism and boost the share price, and the Bank One deal did precisely that. When the deal was announced, analysts – as well as the JPMorgan Chase staff – seized on the fact that the merger brought with it the brash financier Jamie Dimon, who had famously helped to build the Citigroup financial empire back in the 1990s.

In early 2004, Dimon was running Bank One, and under the terms of the merger he would technically be junior to Harrison. Dimon was named Chief Operating Officer and President, while Harrison held the post of CEO. But the deal also stipulated that when Harrison, who was sixty, retired in two years, Dimon would take over. Until then, Dimon would be paid 90 per cent of whatever Harrison earned, a deal that analysts guessed would give Dimon a pay package of around $20 million a year. 'Everybody eventually reports to me, but Jamie [Dimon] is the President, COO,' Harrison smoothly explained. 'He [Dimon] is running the retail side of the bank, and he's also running the finance and risk-management function . . . it was a good way to segment responsibilities.'

Wall Street was almost ghoulishly fascinated. The two leaders were near opposites: Dimon was a hard-talking, fast-acting New Yorker: the 'boy wonder from Queens', as *Fortune* magazine dubbed him; Harrison was described by the same magazine as a 'courtly Southern gentleman'. The only thing they clearly shared was a history of frenetically forging bank mergers.

Dimon had built his career by joining with Sandy Weill to gobble up Salomon Brothers, Citibank and others to forge the Citigroup empire. He also had a long history of ousting the heads of the companies he took over. Inside JPMorgan Chase, the rumour mill speculated about just how long Harrison would survive. 'Everybody's talking about Dimon being the CEO,' a reporter pointed out to Harrison shortly after the deal was announced. 'Does it bother you? . . . do you feel that in some regard you're stalled for the next two years?' Harrison batted the question away.

At the time of the merger, Dimon was only forty-seven, a good thirteen years younger than Harrison. But he had already generated more legends than Wall Street financiers twice his age. He grew up in Queens, New York, in a family of Greek immigrants from Smyrna. His grandfather worked as a small-time broker, and Dimon's father, Theodore, took a similar job on Wall Street, eventually working for Salomon Brothers. As a child, Dimon spent summers working in his father and grandfather's offices. His father's well-paid job also afforded Dimon a good education. He attended Browning School, a smart prep school in the Upper East Side, then majored in psychology and economics at Tufts University and completed his studies with an MBA from Harvard.

On graduation from Harvard in 1982, at the age of twenty-six, he was offered jobs at Goldman Sachs and Morgan Stanley, but he turned those elite positions down in favour of joining up with Sandy Weill. A friend of his father, Weill was an aggressive, up-and-coming financier who was working at American Express. Dimon's choice was an extraordinarily bold punt. Weill was a highly controversial figure on Wall Street, and something of an outsider. But he was also forceful, entrepreneurial and highly ambitious, qualities Dimon admired.

When Weill was ousted from American Express a couple of years later, the two men embarked on an extraordinary acquisition spree. First they teamed up to purchase Commercial Credit, a floundering consumer loan company, which they used as a vehicle for grabbing several other firms. Finally, in the late 1990s they implemented their biggest coup of all, acquiring Travelers Insurance to create the Citigroup conglomerate, just as the Glass-Steagall rules were being swept away.

The streak was a stunning triumph, but their story soon took

a Shakespearian turn. Outsiders often described their relationship as being like father and son, since it appeared emotionally
intense. Journalists also tended to assume that it was Weill pushing through the deals. Dimon, though, vehemently disputed that
Weill was a father figure. He regarded the older man as a manager, and not a very good one at that. He also insisted that he
was as responsible as Weill for developing strategy, if not more so.
His close friends at Citigroup, such as Steve Black, were apt to
agree.

As the 1990s wore on, the relationship between Weill and
Dimon steadily deteriorated, marred by numerous fights. One
such clash started in 1995 after Dimon refused to promote Weill's
daughter, Jessica Bibliowicz, who was working at Citigroup.
Eventually the atmosphere soured so badly that Dimon left
Citigroup. A sixteen-year partnership came to an abrupt end.

For more than a year, Dimon hung in limbo, without a job.
So far did he vanish from view that some Wall Street commen-
tators suggested that his career had been completely derailed.
Then in 2000 he accepted the job of running ailing Bank One.
It was one of the smartest strategic moves Dimon ever made.

Bank One, like Chase Manhattan, was the unwieldy product
of three Midwest banks that had been carelessly cobbled together
during the 1990s merger mania. When Dimon arrived in
Chicago the company was almost bankrupt, weighed down with
internet-related loans that were imploding and a bloated cost
structure. In short order Dimon fired the old management,
installed new bankers, including some from Citigroup, slashed
expenses by 17 per cent – $1.5 billion – and transformed the
loan book. He also radically reorganized the retail banking operation to make it more customer-friendly. By 2003, the bank was
reporting a $3.5 billion profit, up from a $511 million loss in
2000. The turnaround was sweet revenge. Then the fates played
into his hands again.

As the reverberations of the internet bust and the Enron and

WorldCom scandals pounded Wall Street, Citigroup was hit hard, and Sandy Weill's reputation was badly damaged. In October 2003 he resigned. Miles away from New York, in Chicago, Dimon was one of the few senior bankers who emerged from those years with a reputation that was not just intact but was soaring. Harrison's decision to reach out to Dimon and Bank One was an exceedingly canny move, analysts agreed. If anyone could restore the reputation and confidence of the damaged JPMorgan Chase brand, it was Dimon.

The question left critically unclear was how Dimon would actually go about restoring the bank's fortunes. Would he go head to head with the Citigroup behemoth he had been instrumental in creating? Or did he have something completely different up his sleeve?

Shortly after arriving at JPMorgan Chase, Dimon flew across the Atlantic to make himself acquainted with the European operations of the bank, including the impressive derivatives empire Bill Winters had built. Winters was now the most senior remaining member of the old Hancock group.

The bankers in London were extremely curious to meet Dimon – and apprehensive too. After three years of bitter infighting with the Chase side of the bank, the 'heritage' (as the former J.P. Morgan bankers were known) Morgan team there was deeply wary of anything in the vein of Chase. Some had decidedly low expectations. 'Not another retail banker from Hicksville, USA!' one muttered to colleagues before Dimon's arrival. In the years before he had arrived at JPMorgan Chase, rumours circulated that suggested that Dimon was no fan of investment banking. This was partly because, back in the late 1990s, Dimon ran Salomon Smith Barney, the investment banking arm of Citigroup, and shut down the US proprietary trading desk. The furious Salomon bankers promptly concluded that Dimon hated traders. Dimon vociferously denied that, pointing out that he had chosen to merge with an investment bank when he and Weill were building up Citigroup. The rumours, though, made some J.P. Morgan bankers wary: they wondered what Dimon would do with their derivatives powerhouse. The London-based bankers had nervously prepared a briefing for Dimon about their successes, sent to him in advance of his trip. By 2004, they had plenty of good news to highlight. Their derivatives business was rapidly expanding, as was their under-writing business. The bank was also in the process of forging a joint venture with Cazenove, the blue-blooded British invest-ment bank, which promised to offer JPMorgan Chase a powerful platform for expanding its advisory and underwriting work in Europe.

Tony Best, a former member of the old J.P. Morgan deriva-tives team, fully expected to spend the morning of Dimon's arrival discussing the briefing he had sent him. Nobody ever dared to assume that a bank head would have had time actually to read a briefing, and the first part of such meetings was usually spent reviewing them. Dimon was different. 'I've read the paper,' he announced abruptly, in his nasal Queens accent, and then asked highly specific questions that indicated he had indeed absorbed the details of the report. He made it a point of pride always to memorize as much of a preparatory paper as he could before a meeting. 'You gotta do homework; I always do my homework,' Dimon liked to say.

For almost an hour Dimon debated the state of the European derivatives market with Best and others. It soon became clear that – contrary to the prior rumours – he knew the minutiae of complex finance. The brainstorming was intense. Then, at the end, the discussion took a completely unexpected turn. 'Do you know what you are paying for these telephones?' he asked, pointing at the phone on the desk. A baffled silence fell. Investment bankers dealing with the esoteric world of derivatives weren't concerned with phone matters. 'I will tell you!' Dimon declared. He loved posing aggressive, rhetorical questions to an audience, to keep them uneasily on their toes. 'The average price of a phone in the London office right now is $22. I have checked and it should be $9. So, listen, I am going to call five vendors and get them to make me a better price. We gotta fix the plumbing first, and then we can worry about everything else!'

Oh my God, some of the London J.P. Morgan bankers thought. They had never experienced anything like Dimon before. In a sense, he seemed to be confirming their worst fears. Or was he? It was clear to Best that Dimon was phenomenally bright: not only had he memorized details about the British telephone system, but he also clearly understood the credit world with its complex acronyms. 'He's not like any leader I have ever met before,' Best confessed to a colleague. The gossip about what Dimon would do with the bank grew intense.

In reality, Dimon's plans were both highly complex and exceedingly simple. Though almost none of the 'heritage' Morgan bankers realized it at the time, Dimon had arrived at JPMorgan Chase with an extensive knowledge of how the old J.P. Morgan worked. That stemmed from a little-known friendship Dimon had forged more than a decade earlier with former CEO Dennis Weatherstone. Back in the early 1990s, J.P. Morgan was a lead banker to Commercial Credit, the unruly financial group that Weill and Dimon had taken over as the first step on their road to creating Citigroup. As a result, Weatherstone had become acquainted with them, and he soon made a point of travelling to the bank's headquarters down in Baltimore on a regular basis, a reflection of Weatherstone's old-fashioned respect for client relationships.

Weatherstone took a particular shine to Dimon, perhaps because he too had started out as something of an outsider. At one stage, Weatherstone even suggested to Weill that he should mentor Dimon, which Weill brushed off. Weatherstone, though, did act as an informal mentor, having long chats with Dimon. 'I adored Dennis Weatherstone – absolutely adored him!' Dimon later recalled. 'Sandy Weill never gave me a piece of advice at all, he just did not do mentoring. But I guess that Weatherstone was a mentor to me in a way, since he really took me under his wing.'

During the course of those conversations, Dimon gained respect for the values Weatherstone stood for. 'They were a good, ethical lot at the old J.P. Morgan. They really believed in trying to do the right thing, in trying to serve clients,' Dimon recalled. However, by the mid-1990s, Dimon was increasingly unimpressed with the commercial results of the bank. He appreciated the bank's impressive history and formidable franchise, but he thought the bank was dangerously arrogant and insular. Subsequently he also became highly critical of the way the merger with Chase had been carried out, generating so much dysfunctional infighting. 'My first impression of [JPMorgan Chase] was that it was completely undisciplined – there was a lot of politics,' Dimon recalled. 'There was not a lot of good there, apart from the investment bank, which had some great embedded businesses. But that was also just really undisciplined. No discipline at all.'

In Dimon's eyes, that lack of discipline was nothing short of a cardinal sin. It was a stance born from a more profound set of attitudes towards the craft of banking. Contrary to his reputation, Dimon had not arrived at JPMorgan ignorant of how the inner details of high finance worked. He had an extremely curious mind that was exceptionally good at absorbing data, with near-photographic powers of recall. He took it as a point of pride to spend time each month studying new topics. 'I love studying reports, new ideas, just love it! You gotta keep challenging yourself,' he liked to say. Along the way, that mind had enabled him to grasp a vast amount of information about how advanced market instruments worked.

When he arrived at Salomon Brothers in the late 1990s he spent hours sitting on the trading desk, analysing the bank's positions. The Salomon Brothers traders initially tried to fob him off by giving him trading records that were presented with such complexity that they were extremely hard to follow. Dimon, though, waded through the data and eventually concluded that the books only held ten, rather similar, strategies. When he arrived at JPMorgan Chase, he repeated the exercise, determined to get his head around the numbers; he was convinced that much of the complexity in the derivatives world was not just misleading but unnecessary. 'People think I don't understand this stuff, because I don't have a trading background. But I understand it better than they think.'

Yet in one sense, Dimon was very different from the men and women who worked in the world of high finance: precisely because he had not built his career in that sphere, he was not overly impressed by the complexities or potential of high finance. He wasn't antagonistic towards financial innovation, but he wasn't reverential either. He believed that the only way to run a bank effectively was to regard it as a business – *nothing more, or less*. The old J.P. Morgan bankers might have believed they were part of a quasi-noble financial guild, while the young derivatives turks of the late twentieth century were driven by a belief that they were building a brave new cyberfinance world. Dimon took a purely pragmatic approach. To him, bankers were neither noble nor Masters of the Universe, they were just business people doing a job, pushing money around the economy as efficiently and effectively as they could. The point of a bank was simply to do that *business*.

'Banking is a bit like running a small retail store,' Dimon sometimes said – he liked the analogy since he considered it to be one 'that even my grandmother can understand'. 'You gotta work out what kind of stuff your customers want. Then you gotta get the stock in, and sell it as quickly as you can, making a profit. If you get it wrong about the inventory, then you make a loss. That applies to trading bonds, or derivatives, or a retail store. It's all about business.'

'And,' he would add, 'you *gotta* have good book-keeping. You can't have side books and back books, or whatever kinda books – you have to know where you stand with all your stock. I have always said that we have got to only have one set of books at JPMorgan Chase and be accurate and comprehensive.'

This no-nonsense approach shaped every aspect of Dimon's strategy. Like any small shopkeeper who needs to keep track of his stock, Dimon was obsessed with knowing every detail of his bank's inventory. He wanted to know exactly how money was – or was not – moving through the bank, and he spent hours examining the IT systems and the trading books. Yet, like a small shopkeeper, Dimon also knew the critical importance of keeping staff and clients happy. He found it hard to tolerate bureaucracy or formality, and preferred to operate with a brash, informal, in-your-face air. 'I always say to people: "Get to the point!" "Say it upfront!" I hate all this messing about,' he liked to say. On a whim, he would wander around the corridors, bouncing up to staff to pepper them with questions about their business, and their deals, and then he'd ask about their families as well. He would also mentally file the details away, to be brought out at a later date.

He showed little respect for traditional hierarchies. At other banks, investment bankers usually commanded far more status than retail bankers, and both were set well above the lowly 'back office' staff involved in the logistics of running the bank. Dimon was acutely aware that all the bank's groups were crucial for moving his financial 'stock' around, and making it pay. 'How complex do you think it is to run a credit card business?' he sometimes liked to challenge his listeners, when the subject of financial innovation came up. 'Let me tell you – its friggin' complex!

Getting to grips with credit cards is one of the most complicated challenges you get in banking.'

The same mentality shaped Dimon's attitude towards risk. He didn't view himself as particularly risk-averse. On the contrary, his career showed he could make bold bets, starting with his decision to join with Weill rather than go to Goldman Sachs. However, Dimon believed strongly that risks must be properly *managed*, and he went about the task with the same obsessive attention to detail that a small business owner must pay to cash flow. Indeed, he shared Dennis Weatherstone's fascination with measuring and monitoring risk, and when he spoke about risk management, he often expressed sentiments that Hancock and other former J.P. Morgan bankers might have voiced. He was no fan of leaving the task to a dedicated risk department.

One of Dimon's favourite phrases was 'fortress balance sheet', shorthand for the idea that a bank should always maintain a large reserve of spare capital in order to cope with unforeseen shocks. 'We have got to have a fortress balance sheet!' he kept drilling into his staff. 'No one has the right to not assume that the business cycle will turn! Every five years or so, you have got to assume that something bad will happen.'

Within weeks of his arrival at JPMorgan Chase, Dimon started putting his ideas into action. True to his word, he forced the London office to cut a new deal with its telephone suppliers. But that was just the start. As Dimon swept through the bank, peering into corners, he initiated a blitz of cost-cutting measures, and news of them spread through the organization at lightning speed.

He declared that employees must start buying their own cellphones and banned the bank from paying for golf club memberships. As the measures spread, wild rumours about what else Dimon planned to do swept through the bank. One (false) story claimed that he was monitoring which bankers were booking taxis and then running up bills by leaving them waiting, idle. It was even whispered that Dimon was tracking the size of the hamburgers in the staff canteen, with a view to cutting those down too.

Many of these stories were fallacious. (Dimon never inspected the hamburgers.) But that served his aims. As the stories spread they evoked so much fear that bankers started cutting costs pre-emptively. In the first year, the bank's operating committee – its most senior management group – implemented three billion dollars of cost savings. That was reinvested elsewhere. The Chase retail bank branches were refurbished. The investment bank started recruiting staff to fill the gaps created by the exodus of former J.P. Morgan employees. Some $1.5 billion was spent on data centres and another billion on technology at the investment bank.

The technology programme was particularly close to Dimon's heart. On his first trip to London he made an unusual detour. Instead of heading first to the headquarters in the City, near the Barbican, he went straight to Bournemouth, to the head-quarters of the bank's UK IT operations. There he convened a town hall and spent a couple of hours discussing the bank's IT infrastructure.

The British IT specialists were astonished. In most banks, the support staff were either patronized or completely ignored. Dimon was convinced, though, that there was no chance of making the merger at JPMorgan Chase work better if he could-n't streamline the IT sector. Dimon was convinced that the infrastructure issues were far too important to outsource. Before his appointment, Harrison had struck a massive $5 billion IT outsourcing deal with IBM, one of the largest of its kind in the financial industry. By mid-September, Dimon had scrapped the contract and brought IT back in-house, where he could keep it right under his nose.

He also reorganized the human infrastructure. In the four years before Dimon arrived, managers who worked for the

separate parts of the JPMorgan Chase empire had rarely interacted face to face; most cross-department communication –
what little there was of it – was conducted by phone or email.
Soon after his arrival, Dimon created a new, dedicated managing
directors' dining room, to force the different department heads
to meet face to face, over lunch, several times a week. 'You have
to *talk* to people, look 'em in the eye!' he explained.

He also convened a meeting of the operating committee and
demanded that everyone reveal exactly what the most senior
three hundred employees were paid, by name – and in front of
colleagues from other departments. That was revolutionary. At
JPMorgan, like almost every other bank, pay levels were a closely
guarded secret. But Dimon was determined to break down the
hierarchies of status. The new bank, he insisted, should be a
meritocracy: the whole staff judged purely on performance. To
ram that home, he declared the end of employment contracts
with special side deals. All employees would now have a single,
basic contract. The only exception, Dimon declared with a rare
flash of socialist principles, was health insurance, where the best-
paid employees were ordered to pay a far higher set of medical
premiums to subsidize the lowest-paid. 'There are no side deals
in this company, no special deals,' Dimon said.

The result was a shifting of pay levels and status within the
empire. The risk department benefited considerably. In Wall
Street banks, the so-called compliance, control and risk departments – those charged with checking that bankers obeyed the
rules and with monitoring the overall level of risk in the bank –
usually commanded lower status and pay than the bankers. They
also lacked power because they did not generate revenues themselves. Dimon raised the pay of the personnel monitoring risk, so
that it was even attractive enough to persuade some traders to
move across into those functions. He also made it clear that the
risk and compliance personnel carried real clout. Hordes of staff
were placed on training courses organized by the risk department,

and senior managers were told to attend risk meetings. Dimon insisted that the staff should think about risk in a truly holistic manner. It was not enough, he declared, to look at the dangers that might beset narrow 'silos' of the bank, or simply to subcontract risk management to one department. Nor could risk be reduced to a few mathematical models.

Fifteen years earlier, when Dennis Weatherstone ran the bank, J.P. Morgan had invented the concept of VaR and then disseminated it to the rest of the industry. It was a notable legacy. However, Dimon had no intention of giving undue veneration to VaR. Like Weatherstone, he deemed mathematical models to be useful tools, but only when they were treated as a compass, not an oracle. Models could not do your thinking for you. The only safe way to use VaR, or so Dimon believed, was alongside numerous other analytical tools – including the human brain.

By late 2004, speculation was rampant that Dimon was about to oust Harrison. 'Yond Cassius has a lean and hungry look . . . such men are dangerous,' Brad Hintz, an analyst at Sanford C. Bernstein, observed, quoting *Julius Caesar*. The prospect delighted many of the J.P. Morgan bankers, particularly the 'heritage' Morgan group. Though at first many of them were wary of Dimon, as the months passed the unease was replaced by respect. On the surface, Dimon was hardly J.P. Morgan material. At weekends he sometimes wore sneakers to the office, and cheerfully ate hamburgers and chips in the bank's elite dining room. He had few qualms about saying 'Bullshit!' But personal style aside, Dimon's banking philosophy jived well with the ethos of the old J.P. Morgan.

Dimon had no interest in turning JPMorgan Chase into the equivalent of a hedge fund, or copying the aggressive trading tactics of brash Goldman Sachs, placing bets with the bank's own money. He was intent to create a solid, balanced business. That was very much in keeping with the J.P. Morgan tradition. Even

Dimon's informality rang true to the old bank, where junior derivatives traders could cheerfully push their most senior boss into a swimming pool and break another's nose without worrying about getting fired.

'In the old J.P. Morgan people would ask about your families but forget to chat about the business. Dimon does both,' Jakob Stott, the London-based banker, observed. But Dimon had no illusions that he could ever create that same old feeling of family and fraternity in a bank as big as JPMorgan Chase. Nor did he want to. He was striving for a meritocracy, not a tradition-bound club where employees were retained for life, irrespective of how they performed.

Some of the employees inside JPMorgan Chase found this change of style unnerving. They grumbled that Dimon seemed so utterly sure of his opinions he could fall prey to hubris, or overreach. A few muttered that the senior management was turning into 'Jamie's club', full of employees deemed loyal to Dimon. Such sniping, though, was not widespread. To many 'heritage' Morgan bankers, the idea of blending Dimon's ruthless discipline and energy with some of the old values of J.P. Morgan seemed very exciting.

As Tony Best from the London office observed, 'When we first met Dimon and he got obsessed with the telephones, we were all a bit shocked. But then we realized he was quite different from anything we had ever seen before, in a good way. He was almost like the leader we had always been waiting for in J.P. Morgan, but never really got.'

As it transpired, the JPMorgan Chase staff would have reason to be grateful that Dimon had arrived on the scene, and held true to his principles of risk management, even as most of the rest of the banking world broke free from all bounds of rational discipline.

CHAPTER EIGHT

Risky Business

In late October 2004, Jamie Dimon and William Harrison reported results for the third quarter of that year, the first joint figures since the Bank One–JPMorgan merger. They were dismal: profits in the third quarter were 13 per cent below the level a year earlier (in itself a bad period), largely due to losses on fixed-income trades. 'Current results were below expectations, primarily due to weak trading results,' Harrison declared in his usual, courtly manner. Dimon was blunt. 'They're *terrible* results!' he declared. 'Terrible!'

Some analysts hoped the results were an aberration, and that the wunderkind Dimon would soon turn the tide. But the next quarter's results were weak too, leaving total 2004 earnings at just $4.5 billion, down from $6.7 billion the previous year. Return on equity was a mere 6 per cent, in a year when the industry average rose to 15.5 per cent. The results improved slightly in the first quarter of 2005, but then deteriorated again in the spring. 'You can almost hear JPMorgan Chase's investors singing "Why are we waiting, oh why are we waiting?" Jamie Dimon's flock of faithful is certainly being tested,' the *Financial Times* observed in

August 2005. 'His huge banking merger is not yet delivering what investors had hoped, and the stock price has not bounced back from the disappointing results of last month, in spite of trading conditions that many reckon are more propitious.'

The bank's staff waited for sparks to fly. In early 2004, a former Bank of America executive named David Coulter had been running the investment bank. Just before Dimon arrived as the new Chief Operating Officer, Coulter was pushed out of that post. Control of the investment bank was handed to the two men who had been working as Coulter's deputies: Steve Black, a former Citigroup banker who had worked with Dimon, and Bill Winters.

The Winters–Black partnership was approved by Dimon. But it struck many observers as odd; indeed, some of their staff started making bets about who which of the two men would be forced out first. The co-heads structure had thus far fuelled vicious infighting and mistrust, and this solution seemed to promise more of the same. For one thing, Black had worked with Dimon during his Citigroup days and was in fact such a close ally that when Weill fired Dimon in late 1998, Black – or 'Blackie,' as Dimon's circle called him – resigned soon after. On the other hand, Winters had no past ties with Dimon, and their temperaments were opposite: Dimon was famously extroverted, Winters shunned the limelight. Outside the bank, few observers had ever even heard of Winters. In addition, Dimon had never shown any public passion for complex financial innovation, which was Winters's strong suit. 'I've got a rock star for a boss now!' Winters sometimes joked to colleagues. 'But at least it takes the spotlight off the rest of us.'

Dimon was savvy enough, though, to appreciate that Winters had skills he needed. For one thing, Winters was running the non-US investment bank empire, which was generating almost half of all the global profits of the investment bank. Much of that revolved around derivatives, debt and fixed-income activity, but

the group also had a significant presence in the foreign exchange
sector and was becoming more prominent in terms of advisory
work. In the autumn of 2004, that latter strand of the business
was given a particular boost when Winters agreed to combine
forces with Cazenove, the highly traditional UK corporate advisory group. That gave JPMorgan access to a host of European
clients that it had never previously been able to reach.

Dimon also knew, though, that Winters was a key link to the
old derivatives heritage of J.P. Morgan. 'Bill [Winters] has been
around since the invention of seamless nylon stockings,' wrote
Ian Kerr, a columnist on *Euroweek*. 'He knows where all the
bodies are buried in that monster derivatives portfolio.'

JPMorgan executives vehemently denied that there were any
such 'monsters'. Yet, Winters certainly knew more about the
portfolio than almost anyone else. He was also intuitively good
at sniffing for risk. That may have stemmed from his unusual life
story. To his colleagues, Winters usually seemed like a classic, all-
American guy. He worked hard, but loved partying with his
'gang' of fellow traders too. In reality, though, his life before J.P.
Morgan had been striking. In his twenties, he had studied international relations at Colgate, hoping to become a diplomat. That
took him to Croatia one summer, where he fell in love with a
local girl. He then moved to the Balkans for a couple of years,
working in a beer bottling factory under the old socialist system,
where he became fluent in Croatian. On returning to the US,
with his new Croatian wife, he applied for a job with J.P.
Morgan, since he needed to earn money. He then swiftly rose
through the derivatives department, using his formidable wits
and drive. But he never took the gilded banking ghetto for
granted. In the early 1990s, a brutal war erupted in the Balkans
which tipped Croatia into turmoil. That showed Winters in a
profound sense that unthinkable things can sometimes occur in
life. Systems can shatter. After that, he was never tempted to
ignore seemingly 'impossible' risks, in finance or anything else.

Winters rarely discussed any of that with colleagues. What they could see, though, was that he was pragmatic, understated and culturally flexible. He understood the value of quietly forging canny, tactical alliances, to survive. So did Black. As a result, and against expectations, the co-heads managed to craft an effective relationship.

Shortly after Dimon announced their joint promotion, the two sat down and Black said to Winters: 'We're big boys – we know that everyone is taking bets on which of us kills the other! Let's show them that we can actually make this partnership work!' Winters said he was on board with that, and then, with a minimum of fuss, they agreed to rules of engagement. First, they would keep their job descriptions deliberately flexible. The staff living in London tended to report first to Winters, while those in New York dealt first with Black, across a range of different sectors. The division of responsibilities was kept deliberately vague, however, to avoid the appearance that either might set out to build an autonomous empire. 'Everyone reports to both of us. They all have a *first* port of call, but that port of call has got to be constantly changing,' Black said.

They also agreed that frequent interchange was vital, even though Black was in the headquarters on Park Avenue and Winters was in London. 'Making this work is really like making a marriage work. You have to think about communication,' Black later observed, with a wry smile. 'At the beginning, we were just too polite to each other. But then we learnt to communicate better, as we went along. We just talked, talked and talked.'

The task that faced them was daunting. On paper, the wider business climate in 2004 should have been playing to all of J.P. Morgan's strengths. The new decade was shaping up to be the Era of Credit, and credit was supposed to be J.P. Morgan's forte. By late 2004, the bank could still claim a leading position in the trading of interest rate derivatives, foreign exchange and

corporate loans, and a respectable operation in the arena of corporate bonds.

But the situation in securitization – the selling of asset-
backed securities – looked poor. When J.P. Morgan and Chase
had merged, both sides believed the combined bank would
dominate the securitization business. Chase was a leader in
lending money to low-rated companies (an activity known as
leveraged finance), and repackaging those loans into bonds: J.P.
Morgan was a blue-chip lender and was skilled at bundling
together pools of derivatives to create structures such as Bistro.
Chase also had extensive experience repackaging other forms of
debt, such as mortgages, credit cards and student loans, into
asset-backed securities. But the dream of dominating the securitization market had come unstuck. In the asset-backed CDO
and CDS business – fast expanding at so many banks – J.P.
Morgan was slipping behind other banks. The bank's hesitance
to get into the repackaging of mortgages was a key reason.

Uneasily, Winters and Black debated how to fight back. It
was clear that securitization was not the *only* source of embar-
rassment. The bank was also weak in the commodities and
equities spheres. But these had never been strengths of either of
the merged banks; the weakness in securitization was all
the more disconcerting because credit was supposed to be J.P.
Morgan's core competence. Or as *Euroweek* tartly noted: 'Given
the profile of JPMorgan as an institution steeped in structured
finance, it really is surprising that the bank [has] failed to hitch
a ride on the great US remortgaging wave.' So Dimon decided
to act.

As 2005 dawned the word went out across the bank that
JPMorgan Chase would get its act together in the credit world.
'Securitization is a priority!' Dimon declared to his staff, and
there was one sector in particular in which the bank *really*
needed to catch up: mortgage finance.

*

JPMorgan ought to have made good time when it set out to raise its profile in the repackaging of mortgage debt. Inside the sprawling empire of JPMorgan Chase sat Chase Home Finance, one of America's largest home loan mortgage originators. But though the volume of mortgages Chase offered had surged as the house boom took off, they were being sold to Lehman Brothers, Bear Stearns and others for their mortgage CDO and CDS assembly lines. That was partly because the JPMorgan side had less experience with mortgage debt than with corporate loans, and was so leery about the risks involved with Bistro-like products concocted from mortgages. Relations between the managers of Chase Home Finance and the J.P. Morgan side also caused delays. The two groups barely communicated, epitomizing the infighting that still plagued the bank. 'It felt like a state of war,' one banker inside Chase Home Finance later recalled.

Dimon resolved to change that; he had no patience with infighting and was determined to create a financial 'production line', similar to those at the other banks, turning the mortgage loans being produced by Chase Home Finance into JPMorgan bonds in a single seamless operation. Dimon sidelined the senior officials from Chase Home Finance and installed a new team who were willing to work with the investment side. Those officials then hooked the two divisions together and created an integrated infrastructure that would allow all parts of the bank to handle the housing market. 'It took us ages to build, but Dimon insisted we needed to get all the systems before doing anything,' Bill King, one of those involved in the integration project, later explained. 'We produced something a bit like a Google machine of mortgages – you could track the public data in any way you wanted.'

By mid-2005, the production line was finally ready to be activated. But in 2006 Dimon started to get cold feet. The US housing market had now been booming for several years. Between 1997 and late 2005 house prices rose more than 80 per cent, according to the Case-Schiller index, with particularly marked increases in California, Florida, Michigan, Colorado, the Northeast corridor and Southwest markets. Some observers worried that the prices were driven by speculative mania; most economists brushed those concerns off. 'There is virtually no risk of a national housing price bubble based on the fundamental demand for housing and predictable economic factors,' David Lereah, the former chief economist of the National Association of Realtors, wrote in 2005, in a self-styled 'anti-bubble' report. Onlookers 'should [not] be concerned that home prices are rising faster than family income . . . A general slowing in the rate of price growth can be expected, but in many areas inventory shortages will persist and home prices are likely to continue to rise above historic norms.'

Ben Bernanke, then chairman of the President's Council of Economic Advisers, said in 2005:

> House prices have risen nearly 25 per cent over the past two years. Although speculative activity has increased in some areas, at a national level these price increases largely reflect strong economic fundamentals, including robust growth in jobs and incomes, low mortgage rates, steady rates of household formation and factors that limit the expansion of housing supply in some areas.

Yet when King and his colleagues scoured their Google-style mortgage database in early 2006, they spotted something odd: some of the data suggested that the pace of defaults on risky mortgages was starting to quicken. That defied the normal economic rules. Mortgage defaults were thought to be triggered by sharp interest rate increases or a slowdown in the economy, or both. Those had been the triggers in previous economic cycles, and those were the eventualities that had been factored into economists' models evaluating the housing market. Neither was

present in 2005. While in the spring of 2004 the Federal
Reserve had started raising the short-term interest rate, jacking
it up from a historic low of 1 per cent to 4 per cent by the end
of 2005, there was still such voracious investor appetite for mortgage-backed bonds that lenders kept extending very cheap loans
to households, confident they could sell those loans as CDO and
CDS fodder. The economy was also growing strongly, with low
jobless rates. So what was causing the default rate to rise?

Baffled, the mortgage group debated the issue, and Dimon
became keenly interested. Over the course of several weeks, Bill
King, who was a key driver behind the creation of the mortgage
pipeline, was summoned so often to meet with senior risk com-
mittees that colleagues asked whether he had been appointed a
formal member of the groups. As far as King could tell, none of
the other banks were responding to the odd pattern in defaults
by switching off their mortgage production lines. On the contrary, Merrill Lynch, Bear Stearns, Citigroup and others were
stepping up their dealings. So were mortgage lenders like
Ameriquest and Countrywide. Yet King was growing more and
more concerned.

Back in the 1990s, when brokers made loans to subprime borrowers, they conducted checks to ensure that the borrowers
would be able to pay off their loans. However, during the boom,
lenders had become a good deal less fussy about demanding that
borrowers prove they had the income to repay the loans. They
had even started offering 'teaser' loans, with fantastically low initial rates – sometimes below 2.5 per cent – that rose in stages to
be quite high, often well above 10 per cent. Many households
taking out these loans could barely meet the 'teaser' payments,
let alone cope with higher rates once they started to kick in.
Neither lenders nor borrowers worried much about the risk,
because it was widely assumed that borrowers would simply refi-
nance their loans at the end of their 'teaser' rate period. After all,
households had refinanced with ease during the first five years of

the decade, often doing so to cash in on some of the perceived
equity they had earned due to the incredible rise in home prices.
In 2005 American households extracted no less than $750 billion
of funds against the value of their homes, compared with $106
billion a decade earlier, of which two-thirds was spent on personal consumption, home improvements and credit card debt.
Lenders also assumed that if borrowers did face problems meeting their mortgage payments they could simply sell their
property, at a profit, and easily repay their loans.

In 2006, though, in San Francisco, Las Vegas, Miami and
other once-hot areas, house prices stalled. Though the slowdown wasn't dramatic, or spread around the whole country, it
nonetheless triggered a wave of subprime defaults. A number of
subprime borrowers who had been depending on the equity in
their homes continuing to rise robustly decided, when faced
with the prospect that their homes might not, after all, be such
reliable cash cows, that they were better off abandoning their
mortgages. Whereas from early 2002 to early 2005 the proportion of subprime borrowers who were delinquent on payments
had fallen from 15 per cent to 9 per cent, by early 2006, the
number had risen to above 12 per cent.

Dimon and the other managers debated what to do. They
were deeply reluctant to abandon the idea of creating a mortgage-repackaging pipeline, but Dimon was also very uneasy. 'I
know about this stuff [consumer lending]!' he would growl at Bill
King, harking back to his days in consumer credit. Eventually a
cautious compromise was reached. The bank maintained its
mortgage 'production line', but the lending unit was told to raise
its underwriting standards and reduce the level of unsold mortgages it held on its books. The JPMorgan managers were
determined not to get caught short if defaults rose any higher.

The bank also turned to the derivatives market to reduce its
risk, by purchasing credit default swaps from other parties which
promised to redeem any default losses on the mortgage bonds it

would begin selling. Such mortgage derivatives had barely existed a few years earlier, but they were among the products that had become so hot in the last years. Increasingly, banks were using them as insurance against losses from their mortgage-repackaging business. Then, in January 2006, an index for tracking these offerings and their values was launched, much like the Dow-Jones, called the ABX. This allowed all those playing in the mortgage-based investing terrain to track prices and get a continuous read on investor sentiment. King and his colleagues dived in, thrilled that they could buy protection against the risk of a possible cascading of defaults. Somewhat to their surprise, they found that even though defaults had started to rise, there was absolutely no shortage of players willing to take the other side of their bets and insure JPMorgan against the danger that the market might turn sour.

At almost all other banks and investment funds, financiers were still hunting for ways to *increase* their exposure to the subprime market, and boost their returns. By early 2006, in fact, CDS contracts looked to many like a particularly attractive way to place bullish bets. The big dirty secret of the securitization world was that there was such a frenetic appetite for more and more subprime loans to repackage into CDOs that the supply of loans had started to lag behind demand. Mortgage derivatives were an easy substitute, since there was no constraint on how many of *those* could be created, or at least not as long as some market players, such as JPMorgan Chase, were eager to hedge their risk by buying them. Ironically, JPMorgan Chase's conservative stance on subprime loans thereby enabled others to continue rolling the dice on the mortgage boom, to a far greater degree than would have been possible if their bets had been limited to the world of tangible bonds. The JPMorgan Chase management thought they had reached a reasonable compromise, but before long they would be forced to revisit their mortgage-repackaging business.

*

In another corner of the bank, Bill Winters had been growing more and more uneasy about the mortgage market for his own set of reasons. Winters knew that the 1990s derivatives team had rejected the notion of putting mortgage loans into Bistro deals, and he respected that judgement call. But with others making so much money out of such a range of mortgage-repackaging products, the pressure was on. Dimon had made it clear he wanted a mortgage production line, so Winters had duly asked his staff to re-examine how to create a profitable business selling mortgage-based CDOs.

When they crunched the numbers, though, they ran into a problem. 'There doesn't seem to be a way to make money on these structures,' Brian Zeitlin, one of the bankers who worked in the CDO division reported. Baffled, Winters told Zeitlin to look again. So many banks were doing a booming business in the field, why couldn't JPMorgan do the same?

Zeitlin and his colleagues conducted more analysis, but kept encountering the same sticking point. When the business was viewed through the prism J.P. Morgan employed to test whether a business was profitable, it just didn't seem to make sense. The issue was the 'spread', or the level of return, on the CDOs. Back in the days when J.P. Morgan had arranged its first Bistro deal, investors holding junior tranches of debt were paid around 375 basis points over Libor – nice compensation for the risk they were assuming. Even the AAA tranches had a spread of 60 basis points, which was a high enough return to enable the bank to sell the notes. The bank had made juicy fees on these sales. The return on the super-senior debt had been dramatically smaller, but the bank had decided to pass that, at a slight loss, to AIG, Swiss Re and others, and continue to crank out deals because the profits from the higher-risk notes were so good.

As interest rates had gone on falling, however, and so many more banks and investment funds began to offer CDOs, the profits to be made from each deal declined. The returns on the underlying loans repackaged into the CDOs had fallen substantially. Whereas loans might have once produced a cash flow of 10 per cent a year, say, it was now just 5 per cent. Worse, banks were competing so fiercely to purchase the raw material needed to create CDOs that the price of that raw material was rising. If a mortgage had a face value of $100,000, say, banks might now pay $102,000 as opposed to $100,500 to buy that loan. They kept making more and more of the purchases anyway because they could still turn a profit from turning around and selling the CDO notes. But the margins were being squeezed. The business had fallen victim to a vicious cycle. Banks and other lenders were issuing more and more mortgages, which were riskier and riskier, so that those loans could be repackaged into more and more CDOs in order to make up for the declining profit margins.

In the process, those selling these products were creating huge masses of super-senior risk, and Winters and his team wondered how the others were coping with the expense of either selling that off or insuring it. The cost of that cut even further into profits. One solution was simply to park the super-senior on J.P. Morgan's books, but Winters didn't like that idea at all. Like Bill Demchak eight years earlier, Winters thought that it was just a bad idea to let assets pile up on the balance sheet. And while Winters was not opposed to taking calculated risks, he always wanted to be properly compensated for doing so. To him, the returns on super-senior were far too low to justify holding it in any appreciable volume.

Some of the Winters staff floated the idea of buying insurance against the super-senior risks, as Demchak's group had arranged with AIG. By 2005 a host of insurance companies were offering that service. Some of the most active were MBIA and Ambac, which were two industry leaders in the so-called 'monolines' niche, companies that were specialized bond insurers. These monolines had first sprung up three decades earlier to offer insurance for bonds issued by government municipalities, but in the 1990s they had started to insure CDO notes.

Back in the 1990s the Demchak team had been cynical about the monolines. They were very thinly capitalized, for one thing. At some of them, the volume of assets they were insuring was 150 times larger than their underlying equity. Demchak had reasoned that with so little in reserves the monolines wouldn't really be able to pay on any of that insurance in the event of the kind of credit shock it would take to produce losses on the senior risk. If that financial disaster ever *did* hit, it would probably be bad enough to simply wipe out the monolines. Buying insurance from them was therefore pointless. Demchak said: 'To us, that business model seemed nuts!' Winters shared that view, preferring to keep any dealings with monolines to a modest level. 'We did not really use monolines [much] because we reasoned that they would not be there whenever you really needed them.' Winters told his team: 'You have got to get rid of the senior debt in a clean sale – until you do that, you cannot do the deals.'

Frustrated, the team began hunting for ways to sell the irritating super-senior risk, but there were few takers. By 2005, the spread on super-senior was around 15 basis points, and few investors wanted assets that yielded so little. Some banks were trying to solve that problem by repackaging super-senior liabilities into new products; in mid-2005, Deutsche Bank launched one, for example, known as 'leveraged super-senior'. Those were generally sold to Canadian and German investors. The banks were also selling super-senior to investment groups, like hedge funds and the proliferation of SIVs closely affiliated to the banks.

But JPMorgan had never created a network of SIVs attached to it. Back in the late 1990s, when Citigroup and other banks started creating SIVs, JPMorgan Chase executives debated whether they should do so too, but in the end opted out. Winters and others calculated that these vehicles were quite risky, because they raised their funding in the short-term commercial paper market. Meanwhile the assets they were selling would pay the bank over a much longer time frame. This mismatch alarmed Winters. Such was his wariness that when he became deputy CEO of the investment bank he slashed the $12 billion of credit lines that JPMorgan had already extended to other banks' SIVs to a mere $500 million. He also campaigned to get rid of an SIV that had come along with the merger with Bank One. 'I could never work out why anyone thought that SIVs were a good idea,' Winters later remarked.

Without an SIV network to take on the super-senior risk it would accrue by cranking up its mortgage-repackaging pipeline, Winters and Zeitlin just couldn't see a way to make the business pay. Reluctantly, Winters told the J.P. Morgan management that the bank should not open the spigots on its pipeline after all. The decision was greatly frustrating, though. The other banks were pushing JPMorgan Chase further and further down the league tables largely due to the bonanza from their mortgage pipelines. So were they just ignoring the risks? Or had they found some alchemy that made the economics of their machines work? Winters simply could not figure it out.

Having spent all his career at J.P. Morgan, Bill Winters assumed that the logic he employed was roughly similar to that prevailing in the other banks. He knew of course that banking cultures varied, but it was fiendishly difficult for anyone ever to know for sure just how *big* the variations might be, and just how crucial decisions were made at other banks. The internal corporate dynamics and incentives schemes of banks were closely guarded secrets, and when staff hopped from one bank to another, they were interviewed by the senior management, to pick their brains in the way that the CIA would have debriefed a defecting KGB spy. It was years before that mystery of what the others were doing was solved, and when the story of what they were up to was revealed, Winters was shocked.

CHAPTER NINE

Leveraging Lunacy

On 13 April 2005, some of the former J.P. Morgan bankers from the old derivatives team assembled at the Acropolis Centre in Nice, in southern France. The occasion was an industry conference to discuss the credit markets. A whole decade had passed since they had helped build the CDS world. Many were both stunned and thrilled by the sheer pace of growth. By mid-2005 there were $12 trillion CDS contracts alone in the market, a sum equivalent to the size of the entire US economy. The CDO market was also exploding. 'The speed of growth is just astonishing, even for those involved,' observed Terri Duhon, who had worked on J.P. Morgan's team in New York. By 2005 she had left ABN AMRO and was working as a consultant in London, giving advice to investors trying to jump into the frenzied business.

Yet Duhon had some qualms. 'There is a type of euphoria about getting into structured credit products right now, and so you have to ask could we be getting into a state of irrational exuberance?' she remarked. Cynthia McNulty, another former J.P. Morgan banker, agreed. 'There is such a buzz about credit derivative products now that there are hedge funds getting into it without the requisite abilities.'

Ian Sideris, a London-based lawyer who was handling some of the structured products that banks were producing, was also fretting. 'You have to really wonder about the capacity of investors to handle this,' he said at the time. With a grim half-smile, Sideris revealed that he had recently seen deals that were not only being sold to retail investors, but to government bodies, pension funds – and even a charity serving disabled people in Australia. All of those investors, it seemed, were chasing higher returns. Yet few of them, Sideris pointed out, had the ability to fully comprehend these new products. Even some of the bankers seemed overwhelmed.

Those concerns were prescient. A few weeks after the conference in Nice, ratings agencies downgraded the debt of General Motors, taking the markets entirely by surprise. That triggered panic among some investors, and many rushed to sell CDS and CDOs, causing their prices to swing, an eventuality not predicted by the models. JPMorgan Chase, Deutsche Bank and many other banks and funds suffered sizeable losses.

For a few weeks after the turmoil, the banking community engaged in soul-searching. At J.P. Morgan the traders stuck bananas on their desks as a jibe at the so-called 'F9 model monkeys', the mathematical wizards who had created such havoc. (The 'monkeys' who wrote the statistical models tended to use the 'F9' key on the computer when they performed their calculations, giving rise to the tag.) J.P. Morgan, Deutsche Bank and others conducted internal reviews that led them to introduce slight changes in their statistical systems. GLG, one large hedge fund, told its investors that it would use a wider set of data to analyze CDOs in the future.

Within a couple of months, though, the markets rebounded, and the furore died down. Most banks and ratings agencies continued to use the Gaussian copula approach to risk assessment. Having built their structured finance machines, they could not suddenly turn them off, and there was no obvious alternative model on offer. As David Li, the former J.P. Morgan 'quant' pointed out, 'It's not the perfect model . . . [but] there's not a better one yet.' Meanwhile, some bankers comforted themselves with the observation that the industry had been tested and had quickly recovered. 'We have had a shake-up, but that is good in a way,' Tim Frost observed a few months after the storm. 'People have learnt lessons.' Frost liked to quote Friedrich Nietzsche's observation that 'what does not kill us makes us stronger'. He passionately believed in free-market principles, to such an extent that he even stood for election for the British parliament, for the right-wing Conservative party (he lost). As part of that philosophy, he believed that a shakeout would make the credit derivatives markets more vibrant and efficient.

Across the Atlantic, though, one of Frost's former colleagues didn't share his optimism. That man was Andrew Feldstein. Back in the days when the J.P. Morgan team had concocted its derivatives dream, Feldstein had believed deeply in the *intellectual* arguments behind financial innovation. He was utterly convinced that if tools such as derivatives were implemented in a rational, efficient manner, they would vastly improve the financial system and economy. It was the dream that drove them all.

But after living through the mess of the Chase–J.P. Morgan merger, Feldstein became cynical. He still believed that derivatives had the theoretical potential to make markets function better, but in practice, dysfunctional management and warped incentives for traders and the ratings agencies were badly distorting the CDO market. He understood the ways in which the banks were playing around to garner good ratings and make end runs around the regulatory system, and the situation troubled him. But it also presented a trading opportunity.

When he left J.P. Morgan he created a hedge fund, together with two partners, Gery Sampere, a J.P. Morgan analyst, and Stephen Siderow, a McKinsey consultant who had been Feldstein's classmate at Harvard Law School in the class of 1991 (another member of that year was Barack Obama, whom Feldstein supported). They rented a small, windowless room in a skyscraper on Madison Avenue and set up shop under the name BlueMountain Capital. Key to their strategy was placing bets that CDOs were being mispriced.

Feldstein was convinced that banks and funds were miscalculating the true degree of default correlation in loan bundles, and he was convinced that eventually economic reality would hit. The true risk of the CDOs would then become clear, and prices would drop. 'The models are great, but at the end of the day, in credit, anyone relying solely on them will lose,' Feldstein explained soon after he created his fund. 'Those who are successful know this, and overlay their own idiosyncratic views about risk, actual correlation among and between groups of credits and other factors on any model they use.'

But such hedging on the market ironically only further fuelled the boom. After all, for every buyer in a market there must be a seller. A market in any commodity – be it equities, art, or synthetic CDOs – can only operate if there are parties on both sides of the trade. Feldstein and some others putting their money on the contrarian view helped to launch a lively new business of trading in default swaps.

By 2005, there were more tools available to conduct such trading too. In the early years, bankers who wanted to trade credit default swaps generally only used contracts that related to single names. From 2004 onwards, though, indices of credit default swaps sprang up, known as CDX in America, and iTraxx in Europe. They tracked the cost of insuring against default on a basket of companies, offering a handy way for investors to evaluate trends in pricing, in the same way that the S&P 500 shows how the whole equity market is moving. They could also be traded as contracts in their own right.

The ABX index, which tracked the price of derivatives written against risky home equity loans, provided another way for investors to trade, after its launch in January 2006. Other mutations proliferated too. The LCDX was an index of loan derivatives; the TABX tracked derivatives on mortgage tranches; and CMBX was an index of derivatives on commercial mortgages. By 2006, bankers and investors were using all of these indices to trade as if their flashy computing models were infallible. Feldstein and his colleagues at BlueMountain just did not believe they had assessed the true risks. To make the point, he and his colleagues placed an old-fashioned abacus in their office and labelled it 'correlation calculator' as a black joke.

They also constructed an investment strategy to take advantage of the shortcomings of the banks' models. To do this, they quietly constructed CDS portfolios which they traded with different investment banks, and then used detective work to guess how each bank was modelling CDO risk. Then, like hackers tapping into a computer, they hunted for the flaws in those models, which they could exploit. It was not hard to find such weaknesses, since the models varied, sometimes in a haphazard manner. Sometimes the banks' traders guessed what the geeks at BlueMountain were doing. They rarely complained, though. Individual bank traders did not usually have any personal incentive to worry about whether Feldstein was exploiting their models, or not. They got paid according to their trading results, *as measured by the internal models at banks* – and as long as those internal models produced flattering prices, those traders got fat bonuses.

In any case, few managers sitting at the top of the investment banks had much idea what their traders were doing, let alone whether the models were accurate or not.

By 2005, very few men running investment banks had extensive experience in structuring and trading derivatives. The field was just too young to have produced many high-level leaders, and many derivatives experts were too cerebral to play the type of internal corporate political games needed to rise to the top at most banks. Bankers who had started their careers as corporate advisers or salesmen tended to be better at charming their superiors. One exception was Lloyd Blankfein, the CEO of Goldman Sachs; Anshu Jain, the co-CEO of Deutsche's investment bank, was another. But Citigroup, Merrill Lynch, UBS and numerous others were run by former bond and equity salesmen, lawyers, wealth managers and commercial bankers. Such men had little instinctive understanding of the technical details of managing risk. Moreover, the wider competitive climate provided an overwhelming incentive for them to focus on revenues above all else. If they didn't deliver higher revenues, their stock prices would be pummelled. 'Banks now face the challenging task of sustaining their success in creating value,' Boston Consulting Group opined in a report on the industry's performance. 'Continuing to increase profitability remains important but becomes more and more difficult as profitability has already reached a new level.'

The antics of Goldman Sachs had a particularly significant impact on the psychology of many senior bankers. In 2002 and 2003 Goldman Sachs startled its rivals by delivering a hefty increase in profits. In 2004 that winning streak intensified when the brokerage raised its revenues by a third to more than $16 billion – more than any other player. That cranked up the pressure on other banks to deliver equally impressive growth. 'We all got "Goldman envy" – it became like an obsession,' one European bank CEO later recalled.

So, as 'Goldman envy' spread, rivals frantically embraced ideas for boosting profits that in retrospect would look like lunacy.

What was worse, many even stepped up their sales of mortgage-based products after the housing market had begun to turn. Merrill Lynch, the home of the 'thundering herd' of skilled salesmen in the equities world, was one such.

Back in 2003, the bank had appointed a new chief executive officer, Stan O'Neal. He decided to bring Merrill into the securitization business with a vengeance, hiring teams of traders who were ordered to start cranking out masses of CDOs. By 2006, Merrill topped the league table in terms of underwriting CDOs, selling a total of $52 billion that year, up from $2 billion in 2001 (JPMorgan was in seventh place in 2006, selling a mere $22 billion.) The herd had crashed the party in style. But behind the scenes, Merrill was facing the same problem that worried Winters at JPMorgan: what to do with the super-senior debt.

Initially, Merrill solved the problem by buying insurance for its super-senior debt from AIG, just as Demchak's team had done. However, in late 2005 AIG told Merrill it would no longer offer that service. One corner of the AIG empire was involved in extending mortgages, and AIG officials were privately getting alarmed about subprime risk. That left Merrill Lynch's CDO desk with a big headache. But unlike at JPMorgan, that stumbling block was not enough to prompt Merrill Lynch to fold its hand.

The CDO team decided to start keeping the risk on Merrill's books. As the super-senior kept accruing, some of it was insured with monolines, some of it buried in the books. A few bank officials expressed unease. Jeffrey Kronthal, a senior manager, tried to impose a $3–4 billion limit on the amount of super-senior risk that the bank could take on. In the summer of 2006, one trader protested when his colleagues created a $1.5 billion CDO deal called Octans and asked him to put almost $1 billion of that risk on the bank's books. These protests were squashed. The CDO department was determined to keep cutting deals. In

2006 sales of the various CDO notes produced some $700 million worth of fees. Meanwhile the retained super-senior rose by more than $5 billion each quarter.

Very few bankers inside Merrill Lynch had much idea what the CDO desk was doing. At Merrill, as with most Wall Street banks, departments competed viciously for resources and power, and the department that was most profitable usually carried the most clout. As the CDO team posted more and more profits, it became increasingly difficult for other departments, or even the risk controllers, to interfere. O'Neal himself could have weighed in, but he was in no position to discuss the finer details of super-senior risk. The risk department did not even report directly to the board. O'Neal faced absolutely no regulatory pressure to manage the risk with more caution. Far from it. The main regulator of the brokerages was the Securities and Exchange Commission (SEC), which had recently removed some of the old constraints.

Until 2004, the SEC had imposed controls on the amount of assets a brokerage could hold on its balance sheet relative to its core equity. In April of that year, however, the SEC's five commissioners had decided – by a unanimous vote – to lift that so-called 'leverage ratio' control. The ruling drew little attention in the press, since it seemed highly technical, but it had a repercussion: it raised the competitive pressure on the brokerages even further. By 2005 it had become clear that a key reason why Goldman Sachs was producing such stellar earnings was that it had raised its leverage. Because Merrill Lynch and the others came under intense pressure to follow suit, the increased leverage of super-senior risk was tolerated.

The three other major brokerages, Bear Stearns, Morgan Stanley and Lehman Brothers, also built up some super-senior exposure. Bear and Lehman had extensive experience in dealing with mortgage-backed bonds, and they prided themselves on running tight risk controls. As they each cranked up their CDO machines, they realized that super-senior risk was becoming like the toxic by-product of a chemical experiment, or waste from a nuclear reactor. But no good solution occurred to them, and they would not switch off their machines.

Citigroup too was keen to continue to ramp up its production, and as a commercial bank it had plentiful access to the 'raw material' needed to create CDOs. Unlike the brokerages, though, Citi could not park unlimited quantities of super-senior on its balance sheet, since the US regulatory system did still impose a leverage limit on commercial banks: it required them to keep assets below twenty times the value of their equity. Citi decided to circumvent that rule by placing large volumes of its super-senior in an extensive network of SIVs and other off-balance-sheet vehicles that it created. The SIVs were not always eager to buy the risk, so Citi began throwing in a type of 'buyback' sweetener: if the SIVs ever ran into problems with the super-senior notes, Citi itself would buy them back.

Citi's CDO machine began running at such a frenetic speed that by 2007 it had extended such guarantees – internally nicknamed 'liquidity puts' – on $25 billion of super-senior notes. It also held more than $10 billion of the notes on its own books. Almost none of the senior Citi managers knew about the liquidity puts, since Citi ran a power structure that was even more fragmented and tribal than at Merrill Lynch. And Chuck Prince, the Citi CEO, was not a meddler like Jamie Dimon. Prince had trained as a lawyer and he delegated derivatives issues to others.

On the other side of the Atlantic, many banks were doing the same. The senior managers at Deutsche Bank, for the most part, did *not* let their traders put super-senior risk on the bank's books. The German bank had a relatively tight system of internal controls and, just as Bill Winters had concluded, Anshu Jain, the co-head of the investment bank, considered that the paltry returns on super-senior simply didn't compensate for the risks.

However, other banks decided differently. The Royal Bank of Scotland aggressively grew its CDO business, and when some RBS employees expressed unease, they were naysaid. Earlier in the decade Ron den Braber, a statistical expert working in the CDO department, voiced worries that the bank's models were significantly underpricing the risk attached to super-senior. He was prompted to leave the bank. 'I started saying things gently,' den Braber recalled. 'In banks you don't use the word "error", but what I was trying to say was important. The problem is that in banks you have this kind of mentality, this group-think, and people just keep going with what they know, and they don't want to listen to bad news.'

Arguably the most aggressive player of all in Europe was UBS. The Zurich-based group had built its business by acting as a dull but worthy commercial bank, with a formidable private banking franchise. However, during the 1990s merger craze the bank joined with Swiss Bank Corporation and Paine Webber, and built an international capital markets operation that was widely admired for its equity market skills. But UBS – like Merrill – did not have a good franchise handling debt. By 2004, Marcus Ospel, the CEO, was hungry for more. Even in Switzerland, 'Goldman envy' was afoot. Like O'Neal at Merrill, Ospel was convinced that the fastest way for UBS to catch up was to expand its credit business. So the senior management took two momentous steps.

First, they agreed to let a group of UBS's powerful traders create an internal hedge fund, which would be run by John Costas, the former head of the investment bank of UBS. This started life in the summer of 2005, under the name of Dillon Read Capital Management. Second, in the autumn of 2005 the bank implemented a major review of its fixed-income business, hiring consultants from McKinsey and Oliver Wyman. On its advice, UBS decided to expand the securitization business.

On paper, UBS did not seem well placed to make the move.

Though the bank's asset management group had been investing
in American mortgage products for several years, it did not have
its own mortgage-lending operation. To make matters worse,
when Costas created the new hedge fund he took with him 120
of the bank's staff, and these included many of its fixed-income
specialists. Undeterred, the senior management hired new
traders in London and New York and told them to build a CDO
business as fast as possible. By late 2005 UBS was creeping up the
securitization league tables.

When the super-senior problem reared its head the bank first
managed to sell the risk to outside investors. By the middle of the
year, though, the bank had changed tack and was holding on to
it instead. There was no regulatory constraint on doing that
because the Swiss system that governed UBS followed the Basel
Accord, and the Basel rules took a decidedly relaxed attitude
towards assets with high credit ratings, such as super-senior risk.
They stipulated that banks could use their own models to work
out the risk and judge how much capital they needed to set aside.

The UBS risk department used the same fundamental system
for modelling risk, based on the VaR and Gaussian copula techniques, that so many other banks had adopted, and its models
implied that super-senior would never lose more than 2 per cent
of its value, even in a worst-case scenario. So the bank decided it
needed to post only a sliver of capital. Then it went even further
when its CDO traders stumbled on the realization that if they
bought insurance from monolines against that 2 per cent risk, the
super-senior became entirely risk-free. That effectively removed
the need to post any capital at all. The bank could pile as much
super-senior as it wanted on to its books, without constraint.

UBS also engaged in yet another notable means of squeezing
more profit out of its CDO machine. The bank's internal rules
stipulated mark-to-market valuation, meaning that the value of
assets held on the trading book had to be recorded at current
'market' prices. It was still hard to get market prices for senior

CDO notes, since they rarely traded, but what the CDO team started to do was to come up with estimates of what a CDO should be worth using their internal models. Then they would readjust those prices after a time, which with the market still rising, invariably allowed them to report a profit. Those profits were small, but the overall CDO positions were so large that the money added up.

By 2007, the bank would be carrying $50 billion of super-senior assets on its books, most of which sat on the CDO trading desk. Now and then, risk managers expressed surprise as the mountain grew. Their concerns were dismissed. The conservative and bureaucratic UBS managers put great stock in the fact that the super-senior notes carried a 'triple-A' tag. The result was that vast quantities of risk completely disappeared from the bank's internal risk reports. 'Frankly, most of us had not even heard the word "super-senior" until the summer of 2007,' recalled Peter Kurer, a member of the UBS board. 'We were just told by our risk people that these instruments are triple A, like Treasury bonds. People did not ask too many questions.'

By mid-2006, the pressure on Bill Winters's team to make up ground on its rivals was intense. Each year, Oliver Wyman, a consultancy group, conducted an analysis of how all the banks were faring relative to each other. Then it released the results to the banks, in the hope that doing so would prompt them to buy Wyman's services. JPMorgan did not usually succumb to that marketing pitch. When Dimon took over, he had made it clear that he hated the idea of taking advice from such sources. 'Those consultants are a crock of shit!' he sometimes told his staff. To his mind, if a banker needed to take advice from consultants, then that banker was not doing his job.

However, the top managers at JPMorgan found that the reports often provided useful comparative intelligence. Blythe Masters had particular reason to pay attention to what Oliver

Wyman said. By that stage, Masters had moved a long way from
the credit derivatives team. After the JPMorgan Chase merger,
she had been one of the few members of that group who had
the patience and political skills to survive the infighting. So far
did she soar up the corporate hierarchy, that she was appointed
Chief Financial Officer of the investment bank in 2005, at the
age of just thirty-four. It was a striking achievement, and made
her one of the most senior women on Wall Street. By 2005
some of her colleagues were whispering that Masters might possibly be heading for the very top.

As CFO, Masters was responsible for tracking progress relative
to rivals, and presenting that to outside analysts. So in spring of
2006 she met with Nick Studer, one of the consultants at Oliver
Wyman, to discuss Wyman's 'gap analysis' on how JPMorgan
Chase had fared in 2005. This report essentially asked a clutch of
banks to submit data on how their different divisions were performing, which the consultants then used to calculate how the
banks looked relative to each other (on an anonymous basis).
The 2005 scorecard made dismal reading for JPMorgan Chase.
Although the bank was performing well in some areas, such as
foreign exchange or interest rate derivatives, in securitization its
underperformance was getting worse. Equities and commodities
were weak too. As a result, the total revenue gap between
JPMorgan's investment bank and those of its rivals had surged to
around 1.5 billion dollars.

More than a billion! Masters was startled and baffled. She knew
that it would not be easy to placate equity investors in the bank's
stock if they saw that figure. 2005 had been another record year
for the banking world: the largest investment banks had collec-
tively raised their revenues by 31 per cent to $289 billion. In that
time, however, JPMorgan Chase had produced only a modest
rise. So what should J.P. Morgan do? Was it time for the bank to
reconsider entering the mortgage CDO and CDS game?

Once again, Winters asked his team to see if they could work out a way to make mortgage-linked CDOs pay, and Black did the same in New York. Back came the message: there was no sensible way to get rid of super-senior risk. In fact, the problem of super-senior was getting more challenging by the day. As the CDO machine boomed in 2006, it was creating such an extraordinary demand for mortgage and corporate loans that the percentages banks could earn from those loans were falling still further. 'This business just does not make sense,' Winters told his colleagues.

To Winters's relief, Dimon backed him. Dimon was a man with a ferocious grip on detail but he was also willing to delegate decisions to men who could present arguments he respected. 'On CDO of ABS, the reason we didn't get in was due to the basic risk discipline of Winters and Black – they looked at it and just could not work out how to make the business profitable enough for the risks,' Dimon recalled. In addition, Dimon had the supreme self-confidence to go up against analysts and consultants. Irrespective of whether investors were criticizing his strategy, he was *not* going to turn JPMorgan into a pale version of Goldman Sachs, he told his colleagues. 'One of the problems of being a CEO is the constant pressure on you to grow, grow and grow. It is there the whole time,' Dimon recalled. 'But if you are in the risk business you can get into terrible trouble if you just keep growing. As Warren Buffet said, sometimes the best thing you can do is just go to the golf course and do absolutely nothing for a bit.'

Winters and Black duly sat on their hands. Yet each of them was haunted by frustration. So was Masters. She had always prided herself on being a detail-orientated manager: when she ran a business she liked to know every nook and cranny, to check it was done *right*. Back in the 1990s that trait had prompted some colleagues to brand her a 'control freak'. By 2006, most of those colleagues said that her style had mellowed. Like Demchak and others, she had learnt lessons with the passage of time. At the age of thirty-six, she no longer acted as if she needed to win every fight; she had learned to dance flexibly around issues with maturity and a sense of humour. Some of her friends suspected the change also reflected a new sense of peace in her personal life. In the late 1990s she went through a divorce (like several others on the J.P. Morgan team). She subsequently remarried, though, and by 2006 she was spending weekends with her new family on a farm she had acquired close to New York.

She had also become a beacon for other women at J.P. Morgan. By 2006, there were still precious few senior female executives on Wall Street, let alone with a teenage child. Masters felt almost as evangelical about promoting diversity as propagating the derivatives creed. 'In the world I operate in, I stand out for being a woman,' she admitted to womenworking.com, an online publication. 'I believe that a lot of the onus falls on people like myself to help get women into top positions – finding a mentor in her field is one of the most valuable things any young woman can do,' she added, noting that she always advised other women to 'take yourself out of your comfort zone . . . women have to be more assertive than men are accustomed to them being!'

Masters hated leaving a mystery unsolved. She could understand why J.P. Morgan was lagging in commodities and equities. Her failure to work out why the bank was falling behind in the credit world, though, felt like a personal blow. A decade earlier she had helped to create the CDO business, and she had watched with pride as it took off. Now it seemed to have mutated into a phenomenon she could no longer understand. 'How are the other banks doing it? How are they making so much money?' she asked herself over and over again. She could not work it out.

Like Winters, Masters was so steeped in the ways of J.P. Morgan that it never occurred to her that the other banks might simply ignore all the risk controls J.P. Morgan had adhered to.

The thought that they might do so lay too far outside her cognitive map, just as it did for Winters. 'Am I proud of this [failure to guess]? No! Perhaps we should have realized what was going on,' Winters would later say, in a defensive tone. 'Maybe it seems hard to believe, but we *didn't* really understand. Or not until the very end, and by then it was all too late.'

CHAPTER TEN

Tremors

In October 2006, Bill King, the man Jamie Dimon had charged with working out JPMorgan's mortgage pipeline, travelled to Rwanda to participate in a project to help local coffee farmers develop their businesses. One day, after visiting the plantations, he returned to his hotel to hear his boss's voice at the other end of a crackling phone line. 'Billy, I really want to you to watch out for subprime,' Dimon said. 'We need to sell a lot of our positions. I've seen it before. This stuff could go up in smoke!'

King was not too surprised by the intervention. Dimon was a hands-on manager with strong knowledge of the market, who had no qualms about disturbing his employees' holidays if he considered a matter urgent. And by the autumn of 2006, Dimon thought the housing sector was becoming just that.

In the spring of 2006, US house prices had started to slide. 'A housing crisis approaches,' a column in *Barron's* magazine boldly declared by August, pointing out that the median price of new homes had dropped almost 3 per cent in the previous eight months, while sales of new homes had fallen 10 per cent, leaving new home inventories at record levels. 'The national median price of housing will probably fall by close to 30% in the next three years [based on] simple reversion to the mean,' it added, meaning that the steepling prices of the past few years were the result of a bubble. The predictions of doom were derided by the housing and mortgage industry. David Lereah, chief economist of the National Association of Realtors, declared that a 'soft landing' for the market was in sight. Home builders, though, started to slash their forecasts. 'Builders that built speculative homes are trying to move them by offering large incentives and discounts, and some anxious buyers are cancelling contracts for homes already being built,' observed Robert Toll, CEO of luxury home builder Toll Brothers, after its stock crashed 50 per cent for the year by August. *Forbes* magazine tartly observed: 'When even Toll Brothers, the high-end builder, suffers cancelations, you know the real estate boom is over.'

On 6 October, home builders Kara Homes, known for their construction of 'McMansions', filed for bankruptcy protection, less than a month after reporting what it called the 'two most profitable quarters in the history of our company'. The delinquency rate on subprime mortgages rose from 12 per cent to 14 per cent.

Troublesome as they were, these signs of housing strain did nothing to stop the mortgage-based CDO machine. Between October and December 2006 alone, banks issued a record $130 billion worth of CDOs, double the level a year before, and 40 per cent of those were created from asset-backed securities consisting primarily of subprime mortgages. That brought the total sales of cash CDOs to $470 billion for the year. Issuance of derivatives-based CDOs was even higher. One particularly fast area of growth was so-called 'mezzanine structured finance' CDOs, or instruments created from the riskiest pieces of risky ABS. Some $32.5 billion of those were sold in 2006, four times higher than in 2005. Meanwhile, most Wall Street banks were so intent on continuing to grow their businesses that in the summer and autumn of 2006, Merrill Lynch, Morgan Stanley and Bear Stearns each acquired stakes in mid-size mortgage lenders.

By stark contrast, Jamie Dimon was seriously worried. As the winter of 2006 loomed, he held a series of meetings to discuss the mortgage outlook. Should JPMorgan stop mortgage lending? Should the bankers try to hedge it even more? Or was it time to be more aggressive and actively bet on a housing crash – as some hedge funds were doing? The brainstorming was intense, and continued for weeks. Dimon was reluctant to slash mortgage activity too violently, given that the US retail lending market was a key part of JPMorgan Chase's business franchise, and one that he himself had previously targeted for growth. Nor was he keen to make an overt punt on a crash in the housing boom.

Over at Deutsche Bank a group of traders was already taking that tack. As far back as October 2005, Karen Weaver, an analyst in its New York team, had written a hard-hitting report warning of a future mortgage crunch. After that, Greg Lippman, head of the mortgage trading desk, started betting a crash would occur by purchasing ABX contracts that bet on a downturn. Those produced a loss in early 2006, because CDOs were still booming, but Lippman was so convinced that a crash loomed that in 2007 the Deutsche Bank team nevertheless boldly increased its trading bet.

Goldman Sachs was also rolling the dice. During 2005 and most of 2006, the bank had adopted a bullish trading stance towards the mortgage world, believing the house bubble had further to run. At the end of 2006, though, managers decided conditions were changing. In one of the big bold gambits that had made the brokerage so famous, the Goldman traders sold their mortgage positions, sometimes at a loss, and then adopted a bearish stance, using large quantities of the bank's own money to benefit from a crash. 'We could tell that the markets were getting overheated so we took a position in the ABX and other ways,' one senior Goldman trader recalled.

Some of the senior JPMorgan managers thought their bank should do the same. In December, Ownit and Sebring, two mortgage brokerages, collapsed – a signal that housing conditions were worsening. Even so, Dimon remained reluctant to make aggressive trading bets. That flew in the face of JPMorgan tradition and style. 'We are *not* Goldman Sachs,' he told his staff. So the bank concentrated on less dramatic ways of protecting itself. For the second time, Chase Home Finance was told to raise its underwriting standards, and to sell its mortgages on as fast as it could. The investment bank was also told to keep purchasing CDS contracts to gain shelter against mortgage defaults.

By early 2007, the cost of buying that shelter was starting to rise, as more and more bad housing news tumbled out. In late February, the British bank HSBC admitted that mortgage defaults were rising sharply at Household Finance, a Charlotte-based subprime lender it owned. Chillingly, the bank revealed that the behaviour of these defaults was defying the bank's economic models. New Century Financial, another housing lender, issued a similar statement. By late February it had become quite expensive to buy protection against default risk on the BBB portions of CDOs; so costly, in fact, that the price of insurance only made sense if you believed those mortgage bonds were worth just 70 cents on the dollar.

Yet, even amid the unease, the JPMorgan bankers continued to find players willing to write those insurance contracts. 'There were plenty of people on the other side of the trade, which made it easier for us,' Winters later recalled. Some banks were convinced that the decline in valuations on the ABX was extreme. They figured that they could make an easy profit by selling protection they wouldn't ever have to pass on. Analysts at Bear Stearns claimed that the 'true' price of BBB tranches should be 90 cents on the dollar, not the 70 cents they were trading at on the ABX. 'It's time to buy the index,' Gyan Sinha, Bear Stearns's respected mortgage analyst, said. 'The market has overreacted.'

Others institutions continued to write protection against mort-gage default because there was so much momentum behind the CDO machine that it had almost left them on autopilot. They had to keep finding CDS contracts to create CDOs, to keep their investors happy and keep earning fees.

One bank that remained bullish about the market was Merrill Lynch. As spring approached, it kept frenetically creating CDOs, in fact at an accelerating pace. Though the JPMorgan bankers were relieved that others were willing to sell them default pro-tection, they were also baffled. Did Merrill Lynch know something that they did not? Was it trying to prop the market up? From the outside, Merrill appeared to be on quite a roll. Its 2006 results were the best it had ever produced, with net earn-ings running at $7.5 billion, up a staggering 49 per cent for the year. Meanwhile the senior management appeared to be in a cautiously upbeat mood. 'Investment banks have had no choice but to build their risk-taking capabilities,' Dow Kim, co-head of global, and the man behind much of the broker's CDO boom, told a specialist publication in early 2007. 'Clients want more liquidity and capital from their sell-side providers and that trend will continue. We have been very disciplined and have ramped up only in line with our overall growth. We are responding to the new business environment, but we have picked our spots – and a lot of our risk emanates directly from our client business.'

Merrill's upbeat tone was echoed by many across the market. When Boston Consulting Group published its regular capital markets report on 2006, it noted that investment bank revenues overall had surged by 33 per cent to $289 billion, while profits jumped 38 per cent to $90 billion. The report did not point out that those heady profits had only been achieved by the banks leveraging their assets to unprecedented degrees. In 2001, Merrill Lynch's leverage ratio had stood at just x16. By 2007, it was x32. The ratio at Goldman Sachs stood at x25, Morgan Stanley at x33, Bear Stearns at x33 and Lehman Brothers at x29 – all of which were sharply higher too. However, in the new twenty-first-century finance, very few analysts bothered to pay attention to these numbers. They were fixated on the data about revenues and profits. 'The outlook for 2007 is positive . . . due to favourable economic and market conditions,' Boston Global Consultancy declared, echoing the consensus view. It predicted that investment bank revenues would hit $335 billion in 2007, yet another sharp increase.

By the late spring of 2007, Winters and Black were more and more on edge. Their unease reached much further than the mortgage world. In the first six years of the decade, the business of repackaging *corporate* loans and derivatives had also boomed. In 2006 alone, bankers sold $105.8 billion of CDOs made up of risky corporate loans, double the previous year, and seven times the volume at the start of the decade. They also sold $35.6 billion of CDOs built from corporate credit derivatives, ten times the amount sold in 2001. That had prompted manic demand for the raw material needed to build these CDOs, namely loans, bonds and derivatives. As a result, the borrowing costs for companies were tumbling to record lows.

Few mainstream companies responded to the cheap finance by loading up their balance sheets with debt. Memories were too fresh of what had happened in the internet bubble, when companies collapsed under their debt burdens. Private equity companies, though, had no qualms about grabbing every cheap debt deal on offer. They were like the corporate equivalent of subprime mortgage borrowers. Buyout groups needed debt to fund their acquisitions and had every incentive to raise as much finance as they could, as cheaply as possible. Bankers were only too keen to go with that, since doing so provided the perfect raw material out of which they could build corporate CDOs.

By the spring of 2007, the leveraged finance party had grown so riotous that buyout groups were being offered finance on terms that seemed ridiculously lax. Not only were interest rates ultra-low, but bankers were loosening the legal covenants for these deals, giving borrowers an even more generous ride. Like mortgage borrowers, buyout groups gleefully refinanced to cut their borrowing costs. They also loaded up with debt to pay themselves fat bonuses. Unsurprisingly, the buyout deals got bigger too. In 2006, there were $753 billion of leveraged buyouts, half of them conducted in the US – seven times the level seen four years before. So intense was the mania that a host of giant corporations were gobbled up, including Equity Office Properties, Alliance Boots, TXU and HCA.

That trend left J.P. Morgan in a fix. It did not want to turn its back on the corporate lending world, which was supposed to be its core franchise. Many of the largest private equity groups were long-standing clients. Winters and Black didn't want them going elsewhere, and rivals were more than ready to snap them up. Over at Citigroup, CEO Chuck Prince was flamboyant about his eagerness to extend leveraged loans. 'As long as the music is still playing, we are still dancing – and the music is still playing,' he told the *Financial Times* in the summer.

Yet Winters and Black feared that sooner or later some of the buyout groups would end up defaulting on their deals. If that occurred while the debt was still on JPMorgan's books, in the process of being repackaged, it would leave the bank at risk. That 'warehouse' period typically lasted for several weeks, at least. Dimon was also concerned. So, as with mortgages, they embarked on an initiative to trim risk. They did not clamp down on corporate lending altogether. When the total volume of the bank's leveraged loan deals hit $27 billion in the late spring, though, they ordered their desks to start raising underwriting standards. Then they turned a few deals down, even ones involving powerful private equity firms. A deal to finance a leveraged buyout of the UK retail store Boots was nodded through; so was one involving TXU. Deals to finance the buyout of First Data and Archstone, though, were rejected. 'We took ourselves out of five of the ten big private equity deals that spring,' Black later said. 'But that means we *were* in five of those deals, which we regret.'

Notwithstanding those moves, the volume of leveraged loans on JPMorgan's books continued to rise, and in early summer it hit $32 billion. Dimon, Winters and Black decided to go further and implement a series of so-called macroeconomic hedges. Traders were instructed to short the equity markets, betting that stocks would fall, and to take out derivatives contracts betting that corporate and mortgage defaults would rise. Bets were also made that long-term interest rates would rise. If an economic crunch hurt the value of the leveraged loan pile, the bank would offset those losses with these hedges. 'The fact is that every five years or so, something bad happens. Nobody ever has a right to not expect the credit cycle to turn!' Dimon kept saying. It was an observation driven as much by gut feeling as by hard-headed analysis. To Dimon, that feeling was a reason to act.

Unknown to Winters, some of his former J.P. Morgan team-mates were reaching similar conclusions. The cautious attitude towards risk instilled by the J.P. Morgan training seemed to have become imprinted in their DNA. As Bill Demchak at PNC in Pittsburgh tracked the credit boom throughout 2006, he grew deeply alarmed. Late that year, during a regular earnings update with equity market analysts, he declared that PNC was embarking on a radical new policy to shed credit risk from its balance sheet, either by selling loans or by insuring them with credit derivatives as insurance. By the standards of what almost all other regional banks in America were doing at the time – *expanding* their loan exposure, as the markets boomed – the decision was extraordinary. Demchak, though, remembered only too well the devastation of Chase's portfolio after the internet bubble burst, and he was determined to save PNC from that fate.

Then his team went further and put in place a series of macro hedges. Ironically, they were similar to what Winters was doing half a world away. He had never been a close friend of Winters's, and some of Demchak's friends were angry that Winters did not do more to protect Demchak in the merger years. A friend of Demchak's later said: 'I think Winters was quite pleased to see Demchak leave, in some ways, because it boosted his career.' Yet, irrespective of their personal differences, one thing linked them: neither Demchak nor Winters liked taking uncontrolled risks.

Andrew Feldstein was also battening down the hatches at BlueMountain Capital, the hedge fund he had started. He had been expecting a turn in the credit cycle since 2005 and had designed his fund's whole investing strategy around what he believed were price distortions in the credit markets. Having spotted early on the degree to which banks were abusing their CDO machines, in relation to the treatment of super-senior risk and much else, he had placed hefty bets on a downturn in the CDO market.

He hadn't always called the shots right. His bearish stance on the credit markets cost him considerable earnings during 2005 as the markets continued to boom. 'I called the turning point too early,' he later observed, with a wry smile.

Yet Feldstein was more convinced than ever that something must give in the credit world. Unlike Masters and Winters, he had close dealings with the CDO trading desks of numerous banks, and he had spent hours analysing their trades. He had no way of knowing exactly how much super-senior risk the banks were piling on to their balance sheets. That was a closely guarded secret, even within the banks. Yet he could see that it was rising at some banks, and he was convinced that the situation was precarious.

So he also took short positions in the market on the banks he believed were holding the biggest super-senior piles. He also shorted the super-senior tranches held by the banks, and the mezzanine tranches which banks were selling to customers using prices that were distorted by credit ratings. 'In an ideal world, I would like to think that markets are rational and efficient. And in my own career I have tried to promote that,' Feldstein liked to say. 'But until that ideal world arrives, we will also continue to trade.'

From time to time, Feldstein tried to tell some of his old colleagues about the scale of super-senior risk he thought was piling up on the banks' books, but his warnings were met with scepticism. When he dropped hints to Winters about the distortion of model prices, Winters brushed the warnings off. After all, BlueMountain was in the business of trying to make profits from the shortcomings of the investment banks, so Winters was wary of Feldstein's motives.

Feldstein also explained more explicitly to Demchak that numerous banks were keeping piles of super-senior liabilities on their balance sheets. Demchak and Feldstein were friends, and Demchak was a director of BlueMountain. Even so, Demchak found it impossible to believe that the banks could be ignoring the risk controls he took for granted, or that the brilliant mechanism he'd been involved with creating had become so perverted. 'Andrew told me what he thought the banks were doing with their super-senior risk, but I kind of ignored it,' Demchak later said, with a dry, despairing chuckle. 'I just couldn't believe it. Most of us could not.'

By early 2007 most Western policymakers were convinced that the credit cycle had become so extreme that it would inevitably turn soon, leading to ripple effects well beyond the American housing market. But they were at a loss to judge how that might play out. So much of the financial activity of the boom was out of their sight or control. Since 2004, the Fed had been steadily raising interest rates, along with the Bank of England, in a

deliberate effort to prick the bubble. The ECB had belatedly followed suit. Yet, these moves hadn't worked, Instead of rising, the
cost of borrowing had stubbornly continued to *fall* in many corners of the market. In the US and UK government bond sphere,
yields on ten-year bonds even tumbled below short-term bond
yields, creating a bizarre pattern known as an 'inverted yield
curve'. Alan Greenspan dubbed the situation a 'conundrum'.

There were other puzzles too. In previous decades, the price
of assets had been volatile when surprises hit the markets, be that
an oil-price shock, a rate rise or a swing in the housing market.
However, as Basel's BIS noted at the time, the 'striking feature of
financial market behaviour' in the twenty-first century was 'the
low level of price volatility over a wide range of financial assets
and markets'. The prices of almost all assets were rising, while
the cost of borrowing was flat or falling. One troubling result,
policymakers feared, was increasing correlation between the
prices of many different asset classes, which would mean that a
downturn would also be widespread.

Most policymakers and bankers had never seen such eerily
calm markets in their careers, and they were uncertain and
divided about what – if anything – they should do. At one end
of the intellectual spectrum stood senior American officials, who
mostly assumed that the pattern was benign. In January 2006,
Ben Bernanke, an esteemed academic economist, took over at
the Fed from Greenspan. Earlier in the decade, Bernanke had
coined the phrase 'The Great Moderation' to describe the
new twenty-first-century atmosphere of calm. Both he and
Greenspan seemed to think that this 'moderation' had arisen
because central bankers had successfully crushed inflation and
because there was a savings surplus in Asia. Essentially, the argument was that Asian countries were using their foreign exchange
reserves to buy American Treasuries, and keep rates low.

Greenspan and Bernanke were also both keenly aware,
though, that credit prices could not keep rising indefinitely.

'Extended periods of low concern about credit risk have invariably been followed by reversal, with an attendant fall in the prices of risky assets,' Greenspan noted in 2005. However Bernanke and his predecessor also hoped that any 'attendant price fall' would not lead to a financial shock, because the blow would be softened by financial innovation. Back in the 1980s, the Savings and Loans crisis had devastated some banks because they were not able to shed credit risk. By 2007, though, the dominant creed at the Washington Fed and US Treasury was that credit risk had been so widely dispersed, via credit derivatives and CDOs, that any blows would be absorbed.

The innovation evangelists seemed to have history on their side. During the first seven years of the twenty-first century, the financial system had been rocked by repeated shocks, including the attack on the World Trade Center, the collapse of Enron, the implosion of the internet bubble and then the collapse of a $9 billion hedge fund called Amaranth in 2006. Yet on each occasion the system had bounced back fast. Fed officials appeared confident that the same pattern would apply to any losses that might arise from subprime mortgages, or any other shock to the system. So did many international commentators. 'The dispersion of credit risk by banks to a broader and more diverse set of investors, rather than warehousing such risk on their balance sheets, has helped to make the banking and overall financial system more resilient,' the IMF declared in its 2006 annual report. Such dispersion, it added, would help to 'mitigate and absorb shocks to the financial system' with the result that 'improved resilience may be seen in fewer bank failures and more consistent credit provision'.

Not quite everybody, though, adhered to this creed. At the other end of the intellectual spectrum stood officials at the BIS in Basel. The BIS was known as the 'central bankers' bank' because it provided a forum for those bankers to meet and exchange ideas. It held a peculiar structural position in the global banking world, since it had no direct responsibility to voters and politicians but was privy to many central banking secrets. That gave it some freedom of thought, and from 2003 onwards its officials starting expressing views quite different from the Fed's. One of the first clashes occurred on 30 August 2003, at a conference of economists in Jackson Hole, Wyoming, where Bill White and Claudio Borio, the two most senior economists at the BIS, presented a paper warning that not all financial innovation was good. 'The changes in the financial and monetary regime may have potentially increased the scope for financial imbalances to grow during expansionary phases owing to a relaxation of financial and monetary constraints,' Borio, an impish Italian, declared. 'They may have raised the "elasticity" of the economic system, making it more vulnerable to boom and bust cycles . . . [and] could sow the seeds of headwinds and financial stress during the subsequent downswing.'

The audience was dominated by American economists, including both Bernanke and Greenspan, and they were unimpressed. 'People thought Bill [White] was just being alarmist,' one senior American policymaker later recalled. Afterwards Roger Ferguson, the deputy chairman of the Federal Reserve, harangued the two men for being unnecessarily 'gloomy'. Fed officials also pressured them to water down the tone of the reports that the BIS published. White and Borio complied to some extent, and from then on kept their dissent mostly out of public view. After all, the Federal Reserve was a major shareholder of the BIS.

'There was a lot of opposition to what we were saying,' White later recalled. Alan Greenspan commanded such formidable respect and power that he was often dubbed the 'Maestro', and American academics were powerful too. Confronting that was hard, even for the BIS.

White and Borio, though, grew steadily more alarmed. By early 2007 they had become convinced that a key reason for the 'conundrum' Greenspan had identified was that financial institutions had become so highly leveraged in ways policymakers could not see. Far from being the salvation, innovation might be creating new problems, and they impressed those concerns on their colleagues. 'What worries me is what might happen if – or when – the system start to *de*-leverage,' Malcolm Knight, managing director of the BIS, observed in the spring of 2007. Or as White defiantly wrote in the conclusion to the 2007 BIS annual report:

> It would clearly be undesirable, even if it were possible, to roll back the changes that have occurred over the last few decades . . . nevertheless, more scepticism might be expressed about some of the purported benefits of having new players, new instruments and new business models, in particular the 'originate and distribute' approach which has become so widespread. These developments have clear benefits but they may also have side effects, with associated costs.

The views of other Western central bankers and regulators tended to fall somewhere between these two extremes. At the European Central Bank, in Frankfurt, Jean-Claude Trichet appeared sympathetic to the view of the BIS. 'We are currently seeing elements in global financial markets which are not necessarily stable,' he observed in January 2007, at the annual meeting of financiers and global leaders in the Swiss mountain resort of Davos. 'There is now such creativity of new and very sophisticated financial instruments, that we don't know fully where the risks are located. We are trying to understand what is going on but it is a big, big challenge,' he added, with a Gallic shrug. He pointed to the 'low level of rates, spreads and risk premiums' as factors that could trigger a potentially violent 'repricing' of assets.

British regulators seemed even more ambivalent. That partly

reflected a fragmentation in the focus and responsibility of regulators. Until the late 1990s the Bank of England was the body
that was supposed to monitor the health of the financial world.
Back in 1997, however, the new UK Labour government of
Tony Blair announced that it planned to strip the Bank of
England of its responsibility for the micro-level supervision of
banks and hand that instead to a new institution, the Financial
Services Authority (FSA). The reform took a couple of years to
implement. By the time it was in place, though, the Bank had
lost its prior role regulating the banking world; instead, its main
responsibility in the new system was to maintain financial and
economic stability in a general sense. On paper, that still gave the
central bank, some authority in financial matters. But when
Mervyn King was appointed as Governor of the Bank of
England in 2003, the Bank's focus moved away from finance to
monetary policy. King, a cerebral, owlish man, was trained as a
macroeconomist and had been a professor at the London School
of Economics. He was deeply committed to the task of keeping
inflation stable, but knew little about the finer details of credit
markets. Moreover, he initially gave no impression of caring
what happened in the esoteric reaches of cyberfinance either.
Nor did he show much inclination to talk with real bankers:
soon after his arrival, King quietly scrapped a long-standing
practice of calling senior City bankers in for a dinner with the
governor every six months.

Notwithstanding that, some officials inside the Bank doggedly
tried to keep track of what was going on in the credit world.
Paul Tucker, head of markets at the Bank, was one of those, and
by early 2007 his detective work had left him shocked by the
sheer scale of change under way in London's financial sphere.
'[We are living in] the age of what I call Vehicular Finance,' he
told a conference in the spring of that year. 'The key interme-
diaries are no longer just banks, securities dealers, insurance
companies, mutual funds and pension funds. They include hedge

funds of course, but also Collateralized Debt Obligations, specialist Monoline Financial Guarantors, Credit Derivative Product
Companies, Structured Investment Vehicles, Commercial Paper
Conduits, Leverage Buyout Funds – and on and on. These vehicles can fit together like Russian dolls.'

This pattern made Tucker and others a little uneasy, particularly since some of the trends did not entirely seem to make
sense. In April 2007, the Bank pointed out in its Financial
Stability Report that the balance sheets of large financial institutions had more than doubled since the start of the decade, to run
at $22 trillion, while shareholder equity had merely grown from
around $500 billion to around $1 trillion. It was a stunning
increase and – as the Bank admitted – the pattern seemed rather
at odds with the purported aims of the 'originate to distribute'
creed which implied that the banks were supposed to use innovation to shed assets. But the Bank did not urge banks to cut
their balance sheets, partly because it did not really have the
power to act. Under the 'tripartite' system ushered in by the regulatory reforms of 1997, it was the FSA – not the Bank – that
held responsibility for ordering banks to change strategy. And the
FSA, for its part, did not seem eager to change the strategies of
banks. Under the terms of its mandate, it tended to focus on
whether individual banks were complying with the regulatory
rules, as set out in the Basel Accord, rather than look at the
system as a whole. It did not feel any need to look at institutions
that fell outside the official regulatory net, such as SIVs, or the
wider impact of a spiralling bubble in British house prices.

That situation left some officials at the Bank deeply frustrated.
But they were reluctant to ring alarm bells, since it was far from
clear that the patterns developing in the credit world were truly
dangerous. So much seemed unknown – or untested. Or as
Tucker himself noted: 'Over the last year the world has enjoyed
a further period of monetary and financial stability . . . against
that background, banks and dealers have posted fairly remarkable

profits, accumulating more capital resources. Over the coming decade, some currently observable imbalances will plausibly work their way through the system. In ten years' time, we may therefore . . . be better informed on whether the changes in the structure of our financial markets help or hinder the preservation of stability.'

The position of Timothy Geithner, the youthful president of the New York Federal Reserve, was more ambivalent still. Unlike the men running the Fed and the Bank of England, Geithner had no background in academic economics. He arrived at his post in October 2003, aged just forty-two, after a career in the Treasury. Free from rigid economic dogmas, he was a deeply pragmatic man, who sometimes observed that his aim in life was merely to do 'the least bad job possible'. Like almost every other American policymaker and official, Geithner believed that in an ideal world, banking should be based on the principles of free-market competition. In the real world, though, he recognized that governments sometimes needed to jump in. In his eyes, the financial system was often plagued with what he called 'collective action problems' – or cases when the banks were so busy pursuing their own interests, in a competitive and greedy fashion, that they failed to rationally consider long-term outcomes.

Competitive forces, in other words, did *not* always produce efficient or safe results. That view was different from Greenspan's faith in laissez-faire finance. Geithner's approach was much closer to that of the former New York Fed president Jerry Corrigan. That was no coincidence, as after Geithner arrived at his post, he took to calling Corrigan regularly for advice, along with other experienced financiers. Corrigan was only too happy to play the avuncular adviser. He and Geithner not only shared similar attitudes towards the markets, but both had a 'geeky' fascination with the technical details of market infrastructure. 'I guess you could say Corrigan and Geithner are in the same church pew.

Greenspan is not,' observed one senior American official who knew all three well.

The ever-pragmatic Geithner was careful never to express any public sentiment that might dissent from Greenspan's views. Compared to Greenspan, Geithner was not just younger, but he also commanded far less clout and respect. As the decade wore on, though, he became privately uneasy about some of the trends in the credit world. From 2005 onwards he started to call on bankers to prepare for so-called 'fat tails', a statistical term for extremely negative events that occur more often than is implied by the normal 'bell-curve' statistical models that the banks' risk assessments so relied on. In the summer of 2005, Geithner quietly admitted that 'the growth of credit derivatives looks as if it has made the system more stable, but maybe at the price of making the system more unstable at the tail'. Translated from banking jargon, that meant he worried that while the pattern looked good in benign times, if the system was hit by a shock there could be terrible turmoil. 'We just don't know how much leverage is there,' he sighed.

In May 2006 he spelt his concerns out in a public forum. In a prepared speech he said: 'A number of fundamental changes in the US financial system over the past twenty-five years appear to have rendered it able to withstand the stress of a broader array of shocks than was the case in the past . . . [but] confidence in the overall resilience of the financial system needs to be tempered by the realization that there is much we still do not know about the likely sources and consequences of future stress to the system . . . The proliferation of new forms of derivatives and structured financial products has changed the nature of leverage in the financial system. The addition of leverage embedded in financial instruments to balance sheet leverage has made this source of potential risk harder to assess.'

The most tangible sign of unease was that Geithner also clamped down on the trading infrastructure of the credit derivatives world. Back in 1993, the J.P. Morgan bankers who wrote the G30 report had considered and dismissed the idea of instituting a mandatory clearing house for tracking and settling derivatives trades. One huge benefit of a clearing house would have been protecting against undue 'counterparty risk', or the danger that if two institutions traded and one suddenly collapsed mid-trade, the deal could not be completed. The clearing house idea was rejected because the bankers who wrote the G30 report argued that investors had strong enough incentives to monitor that counterparty risk themselves. Their strong bias was for keeping the derivatives markets private, subject only to voluntary oversight.

By late 2004, though, it was clear to Geithner that self-policing had not removed counterparty risk. What particularly alarmed him at the time was the situation in banks' back offices. Though credit derivatives were supposed to be the epitome of efficient 'virtual' banking, many banks were still using faxes to confirm deals. In the early days of the market, that wasn't a problem, but as the markets exploded, the volume of trades overwhelmed the banks' back offices, creating long backlogs in processing the paperwork. By 2004 the delays were so bad that it took almost eighteen working days *on average* for banks to confirm their deals. Worse, a new fashion had started for 'novating' deals, or assigning them to someone else. If bank A cut a CDS deal with bank B, for example, it might later decide to sell that deal to Bank C – without actually telling Bank B. That left vast quantities of deals in a legal limbo land.

In the rational market conceived of by free-market economists, the banks would have responded to this problem by voluntarily investing to create better trading systems. However, the banks weren't doing so. At most banks the derivatives traders had not only no control over the back office, but no desire to sacrifice their profits to pay for infrastructure investment. With the notable exception of Jamie Dimon at JPMorgan, most bank

CEOs also knew very little about trading infrastructure. And no individual bank wanted to stop doing trades until a new system was in place, as that would let its competitors forge ahead. To Geithner, it was a classic case of a 'collective action problem'.

In late 2004 he acted, encouraging Corrigan to head a study of a group of leading Wall Street financiers to examine the state of the complex financial world. By then Corrigan was working as a managing director at Goldman Sachs and had already conducted one such exercise, back in 1999, which set out the lessons to be learned after the LTCM hedge fund collapsed. This second study would have a much wider agenda, analyzing the state of complex finance more generally. When the 300-page report was finally released in the summer of 2005, it duly demanded that banks overhaul their back-office procedures for credit derivatives. 'Dear Hank,' Corrigan wrote in a letter to Henry Paulson, then CEO at Goldman Sachs, that accompanied the report:

> I want to call your particular attention to [our recommendations] which call for urgent industry-wide efforts to cope with serious 'back-office' and potential settlement problems in the credit default swap market and to stop the practice whereby some market participants 'assign' their side of a trade to another institution without the consent of the original counterparty to the trade . . . this practice has the potential to distort the ability of individual institutions to effectively monitor and control their counterparty credit exposures.

In September 2005, Geithner summoned representatives from the fourteen largest Wall Street banks to attend a meeting in the New York Fed. It was the first time the banks had gathered for a collective meeting in the Fed since the implosion of the LTCM hedge fund. Determined to make his point, Geithner solemnly lectured the banks that they had to overhaul their systems, or face a regulatory clampdown. It worked. By the end of 2005, the

average time for confirming trades fell to eleven days; in 2006 it
fell sharply again. Geithner and Corrigan were thrilled. They
appeared to have nipped this problem in the bud with deft
proactive action involving regulators *and* banks. 'Often it takes a
crisis to generate the will and energy needed to solve a problem,'
Geithner observed in an article in late 2006, co-authored with
Callum McCarthy, head of Britain's FSA. 'Here, the industry
deserves credit for acting in advance of a crisis.' British officials
fervently backed what Geithner was doing, as they too had been
worried about the backlogs, but since regulatory responsibility
was split between the Bank and FSA it was unclear who should
clean up the mess.

Yet when Geithner and Corrigan reflected on the backlog
issue in early 2007, they felt little sense of triumph. Clamping
down on backlogs was a relatively easy issue to address. There
was consensus about what needed to be done, and there was also
tangible data that *proved* why everyone needed to act. But what
if the problem in the banks' back offices epitomized a much
bigger problem in the system as a whole? What if 'collective
action problems' were distorting the credit markets in a myriad
other, less transparent ways? Was there anything regulators could
do about those 'collective action' issues? Neither Geithner nor
Corrigan was sure.

On 17 April 2007, Corrigan travelled down to Washington for
a meeting organized by the German finance ministry. That year
the Germans held the revolving chair of the G8 grouping, the
body that brings together leaders from eight of the world's leading industrialized nations for debate. They wanted to use the
gathering to focus on the thorny matter of financial stability.
Like others, German financial officials feared the credit bubble
might be spinning out of control. However, they had an unusually clear idea who might be the culprit – the hedge funds.
Almost a decade earlier, in the autumn of 1998, the financial

system had been rocked to its core when LTCM imploded. LTCM had been leveraged no fewer than one hundred times, and used that money to place massive bets in the interest rate derivatives world, which later turned sour. After that event, banks and regulators had scrutinized the funds, spurred on by the lessons outlined in Corrigan's report. Nonetheless, the Germans remained alarmed by the lack of formal regulation over these funds.

Even if they did not know exactly why credit conditions seemed so extreme, they were convinced that the high-rolling, risk-loving hedge funds must somehow be to blame – and they hoped to persuade the rest of the G8 to regulate them. If nothing else, that would show that global leaders were willing to act to prevent another bubble burst. 'There needs to be a proper debate about what hedge funds are doing,' Peer Steinbrück, the German finance minister, declared.

On a Sunday afternoon the G8 delegates met at the World Bank's headquarters to discuss the German proposals. Among them were senior US officials, including Robert Steel, the US under-secretary, and Tim Geithner. Senior central bankers and treasury officials from Europe also attended, among them Mario Draghi, governor of the Bank of Italy, and Nigel Jenkinson, a senior official at the Bank of England. Some private-sector financiers had been invited too. Corrigan was one. Another was Jim Chanos, the founder of the hedge fund group Kynikos, famous for taking the type of aggressive 'short' positions that the Germans hated.

The delegates trooped into a large conference room in the World Bank. Security was tight. Corrigan was one of the first to speak. With his usual gruff manner he outlined the key issues that were dogging the world of complex credit, in relation to hedge funds and other investors. The good news, he observed, was that trading backlogs were falling. The bad news was that innovation was occurring so fast that it was posing a host of new risk-management challenges. So many, in fact, that Corrigan admitted he was far from sure that the regulators – or even bankers – really knew what risks were building up.

One of the Italian officials jumped in. A few months earlier, he observed, the Bank of Italy had asked twenty-eight financial institutions with operations in Rome to complete an anonymous survey on their level of exposure to credit derivatives and other areas of structured finance. 'But as of now, not one has replied,' he observed. The room erupted in nervous, embarrassed laughter.

Then Chanos was summoned. Steel, of the US Treasury, had asked him to come to make sure that the hedge fund community got a chance to defend itself. The Treasury didn't agree with the Germans that hedge funds were the key problem, and it wasn't keen on regulating them. To do so would fly in the face of Alan Greenspan's argument that it was good to have some freewheeling risk-takers in the system to disperse risk across a wider group of players.

'So what are your views about hedge funds and financial stability?' a senior German official asked Chanos. As succinctly as he could, Chanos tried to defend himself. The hedge funds, he argued, were in the business of taking calculated risks, and precisely because they were in the risk-taking business, they tended to monitor those exposures. Other parts of the financial system, though, were far more dangerous because they were taking risks that nobody could see. 'It's not us you should be worrying about – it's the *banks*!' he declared.

He explained why he was worried. Leverage at investment banks was surging; banks were holding huge piles of opaque credit assets on their books which no one understood; strange CDO and SIV vehicles were springing up with all manner of tentacles into the banks. Worrying about what hedge funds were doing amid all that litany of dangers was like fiddling with the deckchairs while the *Titanic* was heading for the iceberg. 'It is the *regulated* bits of the system you should worry about!' he said, explaining that he was so concerned that his own fund had taken out numerous 'short' positions on the share price of most large investment banks and many monoline insurers. The Germans looked utterly unimpressed. 'Thank you, but do you have anything to say about the risks that hedge funds pose?' one official asked. 'No,' Chanos said, and sat down.

He had the impression that most of the officials around the room had barely heard what he had said, far less agreed with him. In part, the problem was one of data. The main yardstick used by the regulators and central banks to judge if banks were healthy was whether they were meeting the terms of the Basel Accord. All banks needed to set aside capital worth 8 per cent of their assets, and by that measure the banks all looked extremely healthy. In early 2007 British banks had a capital ratio of 12 per cent, while the American ratio was just slightly lower – way above the minimum that regulators required. Given that, it was very hard for regulators to make a case for getting too worried about the banks. What they didn't know, and Chanos had tried to alert them to, was that those capital reserves were only set against a relatively small portion of the banks' true risk exposure, because so much of that risk was tucked out of mind into shadow banks, or only measured using very narrow and flattering tools.

In reality, some of those around the table suspected that the Basel measurements were far from perfect. By 2007, many international banks were using a reformed version of the original Basel Accord, called Basel II, that let banks use their internal systems when deciding how risky assets might be, and thus how much capital was required. If the bank's own models for judging the risk of, say, a CDO were wrong, then the Basel II system would not work and the dangers in the market might be considerable. Corrigan had spent enough time looking at various banks' models to know that they were far from foolproof.

Geithner's repeated warning that banks needed to pay more attention to 'tail risks' or 'fat tails' indicated that he too was uneasy about the modelling. However, vague notions about invisible risk were not enough to force the G8 to act.

When Geithner launched his campaign to clean up trading backlogs, he had been armed with alarming data. Similarly, when the Germans launched their appeals for hedge fund regulation, they had at least had a concrete disaster story to point to in LTCM. But in the case of structured finance, it was hard to point to any numbers that showed why anyone should be worried.

The meeting closed inconclusively. It was clear that the rest of the G8 did not support the German idea of clamping down on hedge funds, but it was also clear that nobody else around the table could articulate any better, proactive ideas about what they should do. As CEO of JPMorgan Chase, Jamie Dimon could impose policy shifts based on a gut feeling that the credit cycle was turning. Central bankers and regulators, by contrast, were trapped in vast bureaucratic machines. They were only equipped to fight the last war. Faced with a financial system that few people seemed to understand any more, the G8 did nothing – other than hope that the losses appearing in the US subprime mortgage world would be quickly absorbed just as the innovation evangelists presumed.

PART THREE

Disaster

CHAPTER ELEVEN

First Failures

The sun slipped slowly down the cerulean Spanish sky. Next to the elegant Barcelona waterfront, hordes of holidaymakers strolled along the beach, enjoying the summer air. A few stragglers could be heard screeching with laughter as they jumped into the sea. Above them, many hundreds of bankers stood on the elegant terrace of a futuristic, gleaming white hotel, staging a so-called 'champagne salute' in celebration of the fact that investment banks had just enjoyed their most lucrative year in history. The date was 11 June 2007, the occasion the annual meeting of the European Securitisation Forum (ESF), the body devoted to promoting the art of securitization in Europe.

Champagne corks popped. Raucous laughter rang out. And as the light faded, a rock band struck up, playing cheesy covers. The band called itself 'D'Leverage' and was composed of bankers from Barclays Capital, Credit Suisse and others. The name was a joke. ('It's meant to be funny – its 'da leverage,' not 'de-leverage,' one of those watching explained.) They were slightly out of tune.

'It's been an extraordinary year!' beamed Rick Watson, the

man who ran the ESF, as the band struck up. Watson had every
reason to be pleased. Back in the 1990s, Europe had had no
trade body like the ESF to champion securitization, and for years
after the ESF sprang to life, its meetings attracted only a thousand bankers or so.

By the time of this gala, however, securitization had spread
like wildfire in Europe, and more than five thousand attendees
had turned up. The meeting carried a lofty title: 'Global Asset
Backed Securitization; Towards a New Dawn!' An exuberant
crowd included smooth-talking, white-toothed salesmen from
large American banks, eagerly selling repackaged mortgage debt;
self-deprecating British traders; and earnest, chain-smoking representatives from German insurance companies and banks. Their
prey included asset managers from Italy, Spain, Germany and
Greece, often decked in elegant pastel colours. A silent gaggle of
Chinese and Singaporeans circulated. It was rumoured they were
furtively buying CDOs to find a home for foreign exchange
reserves. A few regulators could also be spotted, conspicuous in
looking generally more dowdy than the bankers. Some of the
biggest delegations, though, came from the three credit-ratings
agencies, which were drawing fat profits from the CDO boom.
Barcelona was the perfect opportunity to market their skills.

Long queues formed outside the bathrooms, and around the
coffee stations and computer terminals. Bankers jostled in the
corridors on their way to sessions so full that they were forced to
stand in the aisles or squat on the floor. Lively debate ensued
about the American mortgage-backed bond market, the CDO
sector, the SIVs, the state of the Spanish mortgage market and
the outlook for Russian ABS. There was even a high-profile
debate on Islamic finance, in which investing must comply with
the sharia ban on usury. Some hoped Islamic finance would be
a hot new growth area for securitization. 'What we are seeing
right now in the securitization sector is an extraordinary burst of
innovation,' Watson boasted.

But could the party last? Not everyone thought so. In late May, just before the Barcelona conference, the prices of bonds and loans had suffered some drops, implying the credit market had reached a peak. 'What has happened [in recent days] in the bond market suggests we could be at a turning point,' suggested Ganesh Rajendra, head of securitization research at Deutsche Bank. 'There are some signs that the weather is changing,' echoed Alexander Batchvarov, a highly respected senior securitization analyst who worked at Merrill Lynch. 'The market has been growing very fast – it doubled last year. We have to ask whether there will be such a fast pace of growth this year.'

Nobody doubted that *some* growth would occur. Most of the bankers in Barcelona had never worked in the field when it wasn't booming. The ESF organizers were so supremely confident about the future that they announced during the conference that the 2008 gathering would take place in Cannes, a bigger venue, and considerably swankier too. 'We need more space! Next year's conference will be even *bigger*,' Watson effused, as the champagne kept flowing and D'Leverage played on.

The very next day, on 12 June, the news broke in New York that a crisis was erupting at a hedge fund with close links to Bear Stearns. 'Hard hit by turmoil in the market for risky mortgages, a big hedge fund has fallen 23 per cent from the start of the year through late April,' the *Wall Street Journal* reported. 'The fund, called the High-Grade Structured Credit Strategies Enhanced Leverage Fund, is widely exposed to subprime mortgages, or home loans to borrowers with weak credit histories.' The New York-based fund was run by two former Bear bankers, Ralph Cioffi and Matthew Tannin.

At first, few details were reported about what exactly had gone wrong. What was clear, though, was that the fund had been hit by a toxic combination of bad mortgage bets and massive levels of leverage. Cioffi and Tannin had first set up shop back in October 2003, raising $925 million of investor money to create a fund called 'Bear Stearns' High-Grade Structured Credit Strategies'. They then borrowed heavily from banks to buy securities that were described in their marketing literature as 'high quality, floating rate, structured finance securities'. That included asset-backed bonds, CDOs, and bank loans, many of which had been created by Bear, and most of which carried high credit ratings. In 2004, 2005 and 2006, as the credit markets boomed, the strategy produced fat profits, allowing the fund to produce annualized returns of between 13 per cent and 40 per cent. That success was so impressive that in the summer of 2006 the group created a second fund, called the High-Grade Structured Credit Strategies Enhanced Leverage Fund. This version employed similar tactics but was more leveraged, sometimes as much as $20 for every dollar of investor equity.

The second fund also got off to a running start, delivering cumulative returns of 4.4 per cent in the first four months. At the start of 2007, though, things had begun to unravel. As the subprime mortgage market began to turn sour, the price of some mortgage securities and derivatives fell. That wasn't supposed to happen – those products had been risk-proofed according to the models – but the defaults had built up enough that the unthinkable had started to occur.

The two funds tried to hedge themselves by buying protection against further mortgage defaults with ABX derivatives, but they did too little, too late. By February, investors had become so alarmed about the funds' mounting losses that they demanded more than $200 million of their money back. Cioffi and Tannin tried to soothe them, arguing that the funds offered an 'awesome opportunity' and that 'we're very comfortable with where we are'. In private, though, they were concerned. 'I'm fearful of these markets,' Cioffi wrote in an email to a colleague on 15 March 2007, according to documents seized by the FBI. 'It's either a meltdown or the greatest buying opportunity ever, I'm leaning more towards the former.'

In May, the two men admitted that the most highly leveraged fund had lost 6 per cent in April alone. Then, soon after, they revised that estimated loss up to a staggering 19 per cent. Investors were livid: how could Cioffi and Tannin have miscalculated the losses so badly? In reality, it was easy, because working out the 'true' value of the assets held by the funds was fiendishly difficult. Some of the securities the funds held were traded in the open market, so their prices could be tracked, but most CDO products still weren't being traded. If the funds were pursuing a 'buy and hold' strategy, buying assets and retaining them until they expired (usually five years), the lack of price information might not have mattered. But these were hedge funds, and a widespread convention in the hedge fund world dictated that funds give their investors regular reports on the so-called 'mark-to-market' value of their assets. Without that transparency, investors usually wouldn't invest. The Bear Stearns funds, therefore, faced a big problem: how could they find 'market prices' when a true market for their assets didn't exist?

Most funds resolved this dilemma by using models to take account of default patterns and the price of any such instruments that *were* being traded, and extrapolating from that data to create a price. Extrapolating in this manner was not difficult with corporate credit derivatives, since there were plenty of corporate debt instruments that did trade. The mortgage sector, though, was more problematic. Mortgage derivatives had proliferated so fast in such a short time, that it was hard to draw clear links between the price of underlying mortgage loans and linked CDOs. Trading in mortgage bonds, let alone mortgage derivatives, was sparse. The only obvious guide was the ABX index, which had been launched in early 2006. It had provided a gauge of the value of the range of bonds in the CDOs – from BBB to AAA. So what many funds – including the Bear Stearns fund –

did was look at the prices as given by ABX, and then use that to
deduce the prices of the bonds in their own CDOs. During
2006, that had cast a flattering glow on the fund, since the ABX
trades were bullish. By the end of February 2007, though, the
ABX index suggested that the price of BBB subprime mortgage-backed bonds had fallen to around 65 per cent of face
value. To put that another way, the cost of buying insurance via
the ABX had risen so high that the prices only made sense if you
thought the bonds commanded a mere 65 per cent of their face
value. The ABX ticked up again in March, but by June the
implied price of BBB bonds was sliding towards 60 per cent of
face value. Even the implied prices of A and AA instruments
were starting to deteriorate.

As Cioffi and Tannin factored those movements into their
models, the impact was devastating. By early June, the value of
the assets at the most leveraged fund was 23 per cent down,
while the older fund had suffered losses of 5 per cent. Due to
how highly leveraged the newest fund was, it was effectively
bust, and the oldest fund teetered on the edge. *BusinessWeek*
pointed to the trouble as 'another illustration of the danger
facing funds that rely heavily on borrowed money to make
investment bets'.

As the losses mounted, officials at J.P. Morgan's headquarters
on 270 Park Avenue pondered what they should do. When the
two funds had used leverage to place their investment bets, they
had done so by taking out large loans from banks, often on a
short-term basis. J.P. Morgan had extended a hefty amount,
alongside Barclays Capital, Merrill Lynch, Goldman Sachs and
others. The J.P. Morgan management was well aware of the risk
involved, but the bank was also looking to expand its dealings
with hedge funds. To reduce the risk the bank had required Bear
to put up plenty of high-quality collateral against the loans. By
mid-June, Steven Black, co-head of the investment bank, was
worrying whether the bank would be able to get its money

back, and he sent a team to Bear's Madison Avenue offices to assess the situation. Frantically, Bear officials tried to placate them, pleading: 'Just stick with us, and it will all be fine – these are high-quality instruments!' But the JPMorgan risk managers insisted on seeing the accounts, and these suggested the funds were effectively bust.

Black realized that JPMorgan needed to get its money back as fast as possible – or grab the collateral Bear had put up, and sell it off. He called Warren Spector, the powerful and widely respected head of Bear's investment bank, who had built the group's debt markets operation and was one of the few men at Bear who truly understood the full reach of this business. Spector struck a defiant pose: he suggested that JPMorgan was the only bank threatening to call in its loans. He also declared that the two hedge funds would soon recover their losses.

Black was furious. He knew that Merrill Lynch and several of the other creditors were also threatening to call in their loans. As the pressure mounted, Cioffi and the other officials at the Bear funds tried to get some money to repay the loans. They declared they would sell almost $4 billion of their most liquid assets, and Bear traders circulated a list of the securities on the block. It was not enough to placate the banks, though. As the days elapsed, and Merrill Lynch failed to get its money back, Merrill officials told Bear they planned to sell about $400 million worth of Bear's collateral in the open market. Most of that was complex, rarely traded instruments such as CDOs.

That threat sent shockwaves through the market. Nobody had ever tried to sell that many CDOs or mortgage bonds in public before. A firesale of that kind threatened to produce something the CDO world had never seen before: 'true', undeniable, market prices. In theory, that promised to be a very healthy long-term development. After all, the bankers who had invented structured finance had always claimed to be upholding the virtues of free markets and rational pricing. They were supposed to like transparency. In actuality, though, the prospect of an open auction had terrifying short-term implications. Even at the best of times, forced sales hardly achieve good prices; and by mid-June, conditions in the mortgage market were getting worse by the day.

On 15 June, just as Merrill was issuing its firesale threat, Moody's announced that it was cutting its ratings on 131 bonds linked to BBB-rated pieces of subprime debt, and reviewing the ratings on 247 other bonds, all linked to mortgages issued in 2006. The move affected only $3 billion worth of bonds, a tiny proportion of all the $400 billion subprime-linked bonds sold in 2006. Nonetheless it spooked investors so badly that the BBB tranche of the ABX tumbled to 60 per cent of face value.

Moody's admitted that its experts were finding it hard to read the housing-market trends. '[These mortgages] are defaulting at a rate materially higher than original expectations,' it observed. The mood was turning decidedly edgy. 'Negative sentiment [is taking] a firm hold of the [subprime bond] market,' analysts at J.P. Morgan noted. Bankers feared that an auction of any of the CDO products would push prices lower still, and that would have ominous implications, not just for the Bear Stearns funds, but for numerous other investment groups and banks too.

After all, most of them were also marking the value of their CDOs using model prices; if a visibly lower 'market' price emerged, almost anyone holding CDOs would need to record losses. Transparency would be a nasty shock. 'If we end up seeing these assets sold at significantly distressed prices, it will likely cause other funds to have to re-evaluate how effective and fair the values that they have been carrying these securities have been,' said Josh Rosner, a managing director at Graham Fisher, an investment research firm in New York.

For several days, a game of brinkmanship played out. Merrill circulated a list of the CDOs and other securities it wanted to sell and invited bids from investors. J.P. Morgan and Goldman Sachs threatened to do the same. Frantically, Bear tried to dissuade them, pointing out that the banks would also suffer. Merrill Lynch and J.P. Morgan steadfastly insisted they wanted their money back. Eventually, as the tension mounted, a deal of sorts was cut. In late June, Bear Stearns publicly announced that it would provide $3.2 billion in emergency funds to the older of Cioffi's two funds, to prop it up. The other fund would be liquidated. Bear also privately agreed with J.P. Morgan, Bank of America, Merrill Lynch, Goldman Sachs and others that they could recoup their loans, and the banks dropped their firesale threat.

Financiers with any investments linked to the mortgage market breathed a profound sigh of relief. The shock had been averted. Black and his colleagues at J.P. Morgan didn't dare hope, though, that this was more than a temporary reprieve. Even with its lifeline from its mother bank, the remaining Bear fund looked sickly. Moreover, irrespective of the fate of the Bear fund, the drama had shown that a much wider structural threat was hanging over the system. What had doomed the Bear funds was that they were highly leveraged, exposed to long-term mortgage assets, and they had an investor base able to withdraw money at relatively short notice. In banking jargon, the Bear funds were thus plagued by a 'maturity mismatch': they bought long-term mortgage-linked assets that were hard to sell in a hurry, and they funded those purchases by raising short-term debt that could suddenly disappear. To make matters worse, the Bear funds were also expected to mark their assets to market on a regular basis – a market that barely existed.

In the case of Bear, that cocktail had proved poisonous almost as soon as the mortgage markets turned sour in early 2007, because the Bear funds held CDOs that were particularly vulnerable to a mortgage market downturn, and its investors and creditors had panicked at an early stage. However, Bear was in no way unique. On the contrary, the investment landscape was strewn with a host of funds that had used large quantities of leverage to invest in mortgage-linked assets, and had the same maturity mismatch. Some of them had more patient investors, or a better mix of assets, but the structural problem was widespread. And that begged a bigger question: could the problems at the Bear Stearns funds be treated as isolated? Or were they pointing to an epidemic that could erupt across the system as a whole? By late June, few bankers had a clear-cut answer. For their part, Dimon, Winters and Black were starting to get worried. 'This could turn nasty,' Black observed to colleagues.

In mid-July another shockwave hit. Winters was striding through Geneva International Airport on the way to a meeting when he received a phone call from an official at Deutsche Industriebank (IKB), a medium-sized lender based in Düsseldorf, Germany. The group was barely known outside its home country and had specialized in funding medium-sized manufacturing companies. What IKB had to say on that July day had nothing to do with industry, though: the bank was desperate for an emergency credit line, to cover what it described as a 'temporary' funding problem. 'We have a lot of safe securities, but investors are behaving strangely,' a bank official explained. 'Will you help?'

Winters was startled. The problem centred on a couple of investment vehicles run by IKB, known as Rhineland and Rhinebridge. The older of these, Rhineland, had been created five years earlier. Back then, IKB – like many other German banks – had been hunting for ways to diversify its business away from its core franchise of corporate lending, because that was becoming unprofitable. So it established Rhineland to invest in high-quality debt instruments, including mortgage-linked bonds. Rhineland was run as an SIV, which meant that it did not appear on IKB's balance sheet. It funded itself by selling commercial paper notes to investors, including European pension funds and American public sector investment bodies. Robbinsdale Area

Schools district in a north-western suburb of Minneapolis, for example, bought Rhineland commercial paper. So did the Montana Board of Investments.

Between 2002 and 2006, this strategy had delivered a fat stream of profits for IKB. In fact it was so successful that in June 2007 – or shortly before Winters received the phone call – IKB created a second SIV, which was Rhinebridge. Like the first SIV, this second entity enthusiastically bought debt instruments, including mortgage-linked CDOs. That made Western investment banks eager to court the IKB officials. At the ESF conference in Barcelona, for example, American brokers and City bankers flocked around the Germans, in the hope of selling them more bonds. However, as Winters stood in Geneva airport in July it was clear that something had gone badly wrong with the IKB funds. He called his traders in London. 'What's going on?' he asked. 'There's something like a bank run starting in the commercial paper markets,' a trader replied.

That news was alarming. Until now, the commercial paper market had been deemed one of the dullest, and safest, corners of the financial world. It was where General Electric and other blue-chip giants raised the short-term funds that they needed for day-to-day operations. It was also where solid, risk-averse investors tended to put their cash, as an alternative to placing their money on deposit at a bank. Corporate treasurers often bought commercial paper, since those notes tended to produce a return a fraction better than anything found in a bank account. Pension funds sometimes bought commercial paper too. One of the biggest sources of demand for commercial paper, though, came from the giant $3000 billion money-market fund sector.

These funds typically raised money from ordinary retail investors or companies, which tended to treat money-market funds as similar to a bank account: they placed cash there assuming they could always withdraw it, and on short notice. Precisely because money-market funds knew that investors might redeem their cash with little notice, such funds usually only wanted to purchase assets that had a short duration and were safe. Commercial paper fitted the bill perfectly.

The specific corner of the market where IKB raised funds was one subset of this world, though, a mutation known as the 'asset-backed commercial paper' (ABCP) sphere. It took that name because the groups that issued short-term notes there backed them up with 'assets' such as mortgage bonds. The solid-but-dull investors who typically bought such notes usually knew little about how mortgage-backed CDOs worked, let alone about the inner workings of SIVs. That didn't trouble them much, though, because the notes carried high credit ratings, usually the triple-A or double-A level. Money-market fund managers buying the ABCP notes assumed they were as safe as anything that might be issued by corporate giants such as General Electric.

But in mid-July the pillar of faith in the ratings of those bonds started to crack, for several reasons. One was the dismal news about defaults emerging from the mortgage world. Another was the downgrades that the ratings agencies themselves were starting to make. In mid-July, Moody's announced it was cutting its ratings on $5 billion of subprime mortgage bonds. Around the same time, Standard and Poor's placed $7.3 billion of bonds on review for a downgrade. Then the saga of the Bear Stearns funds burst into the news. After the two funds collapsed, it emerged that many of the bonds and CDOs that had wreaked havoc at the fund had carried relatively *high* – not low – credit ratings. Investors in the ABCP market flinched.

Few of them knew for sure whether the type of 'mortgage-backed bonds' the Bear Stearns funds held were similar to those owned by IKB funds, say. Nor did investors know what the price of a CDO 'should' be. So long and complex was the financial chain that linked US households with CDO investors that it was hard for the experts – let alone a non-specialist – to work out how defaults might affect cash flows of CDO investors at the other end of the chain. But the investors who bought ABCP paper bought it *precisely* because they were highly risk-averse. They could not tolerate uncertainty of any kind. So, as the rumours spread about Bear, they took the only step available to eliminate their risk: they stopped buying notes. 'The problem is that people just don't know quite what to trust, or not,' Donald Aiken, head of a large European money-market fund association, explained. 'Probably everything in most of those portfolios [behind commercial paper] is fine, but people don't know for sure, and people don't want to take the risk.'

That buyers' strike left IKB in a fix. In reality, the vast majority of the mortgage assets that the IKB funds held were *not* impaired, in terms of actual defaults on loans in those banks. However, most SIVs – like hedge funds – were required to provide regular updates on the value of the assets they held. Since the ABX was reporting drops in value, investors became utterly unwilling to buy notes issued by the IKB funds, leaving the funds desperate for cash. In theory, they had the right to call on IKB for a back-up emergency loan to keep them afloat, but in practice IKB didn't have the resources to provide that money. The German bank had never laid aside significant capital reserves to cover for the possibility that the funds might need an emergency credit line. The idea that the ABCP market would shut down was inconceivable. Moreover, the Basel rules did not require IKB to have that safety net, since the funds were 'off-balance-sheet' SIVs. Thus while the IKB funds held more than $20 billion of assets, the bank itself had a mere $16 billion liquid assets on its books.

That was where JPMorgan came in. By mid-July, IKB was frantically calling other banks, seeking a loan to plug the gap. 'Will you help?' the IKB officials asked Winters. Winters discussed the loan with his colleagues in London, as well as with Black in New York. He wanted to take the request seriously, as IKB had traditionally been a good client. Winters had always been suspicious of SIVs, though, and the saga at IKB confirmed his doubts. As tactfully as he could, Winters said 'No.'

For a few days, officials at IKB flailed around, trying to find new sources of funds. Eventually the German government stepped in, and forced a group of domestic banks to extend a €3.5 billion lifeline to IKB. That enabled it to prop up its two SIVs. Once again, traders in the mortgage-backed bond markets heaved a sigh of relief. If the IKB funds had collapsed, they would have been forced to engage in a firesale of assets, which would have pushed down CDO prices. The German rescue had – once again – averted that disaster.

Yet, as with the Bear bailout, the move seemed little more than a temporary reprieve. Across the financial system as a whole, tension was rising. Very few investors or bankers who worked outside the commercial paper market really understood what had gone wrong at IKB. Precisely because the commercial paper sector had been so slow-moving and dull in the past, it had been comprehensively ignored by journalists and regulators. The fact that a buyers' strike was under way in the ABCP sector was all but invisible to anybody outside that market. Yet the headlines about IKB showed that *something* was amiss, even if it was barely understood by anyone outside IKB.

Equity investors did not appear excessively alarmed. On 20 July, the S&P 500 and FTSE both hit an all-time high. In the debt world, though, fear was afoot. By the end of July, the ABX was implying that the price of BBB mortgage bonds had tumbled to just 45 per cent of their face value, while even AAA had fallen to 95 per cent. The models had assured that the triple-A tranches had an absolutely minuscule chance of ever losing value; but the ABX was now suggesting otherwise, and that was alarming. The market for corporate credit derivatives was also signalling alarm: by early August, the cost of insuring risky American and European corporate bonds against default had doubled, compared with its level in early July.

In early August, bankers linked to IKB called Winters again. They asked him for advice about what they should do with the mortgage securities on their books. 'Sell your assets *now*,' Winters told them. 'As much as you can!' It was a typical trader's reaction: his years of working in markets had taught him that when crisis strikes, the people who sell *first* get the best price, if they can move ahead of a wave of forced sales. But the IKB officials rejected that idea. To them, the prices being signalled by the ABX just did not make sense. They could not believe that highly rated mortgage assets could be valued at significantly less than face value, at least not for long. They told Winters that they were going to wait it out, until the markets returned to 'normal'.

CHAPTER TWELVE

Panic Takes Hold

Half a world away in Tokyo, watching the IKB drama unfold, Hiroshi Nakaso, a senior official at the Bank of Japan, was struck by déjà vu. Nakaso had never visited IKB, and knew little about how SIVs worked. However, from his vantage point in Tokyo he saw uncanny echoes of what he had observed almost a decade earlier. Back then, in the 1990s, the Japanese banking system had become overloaded with bad loans after a property bubble collapse, sparking a crisis. At the time most American officials blamed the peculiarities of Japanese finance, and criticized the Japanese government for its failure to tackle the trouble at an early stage.

When Nakaso saw what was happening at IKB, it suddenly seemed as if Japan had not been so unique after all. The bailout deal that the German government had cobbled together to prop up IKB looked uncannily similar to measures the Japanese government had used to stave off a collapse of its banks. The investor psychology seemed dangerously similar too. From a distance, Nakaso could sense that disorientation and panic were spreading, creating strange price swings. Investors were starting to lose faith. The shift was subtle, something almost none of the central bankers and regulators who worked in America and Europe had personally ever seen before. But to Nakaso it was profound. 'I see striking similarities today with the early stages of our own financial crisis more than a decade ago,' he told some of his international contacts on 2 August 2002. 'Probably we will have to be prepared for more events to come . . . the crisis management skills of central banks and financial authorities will be truly tested [in the months ahead].'

Nakaso's reaction was shared by other Japanese onlookers. When his counterparts in America or Europe heard such comments, though, most discounted them. They considered it fanciful, if not alarmist, to draw parallels between Japan's woes and the troubles brewing in Western finance. By 2007, American and European financiers took it for granted that their financial system was vastly more sophisticated and efficient than Japan's. There was also an overwhelming assumption in Washington – and London – that any losses in the subprime world were unlikely to cause wider financial shock. In the spring of 2007, Henry Paulson, the US Treasury Secretary, had told Congress that the subprime problem 'appears to be contained'. Bernanke, Federal Reserve governor, repeatedly echoed that line. 'Given the fundamental factors in place that should support the demand for housing, we believe the effect of the troubles in the subprime sector on the broader housing market will likely be limited,' Bernanke observed in a speech before the Federal Reserve of Chicago in May. 'Importantly, we see no serious broader spillover to banks or thrift institutions from the problems in the subprime market; troubled lenders, for the most part, have not been institutions with federally insured deposits.'

In early July, after the collapse of the Bear Stearns funds, Bernanke had slightly changed his tune. 'Rising delinquencies and foreclosures are creating personal, economic and social distress for many homeowners and communities – problems that likely will get worse before they get better,' he testified to Congress on 18 July, suggesting that subprime losses would be 'in the order of around $50 billion to $100 billion'. He stressed, though, that the problem still seemed negligible given the size of the wider banking system. 'It seems very far-fetched to make any parallels with Japan's crisis. The key thing to remember is that these losses are not just held by American banks, as the bad loans were in Japan, but they are dispersed,' one senior American official observed shortly before Bernanke's testimony. Or as Bill Dudley, a senior figure at the New York Federal Reserve, told bankers in early summer: 'This is a correction, but it is not dramatic in light of history . . . it could be over in a matter of weeks.'

As the summer of 2007 wore on, though, the panic in the commercial paper market steadily intensified. Before the summer, ABCP notes typically paid investors between 5 and 10 basis points more than the US overnight dollar borrowing rate. By the start of August that was moving towards 100 basis points, making it absurdly expensive for SIVs to raise funds. Many could not sell notes, even at that exorbitant rate. An entire network of 'shadow banks' was suddenly discovering that its lifeblood had been cut off. Meanwhile the housing market took a decided turn for the worse.

On 6 August, American Home Mortgage Investment Corporation filed for bankruptcy, having suffered substantial losses on its mortgage assets and finding it impossible to sell ABCP notes. 'This is getting serious,' Winters thought. The SIVs alone were estimated to hold almost $400 billion of securities. In truth, only a third of those securities were thought to be directly linked to mortgages. But if the SIVs collapsed, that could spark firesales of assets that would make the drama of the Bear Stearns funds seem trivial.

On the other side of the Atlantic, at Cairn Capital, one of

Winters's former colleagues at JPMorgan, Tim Frost, was also alarmed – albeit for more personal reasons. By 2007 Frost had been working with Cairn for three years. In that period, it had expanded into a formidable operation, which employed over 100 staff and ran some $22 billion of assets spread between two dozen CDO-like structures and a hedge fund. It had moved from its first cramped office into swanky new headquarters in the posh neighbourhood of Knightsbridge, with a fabulous view of London's Hyde Park. The office was open-plan and airy, and the walls showcased a revolving collection of quirky, cutting-edge art, included arresting portraits of unemployed miners. 'It's a warning of what happens if the returns are bad!' the Cairn staff joked to clients. Not that they were: during 2005 and 2006 and early 2007, Cairn produced steady profits in almost every corner of its sprawling empire. It enjoyed a high reputation among investors.

But by early August, ugly storm clouds were building. The problem was an SIV that Cairn had created back in January 2006, called Cairn High Grade Finance. Cairn had tried to run it in a relatively conservative fashion. Unlike some other SIV managers, Frost and his colleagues had been fussy in selecting their mortgage-backed bonds, trying to choose safe assets even when that meant earning lower returns. As a result, the fund had a higher proportion of triple-A assets than any other SIV, and Frost assumed that made the fund almost bulletproof.

Yet Cairn had an Achilles heel. Its SIV – like the IKB vehicles – funded itself in the commercial paper market, and it did not have a committed bank back-up credit line. Many investors presumed that Barclays Capital would be obliged to help the SIV if it ran into crisis, since the British bank had played a central role in creating the fund back at the start of 2006. There was no *legal* commitment, though, for Barclays to help. Like so much else in the shadow banking world, that support was a matter of trust.

Until the summer of 2007, the Cairn managers saw little

reason to worry about that state of affairs. The commercial paper market was so utterly calm that Cairn found it easy to raise funding. The execution was done by another company, known as QSR. 'Quite honestly, [the] funding ordinarily never kept us awake at night,' David Littlewood, one of Frost's partners, later explained. '[It] required very little maintenance apart from agreeing a daily funding strategy with QSR.' In mid-July, however, QSR told Cairn that the commercial paper sector was freezing up. By late July, Cairn could only sell notes at the ruinously high cost of 100 basis points over the risk-free rate of borrowing.

Frantically, Frost and Littlewood tried to discuss with investors what action Cairn could take. They were convinced that their fund was far better than those of rivals. But investors did not wish to hear about all the data that Cairn had to back that up. They were losing any ability to discriminate. Just like consumers who panic during a food-poisoning scare and stop buying all sausages or burgers overnight, ABCP investors had heard that some dodgy assets had got into the securitization chain – and since they could not tell exactly where the rot had ended up, they were boycotting *all* SIV notes.

Shocked, the Cairn partners debated what to do. Some equity investors wanted to sit tight, and try to ride out what they believed would be a short-lived storm. That was what many other shadow banks, not to mention the IKB officials, appeared to be doing. But Frost – like his former boss Winters – had a trader's instinct, honed from years trading risk at JPMorgan. He was convinced Cairn needed to act fast, to salvage whatever it could, rather than just pray that the markets would recover. His partners agreed.

At the beginning of August the senior management of Cairn hunkered down in their Knightsbridge office, turning the largest conference room into a 'war room'. Outside, tourists strolled through Hyde Park licking ice-cream cones and enjoying the summer sun. Inside the Cairn managers frenetically worked the phones, desperately trying to work out what they could do with their crumbling SIV. It was far from clear. In the corporate world there were well established precedents for how to deal with bankruptcy. There were also clear rules about how to handle a failed bank. After all, over previous decades regulators and bankers alike had seen plenty of banks collapse.

However, the problem with SIVs was that nobody had worked out before what to do if they collapsed. They sat in regulatory limbo since they were not covered by any regulatory rules, and there were no precedents for bankers, investors or regulators to follow, either in relation to Cairn itself, or to the system as a whole. 'We are literally reading through our rule book, trying to work out what to do,' confessed one of Frost's former JPMorgan colleagues who ran a rival SIV. In London, Düsseldorf, Frankfurt and New York, the system was heading into uncharted territory.

On the morning of Thursday, 9 August 2007, the European Central Bank in Frankfurt posted a brief and drily worded statement on its website. The gist was that the ECB would provide as much funding as banks might wish to borrow at a rate of 4 per cent, in response to 'tensions in the euro money-markets . . . notwithstanding the normal supply of aggregate euro liquidity'.

Journalists and investors who read the bulletin were bewildered. Central banks normally pump money into financial markets almost by stealth, using long-standing devices such as auctions in which banks each bid for a pre-assigned pot of funds. The ECB, however, was offering the equivalent of an emergency blood transfusion. It seemed to perceive a crisis.

Two hours later, the ECB revealed that forty-nine banks in Europe had demanded – and received – a staggering 94 billion euros of cash, three times the normal level of demand. The last time the ECB had injected that much money into the markets was after the attack on the World Trade Center in 2001. But there was no such obvious disaster rocking the financial world now. The only specific new development that morning was that an asset-management unit linked to BNP Paribas, a large French bank, had announced it was suspending three investment funds that held mortgage-linked bonds because a 'complete evaporation of liquidity' made it impossible to value the mortgage assets. Yet that appeared small-scale compared with what the ECB had done.

Frantically, journalists besieged the ECB's press team with questions: 'What has prompted the ECB to act?' The ECB staff struggled to cope. It was common practice there – in line with most financial institutions in continental Europe – to let its officials go on vacation for several weeks each summer. On 9 August, Jean Claude Trichet, the wily ECB president, was on a holiday in northern France, and most senior officials were on vacation too, including those who would normally run the press team.

'This is just a *fine-tuning* exercise,' a hapless junior press official was instructed to say, over and over again. More specifically, he added, the ECB had noticed in the days leading up to 9 August that the cost of borrowing money in the interbank market had jumped to a level of 4.7 per cent, well above the rate officially set at 4 per cent by the ECB. However, what neither the press officials – nor the senior ECB staff themselves – appeared to be able to explain was *why* the borrowing rate was rising.

If the ECB's move was supposed to calm markets, it disastrously backfired. Before 9 August, most investors had not even realized that the cost of borrowing euros for banks was rising. The ECB's actions blazoned that news on to trading terminals and television screens around the world. Many of the traders and investors who saw the news had no idea what to think. The senior officials at many European banks and investment groups were also on vacation. Uneasily, their deskbound colleagues dispatched emails to holiday destinations around the world. The

gist of those messages usually went: 'Something is really spook-
ing the markets; but we don't know *what*!'

On the other side of the Atlantic, officials at the New York
Fed were spooked too. Ever since the Bear Stearns funds had
imploded in mid-June, central bankers from the largest Western
nations had been holding regular conference calls to discuss the
strains building in the credit world, and to swap information. In
the preceding weeks, Fed officials had noted that conditions in
the credit markets were becoming strained. The Fed had repeatedly discussed these tensions with the ECB, as well as with
officials from the Bank of England, Bank of Japan, Bank of
Canada and the Swiss National Bank. However, the official
mantra at the Fed, as at the Treasury, was that the mortgage
problems were 'contained'. US policymakers did not want to
make any emergency move, since they feared that would do
more harm than good. They were seriously irritated by what the
ECB had done, particularly since the ECB had *not* notified the
Fed about its intervention.

Fed officials debated how to respond. By the afternoon of 9
August, New York time, some ten hours after the ECB had
posted its statement, almost every indicator tracked on the Fed's
computer screens signalled panic. The price of gold was rising,
together with the price of US Treasury bonds, while the price of
risky corporate bonds and mortgage-backed assets was tumbling.
Investors were dumping anything that might contain default risk,
and heading for the safest assets around. Most ominous of all, the
cost of borrowing dollars in the interbank market was also rising.
That implied that banks and other key financial institutions were
reluctant to lend money to each other, either because they
needed that cash, or did not trust each other – or both.

Fed officials did not wish to do anything that would sow further panic; but nor did they want to admit how vexed they felt
with the ECB. So, they aimed for the middle ground. A
few hours after the ECB move, the New York Fed provided

$24 billion worth of daily funds, higher than usual, but not unprecedented. The next day, it offered $36 billion more funds, as the ECB injected another €61 billion. But Fed officials repeatedly stressed to reporters that they did not consider the situation to be an emergency. The mantra – as ever – was that the market turmoil should be a short-lived storm.

British central bankers, though, broke ranks with the ECB in a more pointed manner. The ECB had not warned the Bank of England either that it was planning to unleash so much liquidity, and by the afternoon of that first day, wild rumours were swirling around the London markets that some large European banks were about to collapse. British regulators tried to work out what was going on, but they found it hard because so many bureaucrats in continental Europe were away on holiday. Briefly, they wondered if they should copy the ECB and inject large quantities of funds into the sterling system too. However, Mervyn King, the Bank of England governor, demurred. Back in the days of the credit boom, in the spring of 2007, he had repeatedly warned investors and financiers that they needed to prepare for a future turn in the credit cycle. He usually expressed this in general terms. However, on 21 June 2007, in a speech at London's Mansion House, King had even warned bankers that it was foolish to assume that all triple-A assets were safe. 'The development of complex financial instruments and the spate of loan arrangements without traditional covenants suggest [a] maxim: be cautious about how much you lend, especially when you know rather little about the activities of the borrower,' he declared. 'It may say champagne – AAA – on the label of an increasing number of structured credit instruments. But by the time investors get to what's left in the bottle, it could taste rather flat.'

Now that the fizz had indeed vanished from the markets, King had no sympathy for those who had refused to heed his advice. It served them right, he reckoned, if their over-hyped

innovations were starting to collapse. 'We are certainly not going
to protect people from unwise lending decisions,' he sternly told
British politicians the day before the ECB move, with the
manner of a headmaster lecturing foolish pupils. He saw little
reason to rescue bankers or investors. In any case, he did not see
much chance that problems in the CDO world would ever have
too great an impact on the real economy as a whole.

On 15 August 2007 another tremor hit. Countrywide,
America's largest independent mortgage lender, announced that
the rate of foreclosures and defaults on its portfolio of subprime
loans had risen to the highest levels since 2002, due to 'unprecedented disruptions' in the home-loan market. It also admitted
that unsold mortgages were starting to pile up on its books,
because it could not persuade investors to purchase mortgage-
backed bonds any more. Countrywide's share price crashed 13
per cent in a matter of hours, dragging a host of banking stocks
lower.

The next day, investors were handed a small respite.
Countrywide announced that it had raised an $11 billion loan
from a group of banks, including Bank of America and
JPMorgan, to plug its funding gap. The largest American groups,
like their German counterparts, had realized they could ill afford
to see one player collapse, since that risked setting off a domino
effect. Then, on 17 August, the Federal Reserve took another
step to calm the markets. It cut the so-called 'discount rate' (a
special rate applied to emergency loans that banks might need to
raise) by 50 basis points to 5.75 per cent. This was an effort to
signal that the Fed stood ready to help the banks – if they actually needed support. The equity market signalled a degree of
relief. But, in the ABCP sector, investors stayed stubbornly on
strike.

In mid July there had been around $1200 billion worth of
ABCP notes outstanding in the market; by mid-August the

sector had shrunk to below $1000 billion, because notes were maturing – and investors were refusing to purchase new, replacement, notes. Activity in the mortgage-backed market was drying up too: whereas around $80 billion of notes a month had been sold at the start of the year, in August almost no notes were sold. Liquidity was being sucked out of the system at a startling rate, albeit in a half-hidden manner. This was affecting markets in New York. However, the problem was dire – if not worse – in London. When European financiers had created their complex networks of SIVs and related structures earlier in the decade, they had typically decided to fund these vehicles in dollars, not euros. But it was much harder for London-based banks or other financial groups to get hold of dollars than an American bank, since they did not have access to US bank deposits or the Federal Reserve's funding window. That created a vast currency mismatch, to use banking jargon, that made the dollar squeeze doubly intense for European groups.

As tensions spread, the senior managers in many banks ordered each department to stop lending money to any counterparties that looked at all risky. The panic spread well beyond Europe. Over in Tokyo, a host of large Japanese institutions started to cut their dealings with all European banks due to concerns that those banks faced a liquidity squeeze. Ironically, it was the mirror image of a pattern that had developed a decade earlier, when Japanese banks faced their own crisis and were shunned in global markets. 'People are talking about a German premium or a British premium now,' one Japanese banker observed, referring to the 'premium' that any bank from that country needed to pay in order to raise finance on global markets. Other Asian banks followed suit, cutting lines to Europe. So did some American groups. However, non-American banks also shunned any American groups that were perceived to be heavily exposed to subprime mortgage markets. Distrust was spiralling across borders with stunning speed. And even when financiers were not overtly scared of dealing with each other, many were reluctant to extend loans for fear they might need those funds if they found themselves locked out of markets too.

Just like households which may stockpile baked beans and bottled water if a hurricane approaches, banks were hoarding whatever cash they had. Yet the more they hoarded cash, the higher borrowing costs in the interbank market rose, creating *more* fear. And the more that investors refused to purchase ABCP notes, the more investments with firms that relied on ABCP funding were also shunned, for fear they might collapse. 'The main fear [now is] fear itself,' Matt King, an analyst at Citigroup, noted in a research report issued in London on 16 August. 'Of course there is no fundamental reason why the ABCP buyers should take fright – the assets themselves are generally sound and most of the banks are very well capitalized. But the greater the fear in the system, the greater the potential for problems.'

At the end of the month, economists and central bankers from Europe and America gathered for an annual symposium in Jackson Hole, Wyoming. By then, the fear in the commercial paper market had leaked out into the news. However, economists and policymakers appeared deeply split about what – if anything – could be done. Though the Fed had already cut the discount rate, officials were not eager to start cutting the main federal funds rates, because they were concerned about inflation. Many economists were also opposed to bailing out investors from their foolish mistakes. 'There are a lot of investors who invested on a leveraged basis in high-risk assets,' Michael Mussa, the former chief economist of the IMF tartly observed. 'They are going to have to eat substantial losses and their creditors are going to have eat substantial losses. And as far as I am concerned the proper policy response is "Bon appétit!"' Many economists and policymakers also appeared convinced that any turmoil in the mortgage market would sort itself out fairly soon. 'What we are seeing right now is a total overreaction in terms of expected losses,' insisted Axel Weber, head of the German Bundesbank. He suggested that the most sensible strategy for many institutions might be to wait 'and simply ride it out'.

Yet officials at Pimco, the giant American bond fund, were uneasy. They did not run any SIVs themselves, but they were keenly aware of the interlinkages that were starting to unravel. 'The real issue right now is a run on the shadow banking system, which is about $1.3 trillion in size, funded by commercial paper,' Paul McCulley, a senior Pimco official, told the Jackson Hole conference. 'The key issue [that] is going to come to a head in the next couple of months is that the shadow banking system is going to have to be put on the balance sheet of the real banking system.' The 'real' banks were going to have to bail out their shadowy offspring – or face a terrible chain reaction of collapses. The pattern seen at IKB could be repeated many times. It was a terrifying thought. In theory, the big banks were supposed to have fat capital cushions, but when regulators stipulated how fat those cushions needed to be, they had never given any thought to the $1.3 trillion shadow banking world. 'It is stunning how little many policymakers know about the workings of asset-backed commercial paper (ABCP) and collateralized debt obligations (CDOs),' lamented Carl Tannenbaum, chief economist at LaSalle Bank, the day after the conference ended.

By late August, Tim Frost and the Cairn Capital management team were haggard. The summer heat had turned Hyde Park from verdant green to a parched, dusty brown. Inside the Cairn offices, stress was taking its own toll. For several weeks, Frost and the other managers had lobbied Barclays and other banks for a loan, to plug their funding gap, but Barclays had refused. It was starting to worry about the impact of the mortgage market turmoil on its own portfolio of CDOs and was engaged in a massive – and ill-timed – bidding war with Royal Bank of

Scotland to purchase ABN AMRO, a Dutch group. It did not wish to expose itself to any new credit risk.

Cairn refused to take 'No' for an answer. What would happen, they asked Barclays, if a way could be found to remove any credit risk from a loan, using Frost's beloved credit derivatives? Barclays indicated that it might extend a loan under those circumstances. So Frost and his colleagues worked the phones, trying to find someone willing to write protection on the assets held by the Cairn SIV, using credit derivatives. Many banks were wary of the idea, since they – like Barclays – were battening down the hatches. However, the bankers who traded credit derivatives at the Lehman Brothers' office in London were feeling more bullish than most and agreed to organize a consortium to write the necessary CDS contracts on Cairn's SIV assets, protecting it from the risk of default.

Then Frost got back on the phone and tried to persuade the investors in the Cairn SIV to back the idea – and to pay for the cost of raising that insurance. It was not easy. The investor roster included not just European banks and American asset managers, but a clutch of Asian banks too, and some were reluctant to pay for insurance. 'Can't we just wait this out?' some asked. Like the IKB bankers, they were still assuming that the woes in the mortgage market were temporary. The Cairn managers were adamant: they *had* to restructure its SIV. The charter that governed the SIV stipulated that if the vehicle's funding levels fell below a certain threshold, it would need to start selling off its assets, and that moment was ticking closer.

Finally, on 31 August, a deal was struck: Barclays announced that it would 'provide senior financing' in the form of a loan to the fund, in exchange for getting the loan 'fully hedged'. Frost was elated. Once again it seemed that the magic of derivatives had solved the problem, linking people who wanted to shed risk with those who wanted to roll the dice. He considered the Cairn deal to be as creative and ground-breaking as any he had ever concluded during his days at JPMorgan; to him, this was a prime example of true financial innovation at work.

The crisis seemed to have been averted, at least at Cairn, but ominous portents would soon signal that this was merely the end of the beginning.

CHAPTER THIRTEEN

Bank Run

On the morning of 31 August in Washington – or a few hours after Tim Frost completed the rescue plan for the Cairn fund – President George W. Bush stepped out into the Rose Garden of the White House to meet reporters. He was flanked by the imposing figure of US Treasury Secretary Henry Paulson. All through the long summer, Bush had pointedly avoided getting dragged into the escalating debate about America's troubled subprime market, but by the end of August it was becoming ever harder to maintain the official line that the problems were contained. At one end of the financial system, the funding crisis that had engulfed Cairn was spreading out to hit a host of institutions holding assets linked to subprime debt. At the other end, in the 'real' world, the mortgage picture was steadily deteriorating. The National Association of Realtors finally dropped its bullish stance and admitted that US house prices looked set to post the first annual decline since the Great Depression of the 1930s.

In the subprime world, the mood was particularly grim. At the start of 2007, the rate of default on subprime mortgages had been running at around 13 per cent; by September it was 16 per cent, and rising. What was especially vexing was that it was so difficult to predict how much higher the rate might go. Cycles of default had been seen in the mortgage world before, usually as a result of a recession or sharp rise in interest rates. However, this cycle was not behaving quite as economists had expected.

The economy was *not* in a recession, overall, and unemployment was low, but interest rates had risen sharply on many loans – the average rate on an adjustable mortgage rose from 3.5 per cent in late 2005 to 5 per cent by the autumn of 2007. The result was that households were defaulting in surprisingly large numbers. When economists peered into the data, most blamed the fact that so many households had so overstretched when they took out their loans. Now that house prices were falling they had no incentive to hang on to their homes. It was clear that house prices were the key to the default pattern, but nobody was sure just how far those prices might fall – or how many more defaults that might trigger. 'There's no model for what's happening now in the housing and mortgage industries,' said Josh Rosner of investment research firm Graham Fisher.

That left Bush and Paulson in a bind. They certainly didn't want to see millions of voters thrown out of their homes. Nor did they wish to see the financial crisis spread. Yet Bush hailed from a Republican Party that espoused free-market ideals, and using federal intervention to prevent so-called creative destruction flew in the face of those principles. So, as Bush stood in the Rose Garden in the August sunlight, he tried to steer a middle course. 'Owning a home has always been at the center of the American Dream,' he declared, in his folksy style. '[But] the markets are in a period of transition, as participants reassess and re-price risk [and] one area that has shown particular strain is the mortgage market, especially what's known as the subprime sector of the mortgage market. This market has seen tremendous innovation in recent years, as new lending products make credit available to more people. For the most part, this has been a positive development . . . [but] there's also been some excesses in the lending industry. One of the most troubling developments has been the increase in adjustable-rate mortgages that start out with a very low interest rate and then reset to a higher rate after a few years. This has led some homeowners to take out loans larger than they could afford based on overly optimistic assumptions about the future performance of the housing market. Others may have been confused by the terms of their loan, or misled by irresponsible lenders.'

Bush went on to unveil some modest measures of aid. These included a pledge that the Federal Housing Association would provide some guarantees for mortgages, if the lending industry agreed to modify the terms for households in default. The idea was to keep troubled families in their homes, if possible, but without bailing them out. It was little more than a token show of help. Economists calculated that the measures would apply at best to only around 600,000 of two million-odd households who were close to default. Nonetheless Bush clearly felt loath to do more. 'We've got a role, the government has got a role to play – but it is limited,' he declared. 'It's not the government's job to bail out speculators, or those who made the decision to buy a home they knew they could never afford . . . America's overall economy will remain strong enough to weather any turbulence.' With that, Bush paused for breath. Then a reporter yelled out: 'Sir, what about the hedge funds and banks that are overexposed on the subprime market? That's a bigger problem! Have you got a plan?'

Bush blinked vaguely. 'Thank you!' he said, and then he and Paulson turned to leave.

For a few days after Bush's speech in the Rose Garden, the mood in the financial world perked up. The equity markets rallied, and the tone of the credit markets improved, with declines in the cost of buying protection against the default of corporate and mortgage bonds. Inside Cairn, some managers started to fret that they might have overpaid Lehman Brothers for the CDS protection they had bought in the deal to restructure their SIV. The managers of some rival SIVs quietly dropped plans to conduct similar restructuring deals. Across the industry, bankers began to clutch at straws, hoping that the commercial paper markets would reopen soon, and that the August turmoil would prove a short-lived squall.

The respite barely lasted two weeks. At 8.30 p.m. on 13 September Robert Peston, the gangly business editor of the BBC, appeared on its news channel. Until that point, the BBC had given only cursory coverage to business dealings. On that Thursday night in September, however, Peston had electrifying news to report. In breathy, dramatic tones, he declared that Northern Rock, the fifth-largest British lender, had gone to the Bank of England and asked for emergency support. 'Although the firm remains profitable,' Peston declared, 'the fact that it has had to go cap in hand to the Bank is the most tangible sign that the crisis in financial markets is spilling over into businesses that touch most of our lives.'

It was a damning, shocking statement, and within seconds it had flashed up on trading terminals all over the world. During the summer, most investors had assumed that the problems in the subprime mortgage market would only hurt the shadow banking world, and some specialist mortgage lenders, such as Countrywide. Northern Rock took the crisis into a whole new dimension. It was a large regulated bank, located in Newcastle, hundreds of miles from the high-stakes financial machinations practised in the City of London, or the housing markets of Florida or California. 'The Rock', as it was known locally, extended loans to families all over the UK. It held the savings of millions of British consumers and was deemed eminently safe. Or it had been until Peston's report.

Within minutes of the BBC bulletin, consumers began logging on to Northern Rock's website and withdrawing their cash. The website then crashed, fuelling panic. The next morning, Northern Rock savers flocked to the bank's branch offices, and pictures of terrified savers in a long line in front of the bank beamed on to computers, television screens, BlackBerries and mobile phones across the world. By mid-morning, a full-scale bank run was under way. Never before had so many terrified consumers and investors seen a bank run in action, in real time. Technology was helping to spread the panic.

What brought Northern Rock down was another variant of the woes that had beset IKB and Cairn. At the turn of the century, the bank had embraced securitization with a vengeance, raising funds by selling masses of mortgage-backed bonds to investors all over the world. By 2007, less than a quarter of Northern Rock's funding came from retail deposits, with the rest raised by securitization.

Because the bank was securitizing its mortgages with off-balance-sheet vehicles, it did not need to hold a large volume of capital reserves against those loans, and it could extend about three times more mortgages, per unit of capital, than in its pre-securitization days. By 2007 Northern Rock had trebled its share of the UK mortgage market, accounting for 18.9 per cent of all mortgages, and was still hungry for more. At the start of that year its website cheerfully told consumers that 'if your wallet has taken a beating over the festive season, a new loan from Northern Rock could be the perfect way to sort things out'. When the money-markets seized up in August 2007, though, Northern Rock discovered that its main funding source had frozen.

For a few days, officials cast around to see whether any large UK banks would be willing to buy Northern Rock or club together to offer a loan. Lloyds TSB, one large lender, seemed interested in a deal. However, it refused to commit itself unless the Bank of England offered a loan to the group, and Mervyn King, the Bank governor, was unwilling to do that. King worried that offering aid of that sort might contravene the laws that set out what the Bank could – or could not – do in a crisis.

For days British banking authorities searched for ways to save the bank. Then, on Monday afternoon, 17 September, a full four days after Peston's newsbreak, the British government stepped in to stop the bank run. The government would guarantee *all* remaining Northern Rock deposits and the Bank would provide enough loans to keep the lender operating, and extend the same support to other banks too, if necessary. As Peston had pointed out in his first BBC bulletin, Northern Rock's fate showed that the impact of the subprime crisis was spreading inexorably into the 'real' banking system. That posed a troubling question: just how much further might the shocks spread?

A couple of days after the Northern Rock drama, senior officials at JPMorgan Chase's offices in New York received a surprising telephone call from the Treasury in Washington: could they attend a voluntary meeting to discuss the state of the shadow banks? 'We'll buy the coffee!' a Treasury official cheerfully remarked, a coded way of saying that though the Treasury would host the affair, it did not plan to dictate terms to the banks; it was their job to find a solution to the problem.

John Kodweis, a senior JPMorgan official who was an expert in securitization, attended the meeting, which was held in a large, ornate room at the Treasury. Representatives from Bank of America, Lehman Brothers, Citigroup, Bear Stearns, Merrill Lynch and Goldman Sachs came. Kodweis arrived expecting that all the banks would be engaging in preliminary discussions, 'over coffee', as the Treasury officials had said. The Citigroup representatives, though, had arrived with a fifteen-page PowerPoint presentation. The gist of Citi's message was that it wanted all the big banks to band together to create a *collective* vehicle to buy up the assets held by the shadow banks, with tacit government support.

The move marked another crucial shift in the crisis. Until that point, the American government had insisted that it did not want to get directly involved in trying to bail out SIVs, or any other shadowy vehicles. Tradition dictated that only certain institutions in the financial system were so large, and their services so vital to the economy, that they must never be allowed to fail. The rest were not protected by any state-sponsored safety net. Shadow banks fell into the second camp, meaning that the Treasury – let alone the Fed – did not have any mandate to intervene. In banking jargon, these entities did not have any official 'lender of last resort'.

Yet the more the crisis spread, the more it was becoming clear that shadow banks were so entwined with 'real' banks that a collapse could damage parts of the system that *did* fall under government control. Citi itself had created seven shadow banks, and by 2007 these held almost $100 billion of assets. The SIVs were also entwined with America's vast £3000 billion money-market fund sector. Most ordinary Americans assumed that money-market funds were as safe as bank deposits. The funds marketed themselves on the mantra that no fund had ever 'broken the buck', or returned less than 100 per cent of money invested. However, these money-market funds were now holding large quantities of notes issued by SIVs and were *not* covered by any federal safety insurance. That created the potential for a chain reaction. If SIVs collapsed, the worry went, money-market funds would suffer losses and consumers would suddenly discover that their super-safe investments were not so safe after all.

Citi hoped to avoid a panic by persuading American banks to act, en masse, to avert widespread SIV collapse. Essentially, the idea was that the banks would purchase some of the assets owned by the SIVs, and put those into a new giant SIV – or 'superfund', as it was dubbed. The plan suggested the superfund would then finance itself by selling new commercial paper notes, backed by the banks. Citi assumed that would make investors more willing to purchase them, since it was taken for granted that the large banks still commanded credibility. Citi also reasoned that if the SIV assets were stored in the superfund for a while, removing the threat of a firesale, then the prices of mortgage-linked securities would stop falling.

Kodweis returned to New York and reported the plan to his colleagues. Should JPMorgan take part? Over in London, Winters's reaction was a swift 'No'. He could understand perfectly well why Citi wanted to create a communal fund. 'But why does JPMorgan need to take part in this?' Winters asked. After all, he reasoned, nobody had forced Citi to create all of its shadow banks. That had been their own choice, and a choice that JPMorgan itself had notably not made. He did not see why JPMorgan should bail out a rival, or expose itself to new risk by underwriting a superfund. He also had a nasty feeling that if JPMorgan did provide a backstop credit line to the superfund, it would face new losses further down the road. The JPMorgan officials duly told the Treasury they would not participate.

The Treasury, however, was persistent. 'We *really* want you to take part!' the message came back. Winters continued to resist. If Citi needed the scheme so badly, he asked, why couldn't Citi organize it all? Why lean on a bank with no shadow banks of its own? The US officials let it be known that *that* was the whole point: the Treasury wanted JPMorgan to help lead the scheme precisely because it had relatively clean hands. Robert Steel, the under-secretary of the US Treasury, called senior JPMorgan officials to press the point. He argued that the financial system had become infected with the banking equivalent of 'mad cow disease'; there was now so much consumer anxiety that everyone had to fight back. Then Henry Paulson spoke to Jamie Dimon directly, asking him to get on board. 'We are being drafted!' Kodweis grimly joked to his colleagues.

Over in London, Winters realized he was fighting a losing battle. Dimon was a savvy operator and he could see which way the political wind was blowing in Washington. 'We need to do the right thing! This is about being a good citizen,' he declared. In the end, JPMorgan told the Treasury that it would take part. Winters was determined at least to avoid exposing the bank to risk, and he insisted that JPMorgan would not provide any credit lines to the superfund unless it could control the design of the scheme. The JPMorgan bankers did not entirely trust the Citi financiers who had drawn up the initial plan. They were led by a banker who was a general expert in restructuring, rather than a specialist on CDOs. His previous job had been to reorganize Iraqi debt.

After days of wrangling, Citi and JPMorgan issued a joint press release on 14 October announcing the launch of a 'Master Liquidity Enhancement Conduit', or M-Lec, the technical term for the superfund. Bank of America put its name on the press release too; it did not have a particularly large presence in the structured credit world, but it did have a network of money-market funds exposed to SIV failure. Treasury officials had decided at the last minute that it would be better to get a third bank on board, to give the impression that it was an industry-wide scheme, and Bank of America was a good pick.

Paulson and Steel pronounced their backing for the plan, fervently denying that it was any form of 'bailout'. 'I don't know how anyone could characterize it as a bailout,' Steel testily responded to reporters' questions. 'There's no federal money and there's no federal organization. We were the original convener and now the market participants are off developing a strategy themselves . . . We didn't bring the people together with an idea, we brought them together to get their ideas. I think that is an important distinction.' Irrespective of whether the government had formally organized the scheme, a great deal was riding on it. 'We really don't have a lot of time to get this sorted,' Steel confessed.

If any evidence was needed that time was running out, the ratings agencies were ready to supply it. On 11 October, just as Citi and JPMorgan were fine-tuning their M-Lec announcement, Moody's cut its ratings on some $32 billion worth of mortgage-backed bonds. Those had largely been issued in 2006 and had previously carried medium-risk ratings of around single A or BB. The agency also warned that it might downgrade more than $20 billion of mortgage-backed bonds that carried the triple-A stamp, and downgrade CDOs composed of those bonds too. All told, the cuts affected a hefty $50 billion of securities.

That was alarming for investors. Worse still, Moody's seemed unsure how much further the downgrades might go. 'The performance, particularly in the US housing [and] mortgage sector, [has been] deteriorating more quickly and more deeply than the ratings agencies or most other participants in the market anticipated,' Raymond McDaniel, CEO of Moody's, told the *Financial Times* on 12 October. 'We [have been] adjusting standards, making our credit criteria more stringent, but the incremental moves [have been] rather overwhelmed by the pace and magnitude of the deterioration in the US housing market.' That was a bland way of saying that the subprime mortgage market was not behaving as the models had predicted. The 'class of 2005 and 2006' borrowers were defaulting at a dramatically faster pace than households who had taken out mortgages before those dates. There were also variations even between mortgage lenders. By September 2007 more than 30 per cent of the subprime mortgage loans issued in late 2005 by Fremont, a California mortgage lender, were in default. At Countrywide and Wells Fargo, the default rate for the same vintage was 'only' 15 per cent.

A particularly pernicious aspect of the defaults was that when this new breed of subprime borrowers walked away from their homes, they often left them in such a bad state that it was hard for lenders to realize any value from the repossessed properties. Until the autumn of 2007, Moody's had assumed, on the basis of past housing cycles, that lenders could recoup 70 per cent of their loans in case of default. By October 2007 it had slashed that projection to just 40 per cent.

To add to the confusion, by the autumn of 2007 it seemed that in some neighbourhoods of the US, feedback loops were developing that threw the ratings agencies' models off even further. As house prices fell, defaults were rising to such a degree that they were blighting entire neighbourhoods. That was pushing house prices lower still, sparking yet *more* defaults. This vicious cycle had never been witnessed in the world of corporate defaults; nor did it fit the logic of the 'bell-curve' technique central to the statistical risk assessment systems so pervasive inside banks and ratings agencies.

Predicting default rates was proving baffling enough, but it was even harder to guess how defaults would impact CDOs at the other end of the chain. The basic concept behind the tranches in CDOs was that when mortgage borrowers paid back their loans, the cash from those repayments would flow into the different tranches like a river pouring down a waterfall into several stacked buckets. The 'senior' tranche would be paid first, and when those note holders had received their due, the cash would spill down to the mezzanine tranche, and so on, to the junior level. If the flows ran a little dry because mortgage borrowers were skipping repayments, there would not be enough to fill the bottom bucket. But as long as some water flowed, the senior note holders were safe.

In real life, though, it was proving difficult to work out precisely how and when changes in cash flows would affect the various buckets under the waterfall. For one thing, there was a time-lag problem. When households went into default, the delinquency process could last for months, a sort of limbo for cash flow. When losses reached a certain, predetermined level, the trustees of a CDO were supposed immediately to declare an 'event of default' and repay assets to note holders. But that process could also take months. On top of that, different CDOs had subtly different rules about how their 'waterfalls' worked, in terms of who received what when. Even worse was the complexity of trying to determine how cash should flow within the CDOs of CDOs.

When the J.P. Morgan team had created Bistro, it bundled up loans of a well-diversified pool of companies specifically to minimize the chance of widespread defaults. In making mortgage CDOs, bankers had similarly tried to diversify, by including loans from numerous regions of the US. The common assumption was that even if one region suffered a housing bust, the property market would never collapse across the country as a whole. But by the autumn of 2007 it had become clear that this diversification theory wasn't working in the subprime mortgage world. Defaults were rising in all regions.

The problem of cash flow was particularly vexing for those managing what had become an especially popular type of CDO during 2005 and 2006, those known as 'mezzanine CDO of ABS'. These were made up out of *only* mezzanine notes – or those rated around BBB. Bankers liked to claim that there was still a high level of diversification in these structures because the mezzanine notes were linked to the loans of a vast pool of different households. In practice, though, because they were all in the mezzanine tranche, they all would be hit by default losses at once. Any 'diversification' was an illusion.

For all of these reasons, the ratings agencies felt forced to continue slashing ratings. A few days after Moody's cut its ratings, Standard and Poor's put 590 CDO tranches on review for a downgrade. It also cut the rating on $3.7 billion of CDOs. Then

Fitch, the third-smallest ratings agency, warned it might cut the ratings on $37 billion of CDOs. Most chilling of all, the agencies warned that these reviews did not just affect the junior tranches of CDO debt. The senior, or supposedly safe, triple-A, CDO debt was at risk for downgrades as well. 'Whereas in a CLO [a CDO built of corporate loans] it is unlikely that all the loans default simultaneously, the additional layer of securitization . . . in a CDO of ABS has led to an all-or-nothing scenario,' pointed out Matt King, analyst at Citigroup, in a research note. 'It is this all-or-nothing which is now causing significant downgrades to CDO of ABS tranches, in particular to the most senior ones.'

It was shocking news for investors. After all, the entire structured credit edifice had been built on the assumption that AAA was ultra-safe, and AA almost rock-solid too. Now that pillar of faith was crumbling. It was impossible for anyone to know exactly how the downgrades might affect the value of particular CDOs. By the autumn of 2007, these were still not being widely traded, partly because bankers and policymakers had made such frantic efforts in previous months to prevent any public firesales of CDO assets. But the behaviour of the ABX index was readily visible, and by mid-October, the BBB component of this index had tumbled to 30 per cent of its face value, down from 95 per cent at the start of the year. Most ominously of all, the AAA tranche of the ABX was trading at around 90 per cent of face value, while the AA was falling towards 80 per cent. To a casual observer, such dips might not have looked extreme. However, bankers and investors had always assumed that the prices of AAA or AA assets would never move at all. They were utterly unprepared for the damage that such price falls might inflict.

On 4 November, Bill Demchak dialled into a conference call arranged by the mighty Citigroup. From his perch at PNC in Pittsburgh, Demchak had spent the autumn following the events in the CDO world with mounting alarm. Back in 2006, when

his team at PNC had made the ballsy decision to start cutting the
bank's credit risk, Demchak had done so largely because he reckoned that conditions in the *corporate* loan market looked
dangerous. He assumed that when the credit bubble went 'pop,'
it would be that area where the pain would be felt first. By the
autumn of 2007, it was becoming clear that Demchak's predic-
tion had been only half right. Conditions in the corporate loan
market had indeed turned worse, because investors had become
reluctant to purchase CDOs built out of risky corporate loans.
The banks were left with some $400 billion worth of unsold
corporate loans on their books, stuck in the securitization
pipeline. What was worse, the price of those loans had fallen
sharply (meaning that the cost of borrowing money for risky
companies had risen, since the two move in opposite directions).

Demchak had expected as much. But by November 2007, he
could see other problems brewing. In the middle of October,
Citigroup had revealed that its net income had slumped from
$6.2 billion in the second quarter of the year to $2.1 billion. The
reason, it reported, was that it had been forced to write down
the value of its corporate and mortgage assets by $5.7 billion.
That number looked very large, but most analysts were not too
surprised. Citi had a vast loan book, and other banks were
announcing similar losses. On 4 November, though, Citi suddenly warned that it would report more losses of between $8
billion and $11 billion. That was such shocking news that Citi
CEO Chuck Prince announced that he would resign. It was also
baffling to analysts. Citi was supposed to be expert at measuring
credit risk. So how did the bank manage to misjudge its losses so
badly? And why was it still so uncertain about the total bill?

Demchak dialled into the conference call eager to find out.
'The issue is super-senior,' one of the senior executives
explained. The problem, he added, was that the bank held on its
books $43 billion worth of super-senior risk, linked to CDOs
backed by mortgage debt. Citi had previously assumed that the

value of those assets was 100 per cent of face value; now the price was falling.

Super-senior? Demchak could hardly believe what he had heard. Almost a full decade had passed since Varikooty, Demchak and the rest of the group had invented the term. Back then, the term had seemed like a geeky in-joke; a concept so quirky and obscure that only a few technical experts knew what it meant.

Now the Citi executives had casually tossed the word 'super-senior' into a conference call with hundreds of mainstream investors, analysts and financiers. Demchak didn't know whether to laugh, cry, or just shake his head in wonder. In other circumstances, he might have felt almost proud that his team's once-obscure brainchild had suddenly burst into the limelight. In reality, though, he was overwhelmed with horror. The way Citi told the story, super-senior had turned into a scourge that had created most of its unexpected losses.

'How could this happen?' Demchak wondered. Back in the days when he had been chasing his credit derivatives dreams at J.P. Morgan, his team had considered super-senior to be so safe that it was 'more than triple A'. Even though Demchak himself had gone to great lengths to sell J.P. Morgan's super-senior risk to AIG and other insurance groups, he had never imagined for a second that super-senior debt could pose more than a moderate level of risk. Nor had he guessed that Citi was holding so much on its own balance sheet. Citi had never discussed the issue in conference calls before nor highlighted it in previous corporate reports. 'How did this happen?' Demchak asked himself again and again. As he listened to the rest of the call, he got the distinct impression that the Citi managers were almost as baffled as he was.

One clue to what had gone so terribly wrong at Citi could be found in the dry details of the technical statement the bank issued that day, and then filed with the Securities and Exchange

Commission. The statement noted that Citi had $55 billion of exposures to the subprime market sitting on its books, of which $43 billion was in the form of super-senior risk attached to CDO of ABS. That was a staggeringly large number, made doubly shocking because it had never been highlighted in any report that Citi had previously issued. Out of the $43 billion, around $18 billion was linked to investment-grade and mezzanine CDO of ABS, which Citi had retained on its balance sheet, either because it was in the process of creating CDOs, or because it had nowhere else to park it as it cranked up its CDO machine back in 2006 and 2007.

Citi's exposure to the strike in the commercial paper market was also staggering. Another $25 billion of the bank's total exposure was 'commercial paper principally secured by super-senior tranches of high-grade ABS CDOs', Citi explained. Back in 2005 and 2006, when CDOs were booming, Citi had sold a large volume of super-senior liabilities to SIVs and conduits. To encourage buyers, the bank had often provided a sweetener, nicknamed a 'liquidity put', that guaranteed that if the shadow banks ever faced problems financing that debt Citi would either take it back or provide financing. Before the summer of 2007, nobody in Citi ever expected those liquidity puts to be exercised, but in July, when the money-market crisis exploded, the SIVs and conduits had duly handed the super-senior risk back to Citi. As a result, Citi's super-senior exposure had more than doubled in just a few weeks.

By mid-October, after the ratings agencies had cut the ratings on CDOs and prices had fallen on the ABX, Citi's management had come under pressure to revalue its CDO holdings, leading to the series of write-downs.

To most Citi executives, the bottom-line hit was as stunning as if the ground had opened up under the bank. On the day of the last announcement, Jamie Dimon bumped into a former senior colleague at Citi. 'How did this happen?' Dimon asked as

gently as he could. 'We are not entirely sure ourselves,' the man
replied. Dimon had no reason to doubt him. By 2007, Citi was
operated as a vast empire of business silos, which tended to be so
fragmented – and feuding – that they rarely interacted. As a
result, few of the bankers outside the CDO silo knew the details
of how the securitization machine worked, let alone of the exis-
tence of the liquidity puts. 'Perhaps there were a dozen people in
the bank who really understood all this before – I doubt it was
more,' one senior Citi manager later recalled bitterly.

Investors were also shocked. Back in July, Citi had been on a
roll, posting record profits and holding an extremely large capital cushion. Now the super-senior disaster was blasting through
that capital cushion, and Citi was looking befuddled.

More frightening still, Citi's woes were hardly unique. In early
October, Merrill Lynch unveiled a $5.5 billion write-down on
its credit assets. Again, analysts weren't unduly concerned at first.
But in late October, Merrill raised the estimate to $8.4 billion,
large enough to force Stan O'Neal, the hard-charging CEO of
Merrill, to resign as well. Unlike Citi, Merrill's problems didn't
stem from liquidity puts offered to SIVs. Most of Merrill's super-
senior woes arose from the CDO notes that Merrill had decided
to retain on its own balance sheet. Merrill had assumed it would
be protected from any losses on super-senior because it had
insured so much of that risk with monoline insurance groups.
But as the pain in the mortgage market intensified, monolines
were reeling. Just as Bill Demchak had anticipated a decade
before, the 'insurance' monolines offered were starting to look
chimerical. That was one reason why, under pressure from its
auditors, Merrill had downgraded the value of its super-senior
assets so dramatically.

The losses at UBS were arguably even more shocking. In early
October, the bank had announced it was writing off approximately $3.4 billion in mortgage-linked losses. Investors were
stunned, but they also congratulated the bank for having the

courage to come clean. By late October, though, the bank was indicating to analysts that it would soon need to revise that loss up considerably, and in December it announced another $10 billion of write-downs. As with Merrill Lynch and Citi, the scourge was super-senior CDOs. Back at the start of 2005, the Swiss bank had barely held a single super-senior CDO note on its books. By early 2007, its CDO business had grown at such a furious speed that it was holding $50 billion super-senior notes.

By late November, the banking sector was barrelling into a full-blown crisis. Bank share prices were tumbling at a startling rate. Since June alone, more than $240 billion had been wiped out of the market capitalization of the largest dozen Wall Street banks. The cost of purchasing protection against default was spiralling upwards. Worse still, it appeared that the banks no longer really trusted each other. The cost of borrowing funds in the interbank market was also rising. Banks were so nervous about the prospect of new shocks that they were either refusing to lend money to each other or were hoarding the cash they had for fear of what lay ahead.

Shocked, some bank executives tried to fight back. Behind the scenes, they asked regulators if they could suspend the mark-to-market accounting rules for a while. To them, it seemed ridiculous that banks were being forced to record these vast, multi-billion-dollar write-downs. There was precious little real-world evidence that the super-senior assets were seriously impaired. Although mortgage default rates were rising at one end of the financial chain, most CDOs had *not* yet tipped into a formal event of default, and most investors holding senior CDO notes were still receiving their regular interest payments. Insofar as the value of CDOs was shrinking, those losses were theoretical. 'This is mark-to-market accounting gone mad! If we stick to these principles we will end up destroying banks for no good reason at all,' complained a senior executive at one of the banks most badly afflicted by super-senior losses.

The regulators, though, showed absolutely no willingness to drop mark-to-market principles. Changing the accounting rules halfway through a bout of banking turmoil, they feared, was likely to make investors even more nervous, particularly given that Western bankers and regulators had championed 'transparency' with such enthusiasm in previous years. The auditors of the banks were even less willing to take a lenient stance. A few short years earlier, the audit profession had suffered a brutal shock when the revered accounting firm Arthur Andersen went out of business due to accusations of being lax in auditing Enron. Auditors were determined not to expose themselves to similar risks now. 'We had seen what happened after Enron . . . that made [accountants] really scared,' one anguished senior accountant explained in October. 'The banks really benefited from mark-to-market when the going was good, so to have them claim that we should drop mark-to-market accounting when the prices were falling, looks entirely self-serving . . . no auditor will willingly endorse that.'

The bigger the theoretical losses became, though, the more they started to have an impact on the 'real' world too. Six months earlier, regulators and investors alike had blithely assumed that American and European banks would be extremely well protected from any future turn in the credit cycle. In the first half of 2007, large Western banks had posted record $425 billion in profits, and wielded capital cushions that vastly exceeded the minimum levels required to comply with the Basel Accord. Global banks alone were estimated to hold core capital (known as 'tier one') of $3400 billion. That was why the Federal Reserve and others had been so confident that the banks would be able to absorb the $100 billion-odd hit that was expected to arise from the subprime sector. Moreover, precisely because banks had been slicing and dicing risk so enthusiastically, most regulators and investors had also assumed that banks would be exposed to only a tiny part of any credit losses. Risk was supposedly scattered throughout the system. But the more the subprime scourge hit the banks, the more wrong-headed all those assumptions started to seem.

When the regulators had celebrated the benefits of 'risk dispersion' they had assumed that the banks were selling almost all of their CDO notes to other players. They had not realized that so much super-senior was piling up on some banks' books, in a manner that left those banks exposed to entirely unexpected new concentrations of risk. Worse, as the super-senior losses mounted, they were so gigantic in scale that they were eating through the banks' capital cushions – even though those reserves had appeared to be so impressively large just a few months before.

The SIV problem presented another headache. All through the turmoil of November, the bankers at JPMorgan had struggled to create a workable plan for the superfund to purchase troubled assets held by the SIVs. Behind the scenes, Bob Steel, the Treasury under-secretary, furtively urged them on. The US government had absolutely no desire to see SIVs collapse and embark on a firesale of their assets. Nor did they want the 'real' banks to bail out the SIVs, since that would consume even more of their scarce capital. Yet, as the three-way talks between JPMorgan, Citi and Bank of America unfolded, the group found it impossible to agree on how to proceed. One key sticking point was that nobody was keen to take on the risk of providing big loans to the superfund. By early December the idea was a bust.

Inside JPMorgan, the death of the superfund angered officials. Having been forced to take part against their instincts, they had then devoted hours of management time trying to establish a plan, now all for nought. 'If we were to bill the US Treasury for that wasted time, the bill would be huge!' one JPMorgan banker observed. For other banks, though, the implications were truly grave. Without a superfund to rescue it, Citi faced pressure to take even more SIV assets back on to its balance sheet. So did other large banks. That, coupled with the super-senior write-offs, had a chilling implication: a banking system that had once appeared nearly impregnable looked like it might actually run low on capital.

In late November, Timothy Geithner at the New York Fed placed furtive phone calls to some of the Wall Street banks. The gist of these calls was: 'Can you find more capital? You need to – now!' Frantically, Citi, Merrill and other large banks looked for ways to plug the capital gap, no one even daring to hope that the government would step in. The debates about the superfund and the Northern Rock fiasco left no doubt that the UK and US governments hated the idea of using taxpayer funds to recapital-ize the banks, and there seemed to be little chance of persuading Western investors to do so either.

In mounting desperation, some bankers looked east for help. During the first seven years of the decade, China, Singapore, Korea and the oil-rich countries of the Middle East had all built up large so-called sovereign wealth funds, huge investment funds dedicated to managing pools of government money. By 2007, such funds were estimated to control over $3000 billion of assets, though the precise tally was unknown because the funds were highly secretive. Traditionally, much of their cash had been invested in US Treasury bonds and other safe assets. The funds had shied away from taking direct stakes in American companies, partly because their doing so tended to provoke nationalist ire. However, as the panic intensified on Wall Street and in the City of London, bankers laid aside that concern, and senior deal-makers from Wall Street, London and Zurich hopped on to planes in a frantic effort to persuade Asian and Middle Eastern funds to help.

Citi was the first to clinch a deal. In late November, the Abu Dhabi Investment Fund, the world's biggest sovereign wealth fund, announced plans to inject $7.5 billion into the bank. Soon after, UBS raised $11 billion from the GIC fund of Singapore and Middle Eastern investors. Then Merrill Lynch raised $5 billion from a Chinese government fund, while Morgan Stanley garnered a similar sum from Singapore. It was an extraordinary turn of fortunes. The Western banks had been the ones to bail out their emerging-market counterparts in the past. Humiliating as it may have been, though, bankers were too relieved to have found cash to engage in hand-wringing about the source. 'Huge quantities of money from the emerging world – some $60 billion at the last count – are injecting a measure of stability into the developed world's arteries,' observed analysts at HSBC in late 2007. Regulators were privately relieved as well. 'If the banks are finding fresh sources of capital, then that is very good. They need to recapitalize, as swiftly as they can,' one of America's most senior regulators observed in December 2007. 'Once they have done that, the banking system can then move on. Or that is what we all hope.'

Yet while the capital raising looked impressively large, the losses that continued to mount at the banks were even bigger. As 2008 got under way, UBS, Merrill and Citi all revealed more big write-downs on their holdings of credit assets, taking their collective total to $53 billion – just for those three banks. Super-senior write-downs accounted for a stunning two-thirds of that figure. Gamely, the three all insisted that they were near the end of these write-downs. Nobody quite believed them, though. The essential problem was that the system was becoming trapped in a vicious spiral. The more that the banks revealed losses on super-senior assets – or any other credit assets – the more scared investors became, causing the prices of the assets to fall still further, which forced the banks to make more write-downs. It was a pernicious feedback loop.

As the losses mounted, the former members of the J.P. Morgan swaps team reeled in shock. A full decade had passed since

Demchak's acolytes had invented the seemingly innocuous concept of super-senior, back in the heady days when they were
fervently chasing their credit derivatives dream. In the interven-
ing years, they had scattered, but many still remained friends.
They emailed regularly, and from time to time, some of them
would meet for dinner, or visit each others' vacation homes in
Tuscany, the Hamptons and other choice retreats. When Andrew
Feldstein and Bill Demchak created a project to raise funds for
Darfur refugees, Blythe Masters, Bill Winters and many others
rallied round with donations and support. Like any family, the
group was also driven by petty rivalries, yet they almost never
criticized each other to outsiders. A deep intellectual bond and
remarkable sense of affection still linked most of them.

By late 2007, though, the emails bouncing between their
BlackBerries were expressions of disbelief. Like Demchak, most
of them were stunned that their super-senior brainchild had
become such a rapacious scourge. 'What kind of monster has
been created here?' one of the former J.P. Morgan group wrote
in a heartfelt email to another. 'It's like you've known a cute kid
who then grew up and committed a horrible crime,' another
member of the team commented. 'All this just totally blows your
mind.'

They simply hadn't realized the degree of risk that was building up under all the acronyms. Over at BlueMountain, Feldstein
had spotted at an early stage that banks were stockpiling super-
senior holdings, and he positioned his hedge fund to benefit
when that pattern turned wrong. The strategy paid off handsomely, and in 2007 the three main funds at BlueMountain
posted returns of 45, 34 and 9 per cent. But Feldstein was the
exception. Winters and Masters had never been able to understand why the other banks were so willing to keep cranking up
their CDO machines, and now that the truth had come out,
they were profoundly shocked. They were also indignant and
angry.

It was little comfort to them that the terrible mistakes of others put JPMorgan in a flattering light by comparison. As the losses piled up, confidence was crumbling so thoroughly that all banks were being hurt. A public backlash against all types of complex finance was building. 'It feels like credit derivatives or CDOs have become a dirty word right now,' lamented Tim Frost.

Most of the former J.P. Morgan team considered pointing the finger at derivatives utterly unfair. 'This crisis has *nothing* to do with innovation. It is about excesses in banking,' Winters observed. 'Every four to five years there is a new excess in banking – you had the Asian crisis, then the internet bubble. The problem this time is extraordinary excess in the housing market.' Or as Terri Duhon said: 'When car crashes happen, people don't blame cars or stop driving them, they blame the drivers! Derivatives are the same – it's not the tools at fault, but the people who used those tools.' Hancock was even more adamant. After he left J.P. Morgan back in 2000, he had created a consultancy group that advised governments and companies on how to use innovative financial products, such as derivatives, to their benefit. The other founding members of the group were Roberto Mendoza, another former J.P. Morgan banker, and Robert Merton, the Nobel Prize-winning economist who had helped to create the path-breaking Black–Scholes formula that had played a crucial role in the development of derivatives. For seven long years, Hancock had extolled the virtues of financial innovation, often in the face of client scepticism. Even as the banking world reeled in shock in late 2007, he remained committed to the cause. 'A lot of the problems in structured finance have not been due to too *much* innovation, but a failure to innovate sufficiently,' Hancock observed. 'People have just taken the original Bistro idea, say, added zeros and done it over and over again without really thinking about the limits of diversification as a risk-management tool. There is a big difference between using this structure for corporate loans, as we did at J.P. Morgan, and subprime mortgages!'

As the losses piled up, though, some of the team realized that a number of the assumptions that had driven them a decade ago had been naive. Back in the 1990s the team had all believed, with near-evangelical fervour, that innovation would create a more robust and efficient financial world. Credit derivatives and CDOs, they assumed, would disperse risk. Now it turned out that the risks had not been dispersed at all, but concentrated and concealed. It was a terrible, horrible irony.

'Is there something we could have done to stop all this?' one of the group asked, as Merrill Lynch announced more losses. 'It wasn't our job to stop other banks being so stupid!' another shot back. 'What about the regulators? Where were they?' With every new piece of bad news the sense of shock and anger grew. So did their fears about a looming backlash.

CHAPTER FOURTEEN

Bear Blows Up

On 11 January 2008, JPMorgan Chase burst into the news again. Andy Kuipers, the chief executive of Northern Rock, announced that JPMorgan was buying £2.2 billion of Northern Rock's mortgage loans. 'This is a relatively small transaction, representing around 2 per cent of Northern Rock's gross assets, but it is a positive development in the company's ongoing strategic review,' Kuipers said, noting that the sale 'will allow us to reduce the debt with the Bank of England'.

The significance of Northern Rock's announcement, though, went well beyond Northern Rock's fate. It signalled that JPMorgan Chase was flexing its muscles even as other major banks were furiously trying to shore themselves up. The price at which Bill Winters's team in London had arranged to buy the Northern Rock mortgages was extremely favourable and Winters regarded the deal as one of the sweetest the bank had done for some time. The reason the deal was so great, of course, was that there were precious few other bidders left in the market.

By the start of 2008, write-downs made by Western banks totalled more than $80 billion. To plug that gap, the banks had raised over $60 billion in capital. JPMorgan had not entirely avoided the pain; it had been caught holding tens of billions of dollars of leveraged loans on its books which tumbled in price. The bank also had a large direct exposure to the mortgage market, because it had expanded its home equity loan business back in 2005 and 2006. Tucked away in corners of the JPMorgan Chase empire, there were even a few super-senior firebombs: one corner of the bank, for example, held a few loss-making mort- gage CDOs on its books, which Winters had not known about. As a result, the bank recorded around $1.3 billion of write-downs in the fourth quarter of 2007, cutting net income for the invest- ment bank to just $124 million. But that loss seemed trivial compared with those of most of its competitors.

What JPMorgan did *not* have on its books were the vast piles of super-senior CDO of ABS assets, which were wreaking such havoc at Citi, UBS and Merrill Lynch. Nor did it have a vast network of shadow banks, or credit lines extended to them. It had also gone into the whole crisis with a stronger balance sheet – and a relatively lower level of leverage – than most of its competitors, due to Dimon's obsession with maintaining a 'fortress balance sheet'.

During the previous seven years, JPMorgan staff had become accustomed to feeling like laggards; suddenly they were stars. Most of the JPMorgan managers were reluctant to crow publicly, for fear of tempting fate. They also felt wary of taking credit for things they had *not* done. 'We have made mistakes too,' Winters stressed, whenever asked about the bank's fortunes. 'It is quite wrong to pretend otherwise.'

There was also no denying, though, that the worse the crisis got, the more opportunities presented themselves. The really big question facing the JPMorgan Chase management was whether they should go further with their bottom-fishing and purchase not just some cut-price loans but an entire *bank*. That seemed a natural step for Dimon. After all, he had shot to fame a decade earlier by embarking with Sandy Weill on one of the most extraordinary acquisition frenzies Wall Street had ever seen. Many analysts had assumed that Dimon would crank up acquisitions when he joined JPMorgan, but he had confounded those predictions. During the credit boom, he believed the prices of other financial groups were grossly inflated. By 2008, though, the share prices of most banks had tumbled by more than 20 per cent, one of the sharpest declines on record. Would that be enough to tempt him?

In early 2008, Steve Black repeatedly told analysts that the bank was not actively pursuing mergers. 'We were really not looking to buy anything [in early 2008] – truly,' Black later explained. 'I mean, we had not ruled anything out, but we knew that we would only consider a deal if something was *extremely* cheap.' Yet Dimon was an opportunistic man. So, as the share prices of other banks kept falling, the JPMorgan management kept scanning the horizon, sniffing for opportunity.

On Thursday, 13 March, Dimon was having a private dinner in a favourite Greek restaurant in New York with his parents, wife and daughters to celebrate his fifty-second birthday. Suddenly his private cellphone rang. He was irritated. The cellphone in question was generally only used for family calls or office emergencies, and he had asked his staff to avoid disturbing him that night, unless it was crucial.

On the other end of the line was Dimon's office. They told him that Gary Parr, a senior Lazard banker who was advising Bear, needed to talk urgently. So did Alan Schwartz, the Bear CEO. Their message was shocking. Bear was running so short of liquidity that it would be forced to file for bankruptcy without immediate aid. Would JPMorgan Chase extend that? Schwartz asked.

Dimon was stunned. He was well aware – as was all of Wall Street – that Bear was vulnerable, because of the collapse of its two hedge funds back in June 2007. Dimon had even explored purchasing part of Bear's operations then, but the brokerage had rebuffed those overtures. In the subsequent months, Bear had continued to forge a fiercely independent path, in keeping with its reputation as a scrappy, maverick player. Like most of its rivals, Bear told investors it would bolster its capital base, but in practice its efforts seemed half-hearted. It embarked on discussions with CITIC Securities, a Chinese entity, but never received anything more than a pledged equity swap worth $1 billion.

By late February, this 'tough-it-out' strategy was testing the nerves of Bear's investors and creditors. Bear was known to be a big player in the field of mortgage debt, and it held a large pile of mortgage securities on its book. Throughout the winter of 2007, the Bear management repeatedly insisted that they were managing the risks of those assets well. Investors, though, were uneasy, because market conditions just kept getting worse.

In early January the US government had published weak economic data. Then in mid-January, the credit-ratings agencies started to downgrade their ratings of the giant monoline companies. That had alarming implications for the banks that had purchased monoline 'insurance' to protect their CDO holdings. As investors digested the news, the equity and credit markets slid again, and though the Federal Reserve responded by cutting interest rates twice in late January, by a hefty total of 1.25 percentage points, market anxiety still ran high. Behind the scenes, banks were starting to feel so cash-constrained – and so jumpy about the mortgage market – that they demanded that hedge funds begin posting more collateral when they took out loans.

Many hedge funds could not comply with these tougher demands, which were known in the industry as 'higher haircuts'. So many began selling their assets instead. As they did that, the prices of those assets fell, making the banks even more nervous about lending money to hedge funds. It was another pernicious feedback loop. Investors were spooked so badly that they started to withdraw from the markets, with the result that 'parts of the financial system [were becoming] dysfunctional, causing further financial retrenchment', officials at the BIS noted.

Investors also kept tabs on any financial institutions that looked particularly vulnerable, Bear Stearns was one. Bear's real Achilles heel was its funding base. Because Bear was a brokerage, with no commercial banking operations, it had no stable pool of bank deposits providing cash flow. Traditionally, Bear had raised most of its funding by issuing long-term bonds, but during the first seven years of the decade it had become more reliant on the 'repo', or 'repurchase' market. This is a corner of finance where banks use assets they hold, such as mortgage-backed bonds, as collateral for borrowing money from other investors, for a very short period, often just one or two days. All American brokerages used the repo market, which was one of the largest – but widely ignored – cogs of the Western financial machine. Bear, however, tended to rely more on short-term repo funding than many of its peers, and it tended to post an unusually high proportion of mortgage-backed bonds as collateral.

As the financial woes intensified in early 2008, Bear found raising funds in the repo market increasingly difficult. This development went largely unnoticed by the wider financial community. The repo market – like the commercial paper sector – had traditionally been widely ignored by journalists and regulators alike. A couple of hedge funds in New York did spot the problem, though, and quietly started to pull their assets from Bear. Once that news leaked out more funds reassessed their dealings with Bear. As unease spread, some investors asked Deutsche Bank, Credit Suisse, Goldman Sachs and JPMorgan to replace Bear Stearns as the counterparties to credit derivatives contracts they had written with Bear. This practice was well established in the markets, and usually performed for reasons having nothing to do with the financial health of a counterparty, but as news of this flood of deal changes leaked out, it further fuelled anxiety about Bear's health.

The cost of buying insurance against a default by Bear, with credit default swaps, began to spiral upwards. A year earlier, the annual price of insuring $10 million of Bear bonds had been well under $100,000. By 10 March it was well over $600,000. Officials at Goldman Sachs and Credit Suisse circulated internal emails warning about the counterparty risk posed by Bear, and when news of those leaked out, investors became even more nervous. Then a large hedge fund called Renaissance Technologies pulled its accounts out of Bear, and a snowball of rumors of Bear's demise was set in motion.

Frantically, the senior Bear managers hunted for ways to stop the leakage. On 5 March Bear's cash holdings, on paper, topped $20 billion, and even on 10 March they were $18 billion, but by 11 March Bear's funds had dropped to $10 billion. Had Bear been a commercial bank it could have gone to the Federal Reserve for a loan, as the large commercial banks enjoy 'lender of last resort' facilities and can always ask the Fed for funds in a crisis, as long as they have collateral. This is done either by participating in the regular 'auctions' run by the Fed to pump liquidity into the system, or else by using the so-called 'discount window', which provides additional funds in an emergency. Banks hated resorting to the second option, because it carried a stigma, but facing a true crisis, at least they had the option, and in late 2007 the Fed had introduced a wave of new measures to make the move more attractive. Bear, however, had no access to the window.

On the evening of 12 March, Bear's lawyers called Timothy Geithner at the New York Fed and asked what they should do. The question put Geithner on the spot, because he had no supervisory responsibility over the brokerages. That fell to the Securities and Exchange Commission. What's more, the Fed only had relatively limited data about Bear's business, and

Geithner had no clear mandate to rescue Bear with a loan. He was a deeply pragmatic man, though, and keenly aware of how entwined Bear was with so many other firms, including the large banks. Back in 2005 Geithner had devoted a considerable amount of resources to studying the infrastructure of the credit derivatives world, and what he had learned told him now that if Bear collapsed, the repercussions could reverberate all across the financial world. Though he had spent less time studying the repo market, he could also see that if Bear were to default on its repo contracts, that would prompt investors to panic.

'If Alan Schwartz [the Bear CEO] is worried, he had better call me,' Geithner told Bear's lawyers. The next day Schwartz duly called Geithner. 'So which institutions are you talking to?' Geithner asked. He dearly hoped that Bear might be able to sell itself. A decade earlier, Geithner had worked in Tokyo, as financial attaché to the US embassy, at the dawn of the Japanese banking crisis. The Japanese had dealt with failing banks by persuading a stronger institution to step in, and Geithner hoped such a shotgun marriage could save Bear.

Schwartz told Geithner that there were two possible suitors, JPMorgan Chase and Barclays Capital. 'Better go back and get talking again!' Geithner said. He then asked his staff to independently check whether the two banks really were serious contenders. A few hours later, the answer came back from Barclays that it was not eager to conduct a deal. JPMorgan, though, was a more serious option. It already knew Bear well, since it acted as its clearing bank, settling all of Bear's trades. There were also good strategic reasons for Dimon to purchase Bear. For years, the JPMorgan management had fretted that the bank had a great big hole in its business because it was weak in the equity market and prime brokerage activities compared with rivals. Bear was strong in both. Discreetly, Fed officials encouraged Schwartz to talk to Dimon, prompting Schwartz to interrupt Dimon's birthday dinner.

Dimon didn't jump at the prospect. 'I can't do that,' he told
Schwartz when the Bear CEO asked him to rescue the broker
immediately with a loan or a merger. He was extremely uneasy
about what lay hidden deep inside Bear's books. Having dodged
so many bullets in relation to SIVs and CDOs, he didn't want to
face a cannonade now. But nor did he want to walk away from
a potentially interesting deal. He played for time. He summoned
Steve Black back from a holiday and ordered a large team of
JPMorgan staff to go to Bear to start combing through its books.

The bankers arrived very late on Thursday night. Some had
just climbed out of bed. Within an hour they determined that
the state of Bear's finances was so dire that the brokerage might
default within hours. Dimon and Geithner played for time. On
Friday morning JPMorgan Chase announced that it would
extend a temporary loan to Bear, using funds that the Fed gave
to JPMorgan Chase 'for an initial period of up to twenty-eight
days'. That loan, of around $30 billion, would stave off the risk
of an immediate collapse, while enabling the Fed to channel
money to Bear without breaching its own rules. Then JPMorgan
drafted more staff to analyse the Bear accounts.

The pressure on them was intense. The Fed had suggested at
first that Bear would have up to twenty-eight days to find a new
buyer, but by Friday afternoon that deadline was cut to three
days. Geithner feared that the financial system would tip into
crisis unless a deal was announced before the Asian markets
opened on Monday morning – Sunday evening New York time.
But Bear's books were vast, with huge quantities of CDOs, as
well as a plethora of complex credit derivatives deals. Getting a
handle on what those were worth in just twenty-four hours was
an ordeal by numbers.

All through Saturday, the JPMorgan bankers frenetically
combed through Bear's records. Every few minutes they relayed
their findings over to Winters in London, until he determined
he needed to be in New York and hopped on a flight on Sunday

morning. As he was landing, Dimon and Black were giving Geithner their verdict: there were too many black holes in Bear's books to cut a deal. Winters agreed. 'It just would not be prudent to proceed,' he told his colleagues.

Geithner frantically tried to allay their concerns. By Sunday morning, the situation was dire. The repo market investors who had lent money to Bear included some powerful state-backed Asian institutions, and they were now threatening to pull their loans to *all* American brokers if Bear defaulted on its contracts. That would likely set off a terrible chain reaction. Geithner became more determined than ever to have a deal in place by the time Asian markets opened later that night.

Fed officials feverishly tossed ideas around. Eight years earlier, the large private equity group JC Flowers – which had also been considering making an offer to Bear, but decided against that – had bought a troubled Japanese institution called Long Term Credit Bank, which had murky black holes in its books. The Japanese government had facilitated the deal by offering JC Flowers a quasi-insurance policy that promised to compensate Flowers if the dicey loans at LTCB turned bad.

In the case of Bear, Geithner and the other Fed officials knew it would be impossible to replicate that deal exactly. But what if the Fed were to ring-fence some of the most troubled assets on Bear's balance sheet, providing a guarantee to JPMorgan that it would cover losses on those assets? Dimon, Winters and Black tossed the idea around and told Geithner that if they could buy Bear cheaply enough, they might cut that deal. Geithner duly consulted with Ben Bernanke and Hank Paulson about the tricky matter of an appropriate price for Bear, and returned to Dimon with a proposal: if JPMorgan bought Bear for $2 a share, the Fed would take $30 billion of Bear's assets and place them into a special, ring-fenced vehicle. If those ring-fenced assets lost value, JPMorgan would take the first hit, up to $1 billion. After that, the Fed was on the hook.

The price was startling. Dimon was famous for cutting deals on the cheap, but even he had never expected to see a price quite that low. At the start of the weekend a price of around eight to ten dollars a share had been floated in the discussion between JPMorgan Chase, Bear, the Fed and the Treasury. By Sunday, the JPMorgan Chase side was pushing for a price nearer four dollars. Paulson, though, cut that in half. He seemed determined to avoid giving any impression that the government was bailing Bear out – or its shareholders. At the close of trade on Friday, the share price of Bear Stearns had been around $18 a share. (The previous October it had been trading at around the $131 mark.) At just $2 a share, the offer now valued Bear at just $250 million, considerably less than just the bank's building at 383 Madison Avenue was worth. Ironically, J.P. Morgan had been planning to move its headquarters from midtown to downtown Manhattan. If they purchased Bear and its building, they would have enough space to stay in midtown. 'Frankly, we could probably raise the funds to do this deal just by doing a whip-round inside the company and getting contributions from everyone who hates the idea of having to commute downtown,' one senior J.P. Morgan banker joked to his colleagues.

Shortly before Asian markets opened on Monday morning – or Sunday night in New York – the deal was struck. The Fed also announced plans to extend its liquidity provisions to all of the twenty primary dealers that bought Treasury securities from it, meaning that it was agreeing to provide a safety net for the brokerages, comparable to that for the commercial banks. It was the first time it had employed that measure since the Great Depression.

As news of the deal broke, employees at Bear reacted with sheer fury, stunned at the bargain-basement price. Most of them had large proportions of their wealth tied up in Bear shares, which had now evaporated, and adding salt to the wound was the fact

that if the Fed had only announced its extension of funds to brokers a week earlier, Bear wouldn't have faced collapse. A
two-dollar bill was taped to the front door of their headquarters
on Madison as a potent symbol of their disgust.

Most observers outside Bear, though, reckoned that Geithner
and Dimon had pulled off a stunning coup. While on Monday
morning the stock market gyrated, as investors tried to make
sense of the deal – they traded particularly heavily in the shares of
Lehman Brothers and Merrill Lynch, since they shared many of
Bear's vulnerabilities – by Tuesday anxiety was ebbing. The cost
of borrowing funds in the interbank sector dropped, as did the
price of insuring banks and companies against the risk of default.
The credit markets rallied. Not only had the deal removed the
immediate threat of a Bear collapse, it had shown investors that
the government was willing to intervene forcefully, and that was
starting to shore up market confidence. Then on Tuesday afternoon, further evidence emerged of the government's readiness to
act. The Federal Reserve slashed the prime rate another 75 basis
points, its sixth cut since September, taking it down to 2.25 per
cent, from 5.25 per cent a year before. 'We had been on the brink
of the biggest financial meltdown this country had ever seen, but
I think the Fed has now turned the psychology around,' said
David Jones, chief economist at DMJ Advisors. 'The Fed is saying
it is ready to supply all the emergency credit banks need to get us
out of this crisis.' Echoing the general sense of jubilation, Mark
Zandi, chief economist at Moody's, noted: '[The Fed] was slow
to react to events last summer and fall, but starting this year they
have been very creative.'

Inside JPMorgan, though, reactions to the deal were less jubilant. During the first few months of the credit turmoil, the bank
had largely escaped the media spotlight, because investors and
journalists were focusing on the banks posting large losses. The
Bear deal pushed JPMorgan into the glare. Jamie Dimon's face
splashed on to magazine covers and headlines extolled him as the

'Wunderkind!' and 'The Contendor'. Some pundits delighted in pointing out that Dimon's feats now seemed to be eclipsing even those of his former boss Sandy Weill. Other commentators reached even further back into the past, and drew parallels between Dimon and the mighty J. Pierpont Morgan.

The bank's press team tried to damp down the hype. 'Nobody here wants to be put on a pedestal, and then just get knocked down,' one JPMorgan spokesman commented. The fascination with Dimon, though, would not die away. 'With that one jaw-dropping deal [to purchase Bear], Dimon, like the bank's namesake before him, has become a principal player in the biggest financial drama of his age,' enthused the *New York Times*. 'Like J. Pierpont Morgan, he is capitalizing on the fear and panic that can grip the markets to expand his storied banking empire.'

In reality, though, this 'storied empire' was facing challenges. In the days after the Bear deal, the headaches mounted at an alarming rate. One problem revolved around the contract they had cut with the Fed. When JPMorgan's lawyers combed through the paperwork that they had hastily signed on Sunday, 16 March, they realized that the fine print could potentially expose JPMorgan to more risks than it had anticipated. Alarmed, the JPMorgan team pressed to renegotiate the deal in the following week. The Fed agreed, but as a quid pro quo it suggested that the price of the deal should be raised to $10 a share. That offered a tiny crumb of comfort to Bear shareholders, but it also removed much of the financial cushion in the deal for JPMorgan. On 16 March, Dimon had thought he was acquiring the bank with a cushion of about $5 billion between the sale price and the book value of its assets. By April that cushion was fraying. It later disappeared entirely.

Other blows followed. In the months before Bear had collapsed, the broker had acquired a large number of credit derivatives contracts that were designed to protect it from a downturn in the credit markets. Ironically, in the week after the

Bear deal was announced those contracts produced big losses, because of the sharp rally in credit markets. Then Winters discovered that Bear was taking another set of unanticipated losses linked to a hedge fund. He was also apprised of large backlogs of unconfirmed credit derivatives trades sitting in Bear's back offices. Worst of all, in many cases the Bear management had not made any provisions against possible losses on its derivatives deals.

Cultural differences also came to the fore. The day the merger was struck, the logistics team at JPMorgan ran cables between the two banks to hook up the IT systems. Since their two headquarters were only two blocks apart, that seemed an easy process, but it soon transpired that the computer networks were incompatible. Mixing the human cultures was more difficult. Bear was a scrappy, aggressive bank, where employees were highly competitive with one another and 'ate what they killed', earning bonuses on the revenues they generated. To the JPMorgan staff, the Bear employees seemed dangerously freewheeling; to the Bear staff, JPMorgan felt oppressively dull, if not bureaucratic. In an effort to bridge the gap, Dimon, Winters and Black conducted a series of town halls, and the Bear employees were taken aback. JPMorgan had made regular town halls a point of pride, but the senior executives at Bear were not at all used to taking questions from junior staff. Some Bear staff liked the idea, but others considered it patronizing. 'This is like the Boy Scouts taking over the mob,' some of the JPMorgan staff joked to each other. Nobody was surprised when JPMorgan executives indicated in early April that apart from large numbers of Bear staff in the equities and prime brokerage sectors who would be retained, only a handful of Bear managers would stay on.

Even as the Bear deal calmed the markets, the drama of Bear's collapse sent a chilling message about the vulnerabilities that now plagued the wider system. In previous decades, entities such as

the Bank of England or New York Federal Reserve had tended
to assume that the main focus of regulatory attention should be
on commercial banks, since these were the entities with most
connection to the 'real economy' – and thus needed to be prevented from collapse. In London, for example, the FSA tended
to pay little attention to entities such as hedge funds and SIVs,
since these lay outside the official regulatory net. In America,
that distinction was even more marked as a result of the historical legacy of the Glass–Steagall Act. Though the Fed supervised
commercial banks, it did not monitor the brokers.

The collapse of Bear, though, showed that it was becoming
increasingly hard to state which institutions were 'core' to the
system, and which were not. Banks had become so multifaceted
that they defied easy definitions. (So much so that the Bank of
England had come to refer to them as 'large Complex Financial
Institutions', rather than as 'banks'.) The shadow banking world
in London and New York had swelled to such a monstrous size
that the regulated and unregulated spheres were deeply
entwined, on both sides of the Atlantic. The numbers were staggering. By 2007 the New York Fed calculated that the
combined assets of all the SIVs and similar vehicles came to $2.2
trillion dollars, while hedge funds controlled another $1.8 tril-
lion and the five brokers had $4 trillion on their balance sheet.
The five commercial bank holding companies – the piece of the
system that Geithner oversaw – held just $6 trillion dollars total,
while banks as a whole had $10 trillion of assets. More important
than mere size, though, was that the shadow banks and brokers
were so deeply interconnected with commercial banks through
a fiendishly complex web of trades. Quite apart from whether
they were 'too *big* to fail,' they were too *interconnected* to ignore.

If Bear Stearns teetered, that was no longer a matter of concern for Bear managers alone, or even just the US brokers, it
threatened to shake markets in London, Shanghai, Frankfurt and
Tokyo too. After all, numerous other institutions were also

deeply involved in the repo sector. Entities in London and else-where also had tight connections with Bear in the vast credit derivatives market, since they had written contracts with Bear as a counterparty. If Bear imploded, these entities would conse-quently be left wondering whether or not those contracts would be honoured. After all, the key point about the credit derivatives market in both London and New York was that it did not take place on any centralized exchange or clearing platform (as, say, trading did in the equities world). Back in 1994, the derivatives world had backed away from the idea of alleviating this coun-terparty risk with a centralized exchange. Instead, they had argued that it was better for each player in the market to use legal contracts and self-discipline to make the system safe. But these bilateral tools had not prevented a panic during the Bear drama. As the broker ailed, investors in both New York and London had panicked when they realized the logistical challenges that would arise from any failure. What further stoked the fear was that it was hard to determine how many contracts had ever been written.

So fast had the credit derivatives sector exploded that there was more than $60,000 billion in outstanding CDS trades sitting in the market as a whole. In a strict economic sense, the risk embodied in those contracts was much smaller, at 'just' $14,000 billion, since many of the deals offset each other. Banks would often both buy and sell protection against the default of bonds, at the same time, meaning that the net exposure was cancelled out. But that would still leave a vast pool of potential counter-party risk if parties to a trade failed. Or so the worry went. The CDS market had turned into a vast, opaque spider's web, linking together banks, shadow banks and brokers alike with unfath-omable trades — and fear.

CHAPTER FIFTEEN

Freefall

In the weeks after the Bear collapse, equity markets rallied; the drama seemed almost cathartic, like a ritual sacrifice in which Bear had been slaughtered to atone for the follies of Wall Street. Some commentators argued that the forceful interventions by the NY Fed and the Treasury showed that the system was not repeating the key mistake of Japan's banking crisis, by covering up its rot. The drama was also spurring wide debate about what had gone wrong.

Only a few days after Bear Stearns collapsed, Timothy Geithner had urged his predecessor Jerry Corrigan to organize a 'voluntary' Wall Street report on how complex finance could be made less risky. Corrigan was only too happy to oblige. He had already overseen two earlier studies, one on the lessons from the implosion of Long Term Capital Management, and the second – in 2005, just as the credit bubble was getting under way – on the state of complex finance. Corrigan was convinced that his third report, though, would be the most important. 'We need to ask some important rhetorical questions – like "why did everyone miss the boat?"' he observed. 'I am still mystified by that – that is the big issue. Yes, we knew that risk was mispriced but we did not see what was coming! I don't think anyone really did.'

Corrigan asked Andrew Feldstein to help him write the section on reforms needed for credit derivatives. Though outside Wall Street Feldstein's five-year-old fund, BlueMountain, was little known, by 2008 the fund's credit derivatives book was bigger than that of many banks, which gave Feldstein huge clout in the sector.

Also in the spring of 2008, the Institute for International Finance, a Washington-based think tank, corralled a hundred senior bankers to write a report on the credit dramas. This report argued that the system had to change: it was time to go back to basics, to revert to a simpler, more transparent and more 'honest' style of banking. 'There really is an overriding responsibility for the industry to get its act together now,' observed Charles Dallara, head of the IIF. The IIF had no powers to force banks to clean up their acts, but most of its recommendations were subsequently adopted by the Basel committee of international supervisors, a body that did have the power to set new rules. In late spring, at meetings of the Group of Seven finance ministers, the Basel committee issued its own report, and though it stopped short of recommending a complete rethink of the Basel Accord, as some analysts had hoped it would, it did call on banks to set aside much bigger reserves, to focus more on liquidity issues, and to be far more discriminating in their use of credit ratings.

Even after the turmoil and losses, though, other voices objected strenuously to radical change. Mark Brickell, who had lobbied so vigorously in the 1990s against regulation of derivatives on behalf of the ISDA, spoke on 16 April 2008 at the ISDA's annual meeting in Vienna.

As Brickell stood on the podium in the ballroom of the Vienna Hilton, history weighed on him. ISDA had gathered in the same city two decades earlier and Brickell considered that symbolically appropriate. Vienna was the home of the great free-market economist Friedrich von Hayek, who was also Brickell's hero. '[Twenty years ago] we set out to design a business guided by market discipline because we believed that it should be an even better guide to good behaviour than regulatory proscription,' he observed. 'The credit crunch gives good evidence that market discipline has guided the derivatives business better than regulation has steered housing finance.' Brickell remained as opposed as ever to the idea that governments should intervene. 'Hayek believed that markets would create a rhythm of their own, that they are self-healing. That is something we all should remember and honour today,' he told the audience. 'When governments arrive to help there is always a price to be paid that often takes the form of greater regulation.'

Not all attendees agreed that government scrutiny was wrong. The conference had started with a keynote speech from Paul Calello, the head of the investment bank of Credit Suisse, who had warned: 'We cannot expect "business as usual". There will be new regulation, and there *should* be; voluntary efforts are not enough. This new phenomenon of "too interconnected to fail" is now a permanent part of the financial system.' Some of the ISDA officials were furious, believing Calello had let them down.

In early August, Corrigan himself weighed in with his report, which urged banks to overhaul their risk-management systems, to create a more standardized and transparent set of financial tools, and to move credit derivatives trading on to a centralized clearing platform. And he urged that these things be done within a matter of months. Corrigan wrote in a covering letter to Henry Paulson:

Costly as these reforms will be, those costs will be minuscule compared to the hundreds of billions of dollars of write-downs experienced by financial institutions in recent months, to say nothing of the economic dislocations and distortions triggered by the crisis. [The banking industry] needs a renewed commitment to collective discipline in the spirit of elevated 'financial statesmanship' that recognizes that there are circumstances in which individual institutions must be prepared to put aside specific interests in the name of the common interest.

Corrigan lamented that there appeared to be precious few such bankers left.

Corrigan's urgency was well placed. In the weeks after the Bear–JPMorgan deal, the Libor rate, the key 'litmus test' of borrowing costs, had fallen, but by midsummer it was creeping back up again. Policymakers were alarmed and confused. More trouble seemed imminent.

One issue was that, as the problem came to be described, the tremors on Wall Street and in the City were now reverberating on the high street. Banks buckling under their vast losses were slashing loans not just to hedge funds, but to all sorts of companies. The crucial question now was one of timing: would the banks recover before the credit crunch threw the economy into recession? Solemnly, Paul Tucker, head of markets at the Bank of England, warned that 'we face a race [against time] to see whether financial conditions . . . stabilize before macroeconomic slowdown, here and abroad, raises loan defaults.'

The signs did not bode well for quick recovery. Losses continued to mount. By April, the total loss in the estimated prices of mortgage-linked CDOs and other securities had reached almost $400 billion, a dramatically larger figure than any of the earlier predicted subprime losses, which prompted the International Monetary Fund to estimate that the total 'losses' from the credit crisis could reach $1000 billion. Though some argued that those ABX-based prices had fallen too far, that argument offered little reassurance to investors. Even if prices seemed

absurdly low, relative to fundamentals, there were simply no
buyers for super-senior assets. 'The real problem is the lack of
any buyers for the AAA debt,' explained Rick Watson, head of
the European Securitization Forum. 'That is the biggest issue
dogging the market.'

What was now driving the price of super-senior risk was not
so much 'hard' economic data, which could be plugged into
models, but investor fear, which economists had long ignored in
their modelling. In this new world, the 'quants' were adrift. It
was a terrifying, disorientating seascape, and the banking community was about to suffer a gut-wrenching case of vertigo.

Steve Black was scheduled to play golf on Saturday, 13
September, with some key JPMorgan clients. On Friday morning he called the club to say that he was not sure if he would
play. Six months after the drama of the Bear Stearns deal, he
sensed that more trouble and uncertainty was brewing. On 7
September the Federal Reserve had put the two state-backed
mortgage giants, Fannie Mae and Freddie Mac, under 'conservatorship', a move tantamount to nationalization. By the
summer, confidence that they would be able to weather the
storm of mortgage defaults, and the credit crunch, had started to
slip. The housing market was continuing to crumble, and the
default rate on prime mortgages started to rise. Like the shadow
banks and brokers, Fannie and Freddie had been operating with
very high levels of assets relative to their equity.

The move on 7 September temporarily calmed markets, but
it also stoked more uncertainty about long-term prospects. As
the implications of the conservatorship sank in, many investors
realized they had suffered big losses. In addition, a host of CDS
contracts written on bonds that had been issued by the two
giants defaulted. The state of the housing market was looking
ever more dire, as were the prices of mortgage-linked securities.
By August, average US house prices were 20 per cent below

their level of two years before. However, the housing crisis was no longer just a 'made in America' affair. The UK had also suffered a house price bubble in the first seven years of the decade, which was as extreme as that seen in the US, and by the autumn of 2008 British house prices were collapsing too. That had not yet produced delinquencies anywhere near the scale of the American subprime market. Nevertheless, fears were growing that British and other international banks could soon suffer fresh losses from that market too. And that emphasized a wider point: as the economic pain spread, subprime was no longer the only blow hitting the large banks. Defaults on credit cards, corporate loans and non-US mortgages loomed as well. A new cycle of fear was gaining traction, and bruised investors scanned the banking landscape for omens of new failures.

In early September, Lehman Brothers came into their crosshairs. During the Bear crisis, Lehman's share price had slumped because investors assumed that if Bear collapsed, Lehman would go next. Lehman too had drawn a large portion of its funding from the short-term repo markets, and had large exposure to both the residential mortgage bond sector and commercial real estate. When the Fed rescued Bear, Lehman's share price rebounded, and when the Fed then announced it would extend funding to all brokerages, some bankers joked that the Fed's announcement should be called the 'Save Lehman Act 2008'.

In June the firm shocked observers by announcing a $2.8 billion loss in its second-quarter results, though it swiftly raised $6 billion of capital to shore its base up. Rumours began to spread, though, that the bank was understating the scale of its bad loans. Analysts thought Lehman should allay those concerns by raising more capital, or by merging, but Lehman CEO Richard Fuld refused to do either. Fuld was a fiercely independent character who hated the idea of selling out, and though Lehman executives discussed selling a stake in the company to investors, including the Korean Development Bank, by early September no deal was in the works.

Lehman was bleeding funding by then, and on Wednesday, 10 September, Fuld made one last desperate roll of the dice. The company declared plans to sell its asset management operations and spin out almost $30 billion of mortgage assets into a separate, ring-fenced vehicle. But when bankers at other institutions looked into the nuts and bolts of what Lehman was up to, they spotted a troubling detail. The small print of Lehman's announcement suggested that it was using valuation estimates for its troubled assets much higher than those of other banks. Confidence crumbled. 'What about the rest of the bank's numbers? Can we trust those?' bankers started to ask.

The price of buying protection against a Lehman default, using credit derivatives, rocketed, and investors in the repo market stopped dealing with the bank. In an eerie replay of Bear's collapse, hedge funds moved their money out of the bank, and investors started to assign the credit derivatives contracts they had previously written with Lehman Brothers to other banks.

By Tuesday, 9 September, Black was becoming alarmed about the risks this posed to JPMorgan Chase. Morgan was the broker's clearer, which meant it would be exposed to losses if Lehman suddenly collapsed. To protect itself, Black called Fuld and told him that he wanted Lehman to post an additional $5 billion of collateral. Black promised to work with the broker so that they did not need to find the funds from its capital. Even so, Fuld baulked. Eventually, Black agreed to accept $3 billion.

By Friday, Black was still hoping that Lehman would make it through. After procrastination, he eventually called the golf club and agreed to play the next day as planned. A few minutes later, Dimon burst into his room. 'Guess what? We have got to go down to the Fed to discuss Lehman's.' At 6 p.m., Dimon, Black and more than two dozen other Wall Street dignitaries – with the notable exception of Lehman Brothers – assembled in a large conference room in the Fed headquarters. Once the bankers were assembled, Geithner cut to the chase. Lehman was on the brink of collapse but the government had no appetite to save it with taxpayer funds. Was anyone willing to buy the broker? Or could the banks club together, as they had with LTCM?

Nobody in the room was keen.

When LTCM imploded in 1998, the hole in the fund had been around $4 billion. Most of the banks that participated in the rescue thus needed to produce 'only' $200 million or so. The hole in Lehman's books was feared to be at least $30 billion, or even double that, implying that any rescue would require each bank to fork out several billion dollars. Many of those sitting in the Fed room could not produce that type of cash, even if they had wanted to. They desperately needed more capital themselves.

'But I assume we are going to talk about AIG [too],' Steve Black interjected. Geithner looked irritated. The meeting, he explained, had been called to discuss a solution to the *Lehman* problem. AIG would have to wait.

During the previous year, the health of the mighty AIG insurance group had attracted less attention from investors or journalists than the travails of the big banks. But Black knew that AIG was sitting on a vast position in super-senior risk that was ravaging its balance sheet. What he wanted to know was what did the Fed – or any of the other banks – plan to do about *that*? Without a solution, he feared that AIG could collapse, creating an even bigger shock.

Vikram Pandit, the man who had replaced Charles Prince as Citigroup CEO, jumped in. 'He's right. We need to talk about AIG!' Geithner looked even more irritated. It was bad enough trying to cope with one financial crisis; battling on two different fronts looked almost impossible. He wanted to find a solution to

Lehman Brothers first, and he pushed on. 'There is no political will for a federal bailout,' Geithner said. 'Come back in the morning and be prepared to do something.'

The next day, more than two dozen senior officials from the main Wall Street, British and and continental European banks and brokers assembled at the Fed. Calello from Credit Suisse was there. As he arrived at the Fed, he was struck by a historical irony: almost exactly a decade earlier Calello had rushed down to the Fed at the weekend to discuss the fate of the Long Term Capital Management hedge fund. This time, Calello noted, there were far more European bankers assembling for crisis talks in relation to Lehman. It was a powerful sign of how closely integrated the London and New York markets had become. Why didn't we learn the lessons from before? Calello asked himself.

They split into groups and went to different rooms to discuss options. One gaggle explored the question of whether the banks might coordinate a joint rescue plan, comparable to the LTCM deal. Another debated what would happen if Lehman Brothers filed for bankruptcy. Separately, Fed officials hunted for a purchaser. Two names were floated: Bank of America and Barclays, which had a large investment banking operation, known as Barclays Capital. Barclays Capital CEO Bob Diamond was highly ambitious, and eager to bolster his position in the American markets.

By Saturday evening, after hours of debate fuelled by deliveries of coffee and doughnuts, the bankers had decided that a joint rescue plan was impossible. Bank of America also signalled that it had lost interest in bidding, but to Geithner's relief, Barclays still seemed keen. On Sunday morning, though, an entirely unexpected hitch emerged. To make the deal work, the Fed wanted Barclays to honour all the existing trades attached to Lehman Brothers when the markets opened on Monday morning. Without that guarantee, Geithner feared panic would erupt.

However, British financial regulations stipulated that Barclays would not be allowed to extend that scale of guarantee without asking its shareholders first. At first, Barclays assumed that the Financial Services Authority, the main UK regulator, would be willing to waive that restriction, given the extraordinary circumstances. On Sunday, though, British regulators indicated that they were not willing to bend the rule.

Officials in the Washington Fed and US Treasury were furious. Henry Paulson called senior UK financial officials and implored them to help, but the British dragged their heels. Some US officials suspected that British regulators secretly feared Barclays was too weak to conduct such a large deal. Others blamed Barclays for playing hardball, to win more financial aid.

Frantically, some of the Barclays team asked if the Fed itself could guarantee its trades, or extend a loan for a few days. The British officials raised similar questions. They believed it was up to the *Americans*, not them, to be creative and get the deal done. However, Paulson refused to condone any move that might smack of a bailout. Lately he had been taking political heat for rescuing Bear and for the move to place Fannie and Freddie in 'conservatorship'. He now believed a line should be drawn in the sand.

That left Geithner in a terrible fix. He had scurried to make banks tackle the issue of counterparty risk in the derivatives markets during the summer, but most of the proposed reforms weren't yet in place. The 'chain reaction' problem loomed as large as it had during the crisis at Bear. However, the rules that governed the Fed stipulated that the central bank could only extend loans when they were backed by solid collateral. In the case of Bear, Geithner's officials had deemed that to be the case because Bear had plenty of assets. At Lehman Brothers, though, the black hole appeared to be so vast that Geithner doubted whether the Fed had the legal powers to act without a specific mandate from the Treasury or Congress, and that mandate was not forthcoming.

On Sunday afternoon, Barclays pulled out, leaving a bitter taste on both sides. Geithner was staring at disaster. The Fed officials made one last-ditch attempt to lessen the shock. They urgently summoned all the senior bankers with connections to the derivatives world whom they could find on a Sunday afternoon, placed them in a room and asked them to come clean about any derivatives deals they had that involved Lehman Brothers. The hope was that banks could then cancel some deals, lessening losses. The initiative failed, though, in part because it was impossible to get enough bankers there on such short notice.

On Sunday evening, Dimon convened a meeting of the JPMorgan board and solemnly told them that the Lehman bankruptcy loomed. Geithner had run out of time. 'We think we are going to be fine, in terms of our bank,' Dimon observed, in uncharacteristically sombre tones. 'But it's going to be very, very ugly for others. Worse than anything that any of us have seen in our lives.'

Dimon was right. The bankruptcy of Lehman's was announced late at night on Sunday, 14 September, New York time. As the markets opened for business in Asia and London, it briefly appeared that investors might take the news in their stride, but, as so often in the credit crisis, the initial calm reflected stunned confusion rather than confidence. Market players were trying to assess the logistical complexities created by the collapse, and they began to panic. Ironically, the biggest source of concern was *not* the issue Geithner had long fretted about, namely the challenge of untangling credit derivatives trades. Precisely because the Fed had already issued so many warnings on the matter, most banks and hedge funds had put a plan in place to unwind large volumes of trades. The logistical details of that task were extremely daunting, but the problem had at least been recognized and worked on. It was a '*known* unknown', as some bankers joked, quoting US Defense Secretary Donald Rumsfeld's notorious comment about the chaos of the Iraq War.

What was more frightening was that Lehman's failure had also created '*un*known unknowns', knock-on effects the investment community had not expected. One problem was that in London, dozens of hedge funds suddenly discovered that the failure of Lehman had left their assets frozen. While in New York hedge fund assets tended to be ring-fenced when they were held by a broker, which meant that they could always be reclaimed by the funds in the event of default, in London such assets were not legally ring-fenced. That left the British funds unable to complete numerous trades. Panic ensued. Another unexpected shock hit the $3000 billion American money-market fund sector. In the months before the Lehman collapse, many of these funds had purchased debt issued by Lehman Brothers, assuming that the US government would never let Lehman collapse. Now those funds were nursing substantial losses. On 16 September the $62 billion Reserve Primary Fund, the country's oldest money-market fund, posted a sombre statement on its website. 'The value of the debt securities issued by Lehman Brothers Holdings (face value $785 million) and held by the Primary Fund has been valued at zero effective as of 4 p.m. New York time today,' the fund said. That threatened to spark more panic. America's money-market fund industry had prided itself on *never* 'breaking the buck', and the Reserve had just done so. A run on the money-market funds now seemed likely.

Meanwhile, as Steve Black and Vikram Pandit had anticipated, a crisis had been building at AIG. By the summer of 2007 AIG was holding around $560 billion of super-senior risk, such a gargantuan number, and so little known outside the group, that when some of the former J.P. Morgan team linked to the Bistro trades later saw it, they assumed it was a typo. 'It's got to be fifty-six billion, hasn't it?' one asked.

What was even more alarming was that AIG was ill equipped to handle that risk. Back in the autumn of 2007, when banks started writing down their holdings of super-senior risk, AIG had at first refused to follow suit. Its executives argued that the swings in the ABX bore no relation to economic reality; they believed AIG could afford to take a long-term view because it was an insurance group, not a trading house. Then, on 11 February 2008, AIG had been forced to admit that its auditors, PricewaterhouseCoopers, had discovered a 'material weakness' in its accounts. The problem was that when AIG insured super-senior CDO debt, it often promised to post collateral to back that insurance up. But AIG had not accumulated the reserves it would need to follow through on that commitment in the event of a wave of claims.

By early 2008 AIG was facing an avalanche of claims, which forced the company to announce some $43 billion of write-downs of super-senior assets, even more than at Citigroup and UBS, blasting a hole in its balance sheet. Like the other banks, AIG had frantically tried to plug that gap by issuing fresh shares, and had asked JPMorgan to co-lead that. But when senior JPMorgan bankers looked at AIG's books during the summer, they were so shocked that they secretly threatened to resign from the underwriting deal.

By mid-September AIG faced a new, even more deadly threat. The largest ratings agencies warned that they were considering removing the insurance group's triple-A tag due to the subprime woes. That threatened to create a new squeeze, since AIG would need to post more collateral for its CDS deals if it lost its coveted triple A. Behind the scenes, some large investment banks quietly demanded that AIG produce more collateral. The insurance group, however, did not appear to have that money to hand. It seemed that another default loomed.

That helped to tip the market into freefall. The shock of the Lehman collapse on Sunday night had been devastating by itself. The money-market and AIG woes, though, were combining to produce the perfect market storm. Around the world, stock markets collapsed, wiping $600 billion off global equity prices in the space of just thirty-six hours. By Tuesday, the cost of borrowing funds in the interbank market spiralled so much that quotes became almost theoretical. Institutions were refusing to deal with each other at all. Rumours started to fly that Merrill Lynch and other American financial institutions were on the brink of collapse. The share price of Barclays, Royal Bank of Scotland and HBOS tumbled. Nothing as brutal had been witnessed in the markets since the Wall Street Crash. By Tuesday, 16 September, some traders thought events were even worse than 1929. The machinery of modern finance was seizing up; markets were simply not trading any more, because nobody trusted anyone else. 'If this continues, the next logical step is that the cash eventually stops coming out of the ATM machines,' confessed one senior banker in the City of London. 'If that happens, God help us all.'

As the panic intensified, the turmoil hit not just those markets that had already been buffeted by the subprime crisis, but even those that had hitherto appeared immune. Share prices in emerging markets crashed, as did the stock markets in countries as diverse as Australia, China and Japan. That flew in the face of the received market wisdom. In the previous year, many pundits had suggested that countries such as the 'BRICs' – Brazil, Russia, India and China – should largely be protected from any American subprime woes. The assumption was that the BRICs' internal economic dynamic was so strong that those regions were 'decoupling' from the Western world. But as the market storm intensified in the wake of Lehman's collapse, the 'decoupling' thesis was blasted apart. Investors were cutting credit lines and sold anything they could, irrespective of whether or not it made sense from a rational economic perspective. Moreover, investors had belatedly realized that a sharp downturn in the West could damage emerging markets too.

In Europe, regulators and policymakers seethed in fury and shock. Until the very last minute, most European officials – like investors – had assumed that the American government would find a way to save Lehman. Its failure to do so had tipped the system into a global crisis, the Europeans complained. 'What was horrendous is the decision of Henry Paulson to let Lehman Brothers go – for the equilibrium of the world financial system this was a genuine error,' observed French economy minister Christine Lagarde, reflecting a widespread view. Stung, Geithner tried to explain that he had had no choice. 'The Fed just did not have the legal authority to act,' he told European counterparts. But that cut little ice with the Europeans. All they wanted to know was what the Americans, or anybody else, could do now to prevent a catastrophic meltdown of the entire system.

The answer came in several stages. On the evening of Tuesday, 16 September, the Fed announced that it would extend an $85 billion loan to AIG, in exchange for taking a 79.9 per cent stake in the group. Essentially, that added up to a full-blown national-ization of AIG. It was an extraordinary step, especially given that just forty-eight hours earlier the Fed and Treasury had refused to extend aid to Lehman Brothers. Gamely, the Fed officials tried to explain away the policy contradictions by pointing out that AIG did have assets to post as collateral to any Fed loan, but that was, at best, a fig leaf covering a major policy shift.

The level of state intervention was steadily cranked up, facil-itating many mergers. On Monday, 15th, even before the AIG deal was finagled, Bank of America announced plans to purchase Merrill Lynch. The deal appeared to have been heavily encour-aged by the Fed and Treasury, to avert the risk of Merrill collapsing. On Thursday, 18 September, British authorities unveiled a shotgun marriage of their own. Lloyds TSB, one of the stronger British banks, announced it was taking over the operations of ailing HBOS. The same day, central banks unveiled yet more coordinated liquidity injections, including a deal between the Bank of England and the Fed to pump dollar liquidity into London. British regulators also announced a ban on short-selling of bank shares, in an effort to stem the collapse of share prices. On the other side of the Atlantic, on the same day, the Treasury unveiled a safety net for money-market funds. Once again this used Fed money to stave off a run. Then, at the end of the week, Henry Paulson announced a bold plan by which the Treasury would earmark up to $700 billion in funds to purchase 'troubled assets' from the banks, such as their super-senior holdings. The Troubled Asset Relief Program (TARP) was much like the Treasury's idea for the ill-fated 'superfund', but whereas when the superfund had been proposed a year earlier Paulson had been determined to downplay any suggestion that the government was bailing out the banking system, by 2008 the word 'bailout' was no longer taboo. The fate of TARP, however, would prove fraught with controversy.

Goldman Sachs and Morgan Stanley both applied to change their status from brokers into banks, bringing them more firmly under the Fed umbrella and ending the era of independent investment banks. A few days later, Washington Mutual, once an icon of America's mortgage market and retail financial world, collapsed. The American insurance group FDIC took control of the group, to avert a Northern Rock-style bank run, and quickly sold it to JPMorgan for a knockdown price. Jamie Dimon had always wanted to expand the bank's retail operations in the American Midwest and was thrilled to grab WaMu. Then Citigroup announced a move to purchase the ailing Wachovia group, with US government support, only to be trumped by a rival bid from Wells Fargo. Consolidation was intensifying, day by day, and so was state intervention.

In London, on 29 September the British government nationalized Bradford and Bingley. The next day the German,
Luxembourg and Belgian governments poured money into
Dexia, a European financial giant, to avert its collapse, and the
Irish government guaranteed the deposits of all its banks. A few
days later, Germany unveiled plans to save Hypo Real Estate,
another vast property giant, and the Dutch government nationalized Fortis. Then Iceland nationalized all of its large banks, in
a frantic – and ultimately futile – effort to prevent a full-blown
crisis from engulfing the tiny island. It was a potent reminder
that what had once started with a set of bad loans in the heart-
land of America's mortgage market had now spiralled into a truly
global financial storm.

Behind the scenes, the British government frantically tried to
work out what it should do. During most of the previous year,
the London authorities had appeared on the back foot in their
handling of the crisis. The government's response to the crisis at
Northern Rock had appeared particularly inept. That partly
reflected structural problems created by the 'tripartite' regulatory
structure, which gave the FSA responsibility for micro-level
supervision, and the Bank of England responsibility for macroeconomic financial stability, in a wider sense. In theory, the sides
were supposed to coordinate with each other to prevent issues
from falling through the cracks. In practice, though, communication was poor, and while the Treasury was supposed to have
overall power in this system it seemed too under-resourced to
act. In addition to that, the British government was dogged by
ideological unease. The Labour government had come to power
espousing a relatively free-market, pro-City stance, epitomized
by a 'light-touch' financial regime. The idea of meddling in markets, let alone pouring taxpayer money into banks, sat uneasily
with that stance. Moreover, Mervyn King, Bank governor, had
a strong intellectual dislike of any move to 'bail out' the banks.

He felt he had issued plenty of warnings before the summer of 2007 that the credit bubble would burst, yet those had been ignored. If the government stepped in to rescue bankers from their foolish mistakes after that, they would simply be encouraged to take even *more* risks in the future – or so he feared. To him, that was tantamount to creating 'moral hazard'.

By the autumn of 2008, however, events had become so extreme that even the famously stubborn King had changed his stance. He – like Ben Bernanke of the US Fed – had initially assumed that the impact of subprime losses would be easily contained. By 2008, though, he had grudgingly conceded that he had misread the situation. The scale of leverage in the system was much bigger than he had realized, as was the damage caused by subprime losses. As a result, banks faced not just a 'liquidity problem', in the sense of being unable to fund themselves (as at Northern Rock) but a 'solvency problem' too. Moreover, King could see that problem was not confined to merely one bank. By early September the share price of Royal Bank of Scotland was crashing because investors feared it was running low on capital. HBOS was in a similar fragile state. Even Barclays was beset by intense market doubt. And while some banks – such as Barclays – still appeared to be able to raise money from private investors to plug their capital hole, others could not. Indeed, the only British banks that appeared to have weathered the storm in even a moderately decent shape were Lloyds TSB, HSBC and Standard Chartered – and the last two were, at best, only 'part' British.

In early September, the level of unease had risen so high that officials at the Treasury, Bank and FSA started to furtively toss around the idea of creating a systemic support package for the banks. The shock of the Lehman Brothers collapse in mid-September accelerated those talks. 'For the last three weeks we have been dealing with the gravest financial crisis since 1914. We have been on the precipice,' King admitted a couple weeks after the Lehman Brothers collapse. 'When we started this crisis there was a widespread view that banks were well capitalized. But now we realize that the problem was that assets sitting on their balance sheets which were supposed to be risk-free, carried a lot of risk. Perceptions of the value of those assets and the risks changed radically.' From the stubbornly dogmatic Professor King, it was a rare hint that he had changed his mind.

'What has become clear is that you cannot deal with this problem just by providing more liquidity to the banks. That just addresses the symptoms,' he added. 'You need a fiscal response too.'

On 8 October, Gordon Brown duly unveiled that fiscal response. In a packed House of Commons, he presented a three-part package to shore the banks up. One plank of that package, worth around £200 billion, was designed to inject more liquidity into the money-markets, via the Bank. A second £250 billion measure offered government guarantees for any bonds issued by banks. The third leg was the most eye-catching: the government also promised to take equity stakes in British banks, to boost their capital reserves. Initially, some £25 billion was earmarked for that.

The move was greeted with shock. A year earlier, the government had bailed out Northern Rock by using taxpayer funds. But it was one thing to rescue *one* bank in the heat of a crisis; it was quite another to offer systemic support to numerous banks. This represented a level of government involvement unimaginable just a month before. And when the senior bankers had first heard the idea, on 7 October, most had hated the plan. In an angry meeting, the heads of groups such as RBS insisted that they did not need the capital, and did not wish to face any state meddling. However, when news of the meeting leaked out, the banks' share prices crashed, weakening the bankers' hands. By the time that Brown appeared in Parliament, the banks had reluctantly signed up. 'This plan is designed to put the British banking system on a sounder footing,' he solemnly told the House of Commons. 'This is not a time for conventional thinking or outdated dogma but for fresh and innovative intervention that gets to the heart of the problem.' Or as King later observed: 'We had to get more capital into the banks. Doing it one by one would have been hard. It is clear that does not work . . . We have come into the second phase of this [policy response] which is to have a plan to deal with systemic undercapitalization of the banks.'

On Sunday, 13 October 2008, Jamie Dimon received an urgent phone call from the Treasury Department. 'We need you in Washington tomorrow at 3 p.m.' Paulson was summoning the heads of the nine biggest American banks for yet another meeting. He refused to give a clue about the agenda.

As Dimon and the other CEOs travelled to Washington, they had reason to feel apprehensive. In the previous few weeks a financial hurricane had hit them, bringing such havoc to the financial system as none of them had seen in their lifetimes. Or as the head of the IMF, Dominique Strauss-Kahn, told a Washington meeting just days before: 'Intensifying solvency concerns about a number of the largest US-based and European financial institutions have pushed the global financial system to the brink of systemic meltdown.'

As the nine American CEOs trooped into a gilded room of the US Treasury, few were expecting what they were told. Never before in its history, even during the 1930s Depression, had the US government nationalized large swathes of the banking system. When Paulson had first unveiled his proposal for the TARP he had stressed that the money was intended to help the government to buy assets from the banks, not banks themselves; now he was taking a page from the UK's playbook.

When Dimon and the others sat down at the table in the Treasury conference room, they were presented with pieces of paper that stated they would sell shares of their banks to the government and were forcefully told to sign. This was a 'take it or leave it' deal, Paulson added: either the banks accepted this 'voluntary' infusion of federal money, or they would be left out on a limb, ineligible for support if any future crisis broke. It was clear that the Treasury wanted the banks to act in unison.

As the men sat around the table, Richard Kovacevich, head of Wells Fargo, pointed out that his San Francisco-based bank had escaped the worst of the mortgage-linked woes, and thus did not need help. Kenneth Lewis, head of Bank of America, pointed out that his bank had just raised $10 billion of fresh capital – and so did not need more funds. Some CEOs expressed concern that the measure would lead to unwelcome curbs on banking pay.

Then Dimon chipped in. While he was adamant that JPMorgan Chase did not need the infusion of capital to survive, he granted that Paulson's plan might be a good deal. Dimon knew that some of his competitors would *not* survive without more funds. 'It sounds good,' he said. Around the table, the other eight bankers slowly agreed to get on board. Paulson got his deal.

As the CEOs left the room, some comforted themselves that the deals didn't quite add up to actual nationalization. The government was acquiring just a small stake in their banks, and it did not plan to exercise management control. Yet a Rubicon had been crossed, in America as in the UK. For five long decades, American finance had worshipped at the altar of free-market ideals. So had the City of London. Now those ideals were being ripped apart on both sides of the Atlantic.

What most worried some bankers was that it was crucially unclear just how much further those policies would go. Around the same time as Paulson was meeting the US bankers, the British government was finalizing the details of its bailout plans. This was not at all comforting, for the banks. After looking at the books, the FSA had decided that RBS needed to receive

£20 billion state capital, rather than the £10 billion initially earmarked, while HBOS would receive a £17 billion injection to
facilitate its merger with Lloyds TSB. That bumped the total
level of taxpayer injections up to £37 billion – not £25 billion –
and left the government with a 70 per cent stake in RBS and 40
per cent stake in the new merged Lloyds–HBOS entity too. But
would it stop there? And what price would the government
exact for those funds? Nobody knew. The UK Treasury denied
it planned to exercise management control, or wanted to nation-
alize the entire banking world. Yet the banking problems were
getting worse – and political pressure on the banks was rising.
Politicians demanded that banks start lending to 'British' companies and provide more 'British' mortgages. They demanded
that banking bonuses be scrapped. Sir Fred Goodwin and Andy
Hornby, heads of RBS and HBOS, were peremptorily sacked.
'We are moving into a world of socialist banking, where the government can meddle wherever it wants,' lamented one senior
European bank executive. A new era of finance had dawned –
albeit not one that most bankers had ever expected, far less
wanted, to see.

Epilogue

On 29 January 2009, JPMorgan Chase hosted a cocktail party for two hundred of its key clients and contacts in the elegant surroundings of the Piano Bar, in the smart Swiss ski resort of Davos. The occasion was the much buzzed-about annual gathering of the World Economic Forum, which for the first seven years of the decade had been dominated by the investment banking elite. Goldman Sachs, Barclays, Lehman Brothers and others threw lavish dinners for favoured guests, and bank executives strutted on the conference room stages, extolling the virtues of free markets, globalization and financial innovation. Sleek black limousines whisked them between meetings at hotels in close proximity; they were too grand to trudge through the slush.

This year a funereal mood hung in the crisp mountain air. Almost no banking CEOs attended. John Thain, the former CEO of Merrill Lynch, had been scheduled to host a breakfast but had just been sacked. Bob Diamond, head of Barclays Capital, cancelled his dinner appearance at short notice. Lloyd Blankfein, head of Goldman Sachs, stayed away as a demonstration of cost-cutting. As the American and European public realized the scale of the banks' woes over the winter, and the level of government – read taxpayer – money being used to prop them up, outrage had escalated. The numbers were staggering. By the winter of 2009, economists estimated that mark-to-market losses had almost reached $3 trillion. Banks and insurance companies had already written down more that $1 trillion, and received more than $300 billion of government funds. The balance sheet of the Bank of England was exploding in size – like that of the Federal Reserve – as it scrambled to shore up the money markets. National debts were spiralling too. In the UK alone, economists at Goldman Sachs calculated that Britain would end up spending around £120 billion, or 8 per cent of its GDP, rescuing its banks. The IMF reckoned the bill would be nearer 13 per cent. The *Financial Times* calculated that would push national debt up to £1200 billion, or around 80 per cent of GDP. A similar pattern was developing in America too. Politicians on both sides of the Atlantic were furious. Voters were even more livid. Amid that backlash, few bankers wanted to be seen partying in a Swiss ski resort.

Diamond of Barclays Capital had additional reasons for staying away from Davos. By late January his bank's share price was collapsing in particularly spectacular style, as a new sense of crisis erupted among British banks. Irrespective of all the money that the British government had already earmarked for the banks, investors were becoming increasingly worried that it might not be enough to stop the crisis from spiralling further. 'We are sliding into complete nationalization, but almost in a back-door way,' fretted Vince Cable, the Liberal Democrat politician, who argued that it would be 'more honest' simply to embark on full-scale government control, so that the state sector could at least sort the problems out. The UK Treasury vehemently denied any desire to do that. Instead, it started work on a set of plans to insure the most toxic assets held by banks such as RBS and HBOS. But as the problems grew worse, the sense of investor concern was rising too – not merely about the state of the banks but about whether the British government really had the financial strength to mount a fully fledged rescue mission. 'The balance sheet of RBS is bigger than the UK economy,' fretted Campbell. Barclays, for its part, vehemently denied it needed any help, since it had already raised finance from Middle Eastern investors. But in that febrile climate, Diamond – and the rest of the Barclays team – knew they needed to stay on their home patch, to keep fighting. Even the short trip to Davos seemed a journey too far.

Jamie Dimon was one of the rare exceptions who was willing to appear at the Swiss mountain resort. (The other was Stephen Green, head of HSBC, which had also emerged in better shape than many rivals.) Dimon had never been one to stay in the shadows; outspoken speech was part of his brand. By early 2009, Dimon was trying to speak with more gravitas than he had in his youth. He was keenly aware of the increasingly heavy weight of responsibility falling on his shoulders. Yet he reckoned that *somebody* on Wall Street needed to have the courage to speak up and stand out, if nothing else because he was getting fed up with all the procrastination among the Western governments on how to fix the mess. 'This stuff is getting old! I just wish they would get on with it. Politicians are playing catch as catch can,' Dimon said at one of the events, triggering spontaneous applause. 'I haven't yet seen people get all the right people into the room and close the door and put a solution up on the wall. God knows, some really stupid things were done by American banks and American investment bankers . . . Some stupid things were done . . . but it wasn't just the bankers. Where were the regulators in all this?'

Dimon had the luxury of being able to speak as a survivor. Just before flying to Switzerland, he had unveiled JPMorgan Chase's fourth-quarter results, which showed the bank's profits were just $702 million, 76 per cent down on the previous year, due to a $1.8 billion write-down on its leveraged loans and $1.1 billion losses on mortgage assets. 'It's very disappointing,' Dimon curtly declared, warning that the bank could suffer further significant losses on its mortgage book if house prices kept falling. The bank's share price tumbled as some analysts warned that credit card and student loan losses could emerge too. 'Jamie Dimon is set for a fall,' claimed Charlie Gasparino, a prominent financial commentator, suggesting that it 'will put in question his current status as the king of Wall Street'. Compared with its rivals, though, the bank's position looked dazzling. By January 2009 the US government had dramatically increased its stake in Citigroup, after new credit losses threatened to trigger its collapse. Bank of America had also been bailed out again, when it discovered new rotten assets on the books of Merrill Lynch. As its rivals' share prices collapsed, JPMorgan had become the biggest bank in the world in terms of market capitalization. When an industry dinner was held in London in January to hand out banking prizes, JPMorgan won more categories than any bank had ever done before.

The bank's party in the Piano Bar on the night of Thursday, 29 January, spoke volumes about how the bank's status had changed. The invitations to the event had been designed to carry the ghostly signature of J. Pierpont Morgan, the bank's founder and former Wall Street guru. In the autumn of 2008, the JPMorgan investment bank had rebranded itself as 'J.P. Morgan', in honour of the traditional link with their founder. In a world where investors had lost faith in cyberfinance, J.P. Morgan realized that it was a huge advantage to have such an illustrious history, and an actual legend to promote. The bank had also revived the motto of J. Pierpont's son – J.P. 'Jack' Morgan – that called for 'First-Class Business in a First-Class Way'. It was now being stamped on to internal memos. The 'heritage' Morgan bankers were utterly thrilled.

J.P. Morgan had big plans. During the early years of the

twenty-first century it had watched with awe and envy as Goldman Sachs extended its tentacles into politics and government, often via its powerful network of alumni. J.P. Morgan now planned to emulate that strategy. It started an 'alumni' society, on the suggestion of Andrew Feldstein and other former J.P. Morgan bankers, and had begun cultivating political allies. As J.P. Morgan's guests nibbled on canapés in the Piano Bar, Al Gore, an adviser to the bank, could be seen mingling in the crowds. So could Tony Blair, another well-paid new adviser.

As Bill Winters surveyed the crowds in the Piano Bar, he seemed to harbour mixed emotions about the strange journey he had travelled with the bank. Almost fifteen years had passed since he had first gone down to Boca Raton for that wild weekend of drinking and brainstorming. In some respects, he seemed little changed from the young derivatives trader who had been thrown into the swimming pool. His hair was now flecked with grey, and dark circles ringed his eyes – a testament to months of financial crisis. Yet he still had a fun-loving streak. Given a chance, he laughed, he would be happy to slip out of the formal reception, grab a toboggan and hurtle down the slopes of Davos.

Winters also remained convinced that financial innovation could be a thoroughly good thing. He had seen at first hand the utterly disastrous consequences of innovation used in an unwise manner; but not all the innovations had turned so sour, he insisted. In spite of all the fears of the New York Federal Reserve, the credit derivatives world *had* continued to function during the crisis, even when trading had stopped in almost every other part of the market. Credit derivatives contracts linked to Lehman had settled smoothly too. JPMorgan's own history showed that innovation need not lead to crises. 'I mean we have made plenty of mistakes,' Winters hastily added. As ever, he was wary of sounding upbeat. 'But we made deliberate choices not to do things like CDO of ABS . . . people are sitting around now and saying innovation is bad, that derivatives are this terrible thing, that credit derivatives should be banned. But really this crisis is *not* to do with derivatives. It is about bad mortgage lending, bad risk-management practices, how the innovation was used.'

It was a message, though, that was hard to get across. As Winters circulated at Davos, he had repeatedly tried to explain to people that he still believed that innovation – used correctly – *could* be a good thing. Hardly anyone wanted to listen. What bankers said no longer carried much respect. Time and again in Davos, delegates had lashed out against 'derivatives', and credit derivatives in particular. Wen Jiabao, the Chinese premier, pointedly berated the Western financial world for its lack of self-discipline. Vladimir Putin, his Russian counterpart, scoffed at bankers' use of 'virtual money', noting that 'the pride of Wall Street banks have now ceased to exist'. The optimistic side of Winters liked to hope that the backlash would prove temporary. The realist, though, was dismayed. It looked as if it could take years before the anger subsided. Perhaps longer than any of the original team in Boca Raton remained in their banking careers.

And what of the other members of the old J.P. Morgan group? In late 2008 Winters's former boss Peter Hancock moved to Ohio, to take a job as a vice-chairman of Key Corp, a well-respected regional bank in Cleveland. When he told his former colleagues about the move, some were astounded that such a cerebral, international man would head to Ohio. After Hancock left J.P. Morgan in 2000, though, his career never resumed its former brilliant trajectory. For a few years he ran a consultancy with Roberto Mendoza, another former J.P. Morgan banker, and Robert Merton, the Nobel Prize-winning economist, offering advice on financial innovation. But the venture never truly flourished. Hancock sometimes struggled to convince clients to adopt his wildly creative and innovative ideas, or even to understand how valuable derivatives could be if they were used wisely. He found that lack of comprehension painfully frustrating. He hoped that Cleveland would offer a new chance to implement his vision. 'Watching the financial crisis unfold, I felt that I could be of greater use as a bank executive accountable for ideas and execution, as opposed to being on the sidelines as an adviser,' he explained.

Over in Pittsburgh, Demchak was thriving in the world of regional banking. PNC was one of the winners in the crisis, its losses dramatically smaller than those of its competitors, partly due to Demchak's canny management of the credit portfolio. From time to time, rumours circulated that Demchak was about to be hired back to Wall Street, to help fill in for the dire shortage of experienced executives who both understood how complex finance and derivatives work and had emerged from the crisis with clean hands. Demchak, though, was in no hurry to jump.

In New York, Demchak's good friend Andrew Feldstein continued to run his fund, and to chase his dream of building a better credit derivatives world. The climate, though, was proving extremely challenging. By the end of 2008, BlueMountain had $4.8 billion under management and had outperformed most of its peers. But when the crisis erupted at Lehman Brothers, the entire hedge fund sector witnessed a dramatic outflow of funds. BlueMountain was hit by that trend, ironically because it had produced such good relative returns in 2008 that investors wanted to realize their gains. Eventually the drainage was so bad that BlueMountain was forced to impose a partial 'lock-up', whereby investors are prohibited from withdrawing their funds.

Feldstein remained determined to fight back. 'What we think of as the traditional hedge fund will shrink – that is, hedge funds operating with high degrees of leverage, and with expectations of quarterly redemption,' he observed in early 2009. '[But] I think it is too soon to say whether the alternative investment industry will shrink. Over time, it would be untenable for investors to keep their money in zero-yielding government bonds.'

But Feldstein wasn't expecting a recovery any time soon. Back in the 1990s, he was at college with Barack Obama. 'I was not a close friend of Obama in law school,' he reflected, 'but I did interact with him frequently, especially on the basketball court. You can tell a lot about people by the way they play pick-up basketball – what was very easily recognized about Obama was that he was a leader.' He feared that Obama faced a monumental challenge in repairing the financial sector.

Feldstein was facing his own daunting challenge to create a more rational credit derivatives world. By early 2009, the banking industry had finally started 'tearing up' – or offsetting – derivatives contracts on a large scale, reducing the volume of outstanding deals in the market by more than half. Bankers were starting to adopt a more standardized system for structuring credit derivatives. Progress, however, was patchy and slow. The efforts to build a clearing platform for the credit derivatives world were also lagging, due to internal industry bickering. Jerry Corrigan and Feldstein blamed the problem on a dire lack of 'financial statesmanship', or an inability of banks to think about the public good.

A block away from BlueMountain's offices, at J.P. Morgan's headquarters on 270 Park Avenue, Blythe Masters remained embroiled in her own fights. She was no longer directly involved in the world of structured credit or derivatives, but instead was running the commodities division of J.P. Morgan. Alongside that job, she held the post of chairman of the Securities Industry and Financial Markets Association (SIFMA), the main industry body representing the arena of complex finance. Technically, that made her the most senior Western banker to hold the thankless task of championing the area of finance that was the centre of a violent backlash. It was a tough role. In late 2008, after the

Lehman disaster, Masters started receiving hate mail. One British newspaper dubbed her the woman who created the 'weapons of financial mass destruction'. Angry postings on the internet blamed her for wreaking disaster on the system. 'If the financial world crashes, you'll know who to blame!' shrieked one hysterical blog. Another suggested that the Hollywood actress Tilda Swinton could play Masters in a film about the crash, since they looked similar. When she moved house in early 2009, the gossip column of the *New York Post* gleefully reported that Masters had 'slashed the price of the Reade Street residence to $11.9 million, down from $14 million'.

The vitriol appalled her former colleagues. 'This is obscene. I suspect they are picking on her because she is a woman, because she stands out,' one observed. 'It is a travesty of "justice". Not a single one of us was involved in the transactions that later caused so much damage . . . all of this group are decent human beings.' Masters herself tried to be philosophical. As she had grown older she had developed a growing sense of humour about the absurdities – and unpredictability – of life.

When she addressed a meeting of SIFMA in New York in late 2008, she pointedly referred to herself as 'someone who has been called a weapon of mass destruction!' She knew the public was angry and wanted something to blame, and she could understand that. She was livid herself at how bankers had perverted her derivatives dream. Yet, she – like Winters – continued to hope that something, somehow, of the value of credit derivatives would be salvaged. 'It's probably safe to say that our industry image is at an all-time low,' she admitted, with masterful British understatement, when she addressed the SIFMA conference. As ever, she cut a striking figure. In deference to the dark mood of the times, she wore a sombre, chocolate-brown suit, instead of her usual jewel-toned hues.

'Some in the industry bristle at the suggestion that Wall Street or anyone could have predicted or should have avoided this

meltdown,' she continued, '. . . many players had a role in creating this crisis including lenders, borrowers and regulators . . . But
even if not *all* of the blame that will come should be directed to
our industry, there is unfortunately plenty of blame to go around.'

'Our industry needs to rebuild [its] reputation,' she added,
'and the first step is to acknowledge accountability and to own
the responsibility of rebuilding a more systemically sustainable
business model. Financial engineering was taken to a level of
complexity which was unsustainable. But it is important to dis-
tinguish between tools and their users. We need to remember
that innovation has created tools for *managing* risk.'

She was keenly aware of the ultimate irony of the whole saga.
'The events that have brought us here are a tragedy of unfolding
proportions; it would be a greater tragedy if we fail to learn the
lessons that they offer.'

In London, Tim Frost kept repositioning Cairn Capital.
During the course of 2008, Cairn suffered more blows, as a
clutch of CDOs linked to mortgage securities were declared to
be in an 'event of default'. Yet many other parts of the Cairn
CDO empire that were connected with corporate credit continued to perform. And Frost was finding ways to draw
benefits from all the bitter lessons he had learned. In the last
two years, Cairn had developed an impressive sideline as an
adviser to bankers or investors trying to restructure collapsed
shadow banks. 'We are still the only fund which has successfully managed to restructure [an SIV],' he often said. 'We have
a lot of expertise to offer.' Cairn had snapped up the portfolios
of many ruined CDOs at knockdown prices. In late 2008, the
Bank of England quietly appointed Cairn as an adviser. The
fees on such advisory and restructuring work were paltry compared to what Frost had once hoped to earn from the hedge
fund, but the Bank mandate was a stunning sign of just how
successfully he and his colleagues had managed to find opportunity in adversity.

Terri Duhon's consultancy business was enjoying a flurry of demand, as were advisory services run by Robert Reoch and Charles Pardue. As the full scale of the toxic shock became clear, policymakers and asset managers realized just how little they really knew about CDOs and other complex instruments, and they were frantic to find advisers who knew better and had clean hands. Such people seemed in short supply.

Many of the 'Morgan mafia' remained in close touch by email, trying to make sense of the unfolding drama. Some felt livid about what had happened in the mortgage world. 'The essential question is, what in tarnation led market participants to over-originate subprime mortgages at increasingly silly terms and then warp credit derivative technology into synthetic CDO of ABS when the [over]supply of real mortgages was insufficient to satisfy demand?' raged Feldstein. Some also recognized, though, that ideology was also to blame. 'The economic models that Hancock and Merton and others upheld were right in a sense, but the problem is that they did not give enough emphasis to all the human issues, the regulatory structures and things like that,' observed Masters. 'The idea was that those issues were just "noise" in the models – but that is just dead-arsed wrong. We don't live in that world of perfect economic models.'

For some, the Congressional testimony of Alan Greenspan, the former chairman of the Federal Reserve, in the autumn of 2008, marked an intellectual turning point.

During the previous two decades, Greenspan had vehemently championed unfettered free-market competition, and the argument that markets were not merely efficient, but self-correcting. When Greenspan appeared in front of Washington lawmakers on 24 October 2008, he admitted he was 'in a state of shocked disbelief' and that he had made a 'mistake' in believing that banks would do what was necessary to protect their shareholders and institutions. '[That was] a flaw in the model . . . that defines how the world works,' he declared.

'I think Greenspan is quite right,' one of the former J.P. Morgan team observed shortly after. 'Now it is clear we need a *new* paradigm. But we haven't found it yet, and frankly I don't know where we will.'

Like many of the J.P. Morgan team – and almost everybody else in the Western world – I too am still trying to make sense of the last decade of grotesque financial mistakes. I have found myself drawing on my training as a social anthropologist, before I became a journalist some fifteen years ago. Back in the 1990s, when I first started working as a financial reporter, I used to keep rather quiet about my 'strange' academic background. At that time, it seemed that the only qualifications that commanded respect were degrees in orthodox economics, or an MBA; the craft of social anthropology seemed far too 'hippy' (as one banker caustically observed) to have any bearing on the high-rolling, quantitative world of finance.

These days, though, I realize that the finance world's lack of interest in wider social matters cuts to the very heart of what has gone wrong. What social anthropology teaches is that nothing in society ever exists in a vacuum or in isolation. Holistic analysis that tries to link different parts of a social structure is crucial, be that in respect to wedding rituals or trading floors. Anthropology also instils a sense of scepticism about official rhetoric. In most societies, elites try to maintain their power not simply by garnering wealth, but by dominating the mainstream ideologies, both in terms of what is said, and also what is not discussed. Social 'silences' serve to maintain power structures in ways that participants often barely understand, let alone plan.

That set of ideas may sound excessively abstract (or hippy). But they would seem to be sorely needed now. In recent years, regulators, bankers, politicians, investors and journalists have all failed to employ truly holistic thought – to our collective cost. Bankers have treated their mathematical models as if they were an infallible guide to the future, failing to see that those models were based on a ridiculously limited set of data. A 'silo' mentality has come to rule inside banks, leaving different departments competing for resources, with shockingly little wider vision or oversight. The regulators who were supposed to oversee the banks have mirrored that silo pattern too, in their own fragmented practices. Most pernicious of all, financiers have come to regard banking as a silo in its own right, detached from the rest of society. They have become like the inhabitants of Plato's cave, who could see shadows of outside reality flickering on the walls, but rarely encountered that reality themselves. The chain that linked a synthetic CDO of ABS, say, with a 'real' person was so convoluted it was almost impossible for anybody to fit that into a single cognitive map – be they anthropologist, economist or credit whizz.

Yet the only thing that is more remarkable than this deadly state of affairs was that it went so unnoticed for so long. For my part, I first crashed into the complex financial world back in 2005, when I volunteered to start writing about credit for the *Financial Times*. By 2006, my team had become seriously alarmed by the trends and tried to point out the dangers. It was a lonely endeavour. Most mainstream newspapers all but ignored the credit world until the summer of 2007. So did politicians and non-bankers. Credit was considered too 'boring' or 'technical' to be of interest to amateurs. It was a classic area of social silence. Insofar as any bankers ever reflected on that silence (which very few ever did), most assumed that it suited their purposes well. Freed from external scrutiny, financiers could do almost anything they wished. Locked in their little silos, few could see how the pieces fitted together, or how bloated finance was.

Now, however, it is clear that this lack of holistic thought and debate has had devastating consequences. Regulators have realized, too late, that they were wrong to place so much blind faith in the creed of risk dispersion. Bank executives have been confronted with vast losses created by dysfunctional internal silos. Politicians are facing a debt crisis as an economic boom crumbles to dust. Most tragic of all, millions of ordinary families, who never even knew that CDOs existed, far less dealt with them, have suffered shattering financial blows. They are understandably angry. So am I. It is a terrible, damning indictment of how twenty-first-century Western society works.

In pointing out the cultural issues, I do not mean to suggest that tangible macroeconomic issues were not also crucial too. Excessively loose monetary policy stoked the credit bubble. So did savings imbalances and poor regulatory structures. Those tangible deficiencies must be addressed. Central bankers need to pay more attention to the structure of finance when they set monetary policy. Regulators must monitor banks in a more holistic manner. Banks require bigger capital cushions. Financial products must become simpler and transparent. Many recent innovations, such as mezzanine CDO of ABS, need to die. Others, though, could still be valuable. Nobody would try to ban all prescription drugs or stop all nuclear processing if some innovations malfunctioned. The basic idea that banks should disperse some of their credit risk, or insure against a bond or loan default, still seems valuable.

Yet what is also needed is a wider rethink of the culture of finance. For too many years bankers have treated 'credit' as merely an isolated game of numbers. The roots of the word, though, come from the Latin *credere*, meaning 'to believe'. That is a concept centred on wider social relations, which financiers forget at their peril. After all, if there is one element, above all, that is now needed to restore sanity to banking, it is that policy-makers, bankers and politicians must adopt a more *holistic* vision of finance. In essence, what is needed is a return to the seemingly dull virtues of prudence, moderation, balance and common sense.

Oddly enough, the symbol that J.P. Morgan inadvertently

inherited from Chase Manhattan would seem an appropriate metaphor – the octagonal logo that harked back to the wooden planks once hammered together to make water pipes. The rebranded J.P. Morgan has dropped the logo, which is perhaps a pity. In many ways the craft of finance is not so very different from that of the water industry: both exist in order to push a commodity around the economy, for the benefit of all. If those pipes are wildly inefficient, leaky or costly, then everyone suffers. In the last two decades, as finance spun so far out of control, it stopped being a servant of the economy, rather than its master. That needs to be reversed. Perhaps it is time to stamp an octagonal water symbol over the door of every modern bank as a reminder of the perils of forgetting that money is another vital fluid that must flow freely, and safely, throughout our fragile, interconnected world.

Afterword to the Paperback Edition

In the autumn of 2009, the French Central Bank published some fascinating research on the credit derivatives sector which suggested that JPMorgan Chase accounted for around 30 per cent of the entire global market. It was a striking – and ironic – development. A decade earlier, when the old Bistro team was first developing the credit derivatives sphere, J.P. Morgan had also dominated that sector, accounting for almost half of all the activity. Of course in those early days, the total market was tiny, well under $1 trillion in size. Now, however, it had swelled dramatically – and JPMorgan Chase's market share had surged in the past two years as well.

The bank's return to dominance was partly due to hedge funds dropping out of the sector in the wake of the crisis. However, J.P. Morgan's banking rivals were also dropping out. Some had collapsed, as with Lehman Brothers and Bear Stearns. Others, such as Royal Bank of Scotland, had withdrawn, because the crisis had so badly weakened them. In the new, crisis-ridden world, the strong were becoming stronger, and J.P. Morgan was arguably the strongest of all.

By the autumn of 2009, J.P. Morgan had all but grabbed the top spot on Wall Street, with its only rival being Goldman Sachs. In London, some European banks were trying to snap at its heels. Deutsche Bank and Barclays Capital, for example,

were each trying to expand. However, in 2009 it was
J.P. Morgan that dominated a host of global investment banking
league tables, not just for the underwriting and trading of securities, but advisory services too. Its market capitalisation had
swelled to $170 billion, making it the largest American bank
(and one of the largest in the world). Moreover, its dominant
position was boosting its bottom line: in the third quarter the
bank reported some $3.6 billion in profits, amid a boom in
securities issuance – partly due to banks rushing to raise capital
after the crisis – and a surge in so-called flow business – the
trading of products such as interest rate swaps – as investors tried
to reposition themselves after the financial storm.

That dazzling performance could not entirely detract from
some key problems at the bank. By late 2009 its asset book
remained marred by troubled residential mortgages. JPMorgan
Chase also had a sizeable volume of commercial mortgages and
related securities, which were threatening to produce losses as
commercial real estate prices fell. Perhaps most significantly,
some questions were starting to circulate about Jamie Dimon's
leadership style – both in London and New York.

Outside the bank, Dimon was widely revered for having
brought the company through the crisis so masterfully.
Internally, however, there were concerns among some J.P.
Morgan officials about whether Dimon was becoming over-
bearing – if not, potentially over-confident. One sign of this
emerged in late September, when Dimon suddenly – and
unceremoniously – removed Bill Winters from his position as
co-head of the investment bank, based in London. The move
generated shock both inside and outside the bank, since the
investment bank appeared to have been performing well, particularly in Europe. Indeed, in London, Winters's friends said
that the move had come as a 'complete bolt from the blue' to
Winters too. Steven Black was moved into the position of chairman at the investment bank, but it was made clear that he

would soon retire, effectively indicating that he was being 'kicked upstairs' as well.

Adding to the surprise was that Winters was replaced by Jes Staley, a man who had formerly run the asset management unit of JPMorgan Chase. Staley, like Winters, had previously come from the J.P. Morgan side of the bank. He had joined around the same time as Peter Hancock, in 1979, and then worked in equities and corporate finance. But he had left the investment bank in 1999 to join the asset management unit, and while he was widely respected for his role there, he commanded neither the reputation nor the status in the investment banking world that Winters enjoyed.

For weeks, speculation bubbled about what had sparked the sudden reshuffle. Dimon, for his part, insisted that he had removed Winters simply because he was keen to clarify his succession plans. It was true that Dimon had always insisted that any successor to him needed to have worked in more than one business line – which Staley had notably done. Winters, however, had always made it clear that he did not want to leave the investment bank to do a job in, say, retailing; even if Dimon insisted on that as a precondition for taking a more senior role. However, there was widespread cynicism inside the bank about whether Staley was really being groomed to replace Dimon.

At fifty-three, Staley was relatively old, and the same age as Dimon. And Dimon showed absolutely no sign whatsoever of wishing to relinquish control. Some people wondered if Staley was there simply as a token. Suspicions were also rife that Dimon himself had started to feel irritated – if not threatened – by Winters. Winters had always remained a touch aloof from Dimon, since unlike Black, Staley, or almost every other member of the dominant group at JPMorgan Chase, Winters had not risen through the ranks by virtue of being loyal to Dimon. 'He is his own man, not a member of Jamie's club,' observed one of his friends, 'that is his strength, but also his problem.'

During the middle part of the new decade, Winters's relative independence had not sparked direct conflict or power struggles because he was ensconced in London, far from the New York head office, and thus could run his day-to-day affairs with a natural degree of separation. Black and Winters worked hard to make their odd 'marriage' work, as co-heads of the investment bank. Yet Winters also enjoyed a very strong reputation outside the bank, particularly in Europe, and he was clearly an ambitious man who was jostling – along with a number of others – to rise to the top job.

During the height of the credit crisis, Dimon had not felt able to remove Winters – or to 'clarify his succession plans,' he said – since he knew that could risk destabilising the markets. But by the autumn of 2009, with the markets calming down and J.P. Morgan in a dominant position in the investment banking world, he apparently felt the time was right to act. The irony was bitter: *precisely* because Winters had helped to create a strong bank, with such an utterly dominant position, Dimon felt able to fire him. It was yet another bizarre twist to the saga of the Bistro team.

The new dominance of J.P. Morgan highlights a pressing issue confronting policy makers: namely how to deal with a system so heavily dominated by banks deemed 'too big to fail'. During the second half of the twentieth century, American and British policy makers and financiers had taken it for granted that their economy was based on capitalist principles, and other Continental European policy makers had often adopted these ideas too, albeit to a lesser degree. The workings of the City and Wall Street were thought to epitomise this creed. Moreover, a core tenet of this faith was the idea that free market competition should have a 'winnowing' effect, allowing nimble and innovative market participants to thrive, but pushing weaker competitors to the wall, in a so-called process of 'creative destruction', as it was termed by the economist Josef Schumpeter. By 2009, however, a peculiar irony hung over the system.

Though Wall Street – or the City – had repeatedly preached the gospel of creative destruction to *other* parts of the economy during the twentieth century – urging non-financial sectors to embrace restructuring – policy makers and bankers were unwilling, or unable, to apply that principle to the banks. Back in the autumn of 2007, the British government effectively rescued Northern Rock. The Americans followed suit with Bear Stearns. Then, for a couple of days in the autumn of 2008, it briefly seemed that creative destruction ruled, when Lehman Brothers was allowed to collapse. But financial turmoil erupted because Lehman was so interconnected, through markets such as credit derivatives and repo instruments, that its failure caused a domino effect. When AIG began to crumble so soon thereafter, policy makers on both sides of the Atlantic decided that they could not afford to let free market forces wreak their destruction again. They became convinced that they needed to act to contain the 'too big to fail' and 'too interconnected to fail' problem.

Consequently, during 2009, American and European governments had repeatedly propped up the financial system, using a range of increasingly innovative and dramatic measures including direct capital injections into banks (such as RBS in the UK or Citi in the US); government guarantees for bank bonds; and government schemes to support money markets and purchase toxic assets. The British government unveiled a scheme to insure banks against further losses on toxic assets that they held in their books. Indeed, such was the range of scale of assistance that by the autumn of 2009, the International Monetary Fund estimated that some $11,000 trillion of funds had been pledged by Western governments to support banks (albeit only a proportion of this was actually spent). Relative to GDP, the scale of this aid package was even larger in the UK than the US.

In some respects, it had become clear by late 2009 that this dramatic government intervention had 'worked', at least in that it had stabilized the system and averted further panic. During the summer and early autumn, the mood in the markets had not merely calmed, but turned almost euphoric in some respects. Western equity prices rallied dramatically by more than 60 per cent from their lows; the cost of interbank borrowing tumbled and the price of risky bonds soared. Companies were also issuing bonds and shares again, and there was even some renewed appetite for trading old mortgage-backed securities (although the one part of the market where activity had notably *not* restarted even by late 2009 was in the field of new asset-backed and mortgage securitisation; that remained largely dormant).

Even amid the return to quasi normality, however, deep unease dogged the policy-making world. It was painfully clear to most Western government officials that normalisation had returned because the government was standing firmly behind the financial system. The state had become the central pillar of faith as the other pillars of faith had crumbled, and this situation was inconsistent with any vision of market capitalism, let alone with the principles of basic fairness. After all, the government was essentially propping up the banks, and yet the banks were still, for the most part, in private-sector hands. So while taxpayers were shouldering the risks, bankers or bank shareholders were receiving most of the gains. The government did recoup some of the money it had injected into the banks, but that was modest compared to the entire size of the bailout package. A particularly troubling aspect of this emergency system was that it was not necessarily sustainable, given that Western budget deficits and national debt were skyrocketing. The UK in late 2009 was forecast to be heading for net debt of almost 100 per cent of GDP, with the US heading for a ratio of around 80 per cent. Officials in London, Washington, Brussels – and almost everywhere else – were eager to find a way out.

The crucial question, though, was: *how*? One year after Lehman Brothers' failure, there was little sign that the twin problems of 'too big' and 'too interconnected' to fail had been solved. On the contrary, the problems were arguably getting worse, *precisely* because banking activity had become even more concentrated in the hands of a few, big players.

The failure of JPMorgan Chase, for one, would be so utterly catastrophic that the government could never allow it, and the net result was that J.P. Morgan was now operating with the knowledge that it would have state support. What other constraints on risk-taking could ensure that it wouldn't make moves that would force the government to save it?

Throughout 2009, Western policy makers produced a stream of ideas to combat that problem. One solution, promoted by the American Treasury Department and some European supervisors, was to create a so-called resolution regime, or a process whereby any big bank could be placed into the equivalent of a corporate bankruptcy, in as smooth and efficient manner as possible. This was similar to the system the FDIC was already using for smaller banks when they went bankrupt. Applying this regime to large banks, however, promised to be considerably more complex, not just in the US but Europe too. While the FDIC could take over a small bank with its own resources, taking over the operations of a Citigroup or J.P. Morgan would be far more challenging. An especially pernicious problem was the cross-border nature of most large banks. While Western policy makers knew that they should cooperate to create an international bankruptcy regime, by late 2009, few believed that any global scheme would emerge soon. In attempt to break that impasse, in late 2009, Paul Tucker, the deputy governor of the Bank of England, started to promote the idea of applying 'living wills' to banks. The idea behind this, which was backed by the FSA, was that plans should be created to wind up troubled large

banks, to enable them to fail smoothly. But this seemed unlikely
to bear fruit for several years – prompting some officials such as
Mervyn King, Bank governor, to suggest, almost in despair, that
it might be better to simply break up the biggest banks.

Nevertheless, as the debate raged on, the US Treasury, along
with its European counterparts, emphasised other policy tools
to reduce the risk. During the course of 2009, Western governments made it clear that banks would need to hold much
bigger capital cushions in the future, so that they could absorb
any shocks. Regulators were also preparing to force the banks
to hold large reserves against complex instruments, like CDOs.
Some Western policy makers were even demanding that that
any bank deemed too big to fail should hold reserves even
above these, to make it doubly unlikely that they would
wobble – and giving banks an economic incentive to make
themselves smaller.

Efforts to reduce the interconnectivity problems in the credit
derivatives markets were also launched. The New York Federal
Reserve urged the industry to start cancelling – or 'tearing up' –
overlapping contracts. Treasury and its European counterparts
also urged the industry to move as much activity as possible onto
centralised clearing houses, and this should not be just activity in
the credit derivatives sector, but in most over-the-counter derivatives businesses too. More widely, governments demanded that
banks become far more transparent about how they conducted
complex business, to enable both regulators and outside investors
to assess risks.

The big investment banks initially reacted with considerable
wariness to these changes and proposals. During the first half of
2008, the industry lobbying group ISDA had repeatedly signalled that it was wary of clearing houses. After the Lehman
Brothers collapse, the group had largely dropped that opposition
and thrown its weight behind a campaign to encourage banks to
tear up contracts. To a certain extent, this had born fruit. By the

autumn of 2009 the credit derivatives market seemed to be shrinking by some metrics, with some $31 trillion in outstanding deals by the fall of 2009, half the level of two years earlier. That was primarily because many redundant derivative contracts had been ripped up. The banks had also become far more wary of the deals they made, and there was more transparency in pricing. A new settlement system had been introduced by ISDA which enabled dealers to settle out a credit derivatives contract after a bankruptcy, and by the autumn of 2009, this had been used successfully more than fifty times. A standard system had also been introduced for quoting the prices of a credit default swaps.

Nevertheless, even as some incremental change was introduced – and a debate bubbled on – it remained unclear just how much real change would eventually occur. By late 2009, the large investment banks in London and New York remained vociferously opposed to forcing all activity onto exchanges, a change that threatened to badly reduce their profit margins, and to undermine their control over the business. Some were dragging their feet on the issue of putting all activity onto clearing houses too.

Meanwhile, a sense of bitter irony hung over the credit derivatives world. Back in the 1990s, when Masters, Demchak, Winters, Hancock, Frost and Feldstein pioneered the credit derivatives concept, they had presented it as a tool that could be used to *diversify* credit risk, and spread it around the system. Their vision was of a brave new world where risk would be distributed between a host of investors, banks, hedge funds and corporations. But, by the autumn of 2009 that vision had not been truly realised. One reason was that the corporate sector had never really started to use credit derivatives (in marked contrast say to the situation in the interest rate, commodity or currency derivatives sectors, where corporate users were a significant force). Credit derivatives were essentially a game played by financial companies, parcelling out risks between themselves. And the banking sector was now more concentrated in this sphere, with the top ten banks holding a 90 percent market share in 2009 versus 74 per cent in 2004. Moreover, the most popular type of credit derivatives contracts in the market were those written to guarantee the debt of large banks, or other financial institutions. Large banks were trading with other large banks to bet on whether banks would default or not. As the Banque de France drolly noted, it was a game marked by startling 'circularity'.

Does that render the whole idea of credit derivatives pointless? Have they been so perverted that they have lost their *raison d'être*? These questions remain unanswered. In many ways I – like many policy makers – continue to hope that credit derivatives can be a useful addition to the modern financial toolkit, if only they can be handled more responsibly. Even amid the disaster that has occurred, the fact remains that risk diversification should be a good thing; so too, should be the ability to hedge.

Yet, if I look back over the last fifteen years, and do a rough cost-benefit analysis of whether credit derivatives have been a net positive or not, it is hard to know which side the ledger comes out on. It is certainly true that *some* companies have benefited by being able to hedge risks. JPMorgan Chase is one of those, since it has used credit derivatives to lay off some (albeit not all) of its housing risk. Yet against those positives stands the tale of AIG, which has gobbled up vast quantities of taxpayers funds as a result of partly disguised credit derivatives. And behind AIG stand a clutch of other banks, such as Barclays, Société Générale or Deutsche Bank, which also placed credit derivatives bets with AIG – and which were effectively bailed out by the taxpayer rescue of that insurer too.

Perhaps those risks can be ameliorated by a more responsible new regulatory regime; if so, credit derivatives may yet end up being a force for good. But, as of the end of 2009, it was still unclear whether any of the needed regulatory reforms would be instituted. The dream of the old Bistro team, in other words, was still hanging in the balance; and I suspect it will remain that way for many more years.

Gillian Tett
December 2009

Notes

NOTES ON SOURCES

The primary sources for this book have been extensive interviews with the main characters mentioned in the book, as well as numerous other people, over several years. Except where it is specifically mentioned, the quotes are drawn from author interviews or from author articles already published in the *Financial Times*. I have also drawn heavily from financial reports published by the Bank for International Settlements; International Monetary Fund; European Central Bank and Bank of England, as well as the Capital Markets Monitors published by the Institute for International Finance. Studies conducted by the Counterparty Risk Management Group, the IIF, the Group of Thirty and Basel Committee have also been used, as well as a large range of media sources and reports by financial industry analysts. The research also benefited from a large array of textbooks and popular literature on finance and the recent credit crunch, including (but not exclusively), Tavakoli, J., *Structured Finance & Collateralized Debt Obligations*, John Wiley & Sons, 2003, 2008; Das, Satyajit, *Traders, Guns & Money*, paperback, Pearson, 2006; Morris, Charles, *The Trillion Dollar Meltdown*, Public Affairs, 2008; Bookstaber, Richard, *A Demon of Our Design*, Wiley, 2007; Bernstein, Peter, *Capital Ideas Evolving*, Wiley 2007 and *Against the Gods*, Wiley 1998; Rebonato, Riccardo, *The Plight of the Fortune Tellers*, Princeton University Press 2007, Chernow, Ron, *The House of Morgan*, Grove Press, 2001; Lowenstein, Roger, *When Genius Failed*, HarperCollins, 2001; Soros, George, *The New Paradigm for Financial Markets*, Public Affairs 2008; Shiller, Robert J., *The Subprime Solution*, Princeton, 2008; Davies, Howard and Green, David, *Global Financial Regulation*, Polity, 2008.

CHAPTER ONE

4 **By 1994, the total notional value of derivatives contracts:** Loomis, J. Carol, 'The risk that won't go away', *Fortune*, 7 March 1994.

11 **Versions of derivatives trading have existed for centuries:** Dodd, Randall, 'Backgrounder: Derivatives', *Initiative for Policy Dialogue* <http://www2.gsb.columbia.edu/ipd/j_derivatives.html>.

12 **Salomon Brothers was one of the first:** author interviews; see also Lowenstein, Roger, *When Genius Failed*, Harper Collins, 2001, pp. 103–4.

15 **But J.P. Morgan had always had a transcultural identity:** see Chernow, Ron, *The House of Morgan*, Grove, 2001.

22 **A few months before the Boca off-site:** Loomis, J. Carol, op. cit.

24 **I've known people who worked on the Manhattan project:** Philips, Matthew, 'The monster that ate Wall Street', *Newsweek*, 6 October 2008.

CHAPTER TWO

30 **Out of that, they decided to create an industry body to represent the swaps world:** *ISDA and Risk*, ISDA 20th Anniversary Report, March 2005.

31 **Given the sheer size of the [derivatives] market:** Corrigan, E. Gerald, Speech to New York State Bankers Association dinner, January 1992.

33 **So Weatherstone agreed to chair the G30 report:** *ISDA and Risk*, op. cit., p. 30.

36 **Felix Rohatyn, a legendary Wall Street figure:** Hansell, Saul and Muehring, Kevin, 'Why derivatives rattle the regulators', *Institutional Investor*, September 1992.

39 **I want to produce a guide by practitioners that has so much useful, practical advice that it will be referred to for years to come:** *ISDA and Risk*, op. cit., p. 30.

41 **Brian Quinn, an executive director of the Bank of England said:** Gapper, John, 'International capital markets – bank supervisor calls for tougher futures regulation', *Financial Times*, 29 September 1993.

41 **If the market players continue forward in the spirit of the G30:** Speech by J. Carter Beese at ISDA conference in Washington, 3 November 1993.

42 **The company had made a deal with Bankers Trust:** Essentially, in the first six months, P&G was to pay Bankers Trust a rate of CP (commercial paper) minus 75 basis points. After that, the rate would set at a higher level, close to the floating rate. In return for this initial below-market rate, P&G faced grave uncertainties as to where rates might be six months out. Still, P&G had some insurance against a run-up, in the form of a six-month option to set the rate at any time. The goal of P&G treasury was to get the four and a half years' money at CP-40. And if the interest rates kept falling, then P&G would have enjoyed large costs savings. For full details see <http://www.derivativesstrategy.com/magazine/archive/2000/1100fea3.asp>.

42 **in 1993, Citron's investment pool delivered returns of 8.5 per cent:** Lynch, David J., 'Orange County: How it happened: How golden touch turned into crisis', *USA Today*, 23 December 1994.

43 **The question now is no longer whether regulatory or legislative changes will be made:** Fillion, Roger, 'GAO portrays derivatives as fraught with dangers', *Reuters News Service*, 19 May 1994.

45 **'Derivatives are perfectly legitimate tools to manage risk':** Taylor, Andrew, 'Critical report fuels drive to regulate derivatives', *Congressional Quarterly Weekly Report*, 21 May 1994.

46 **The head of Clinton's new National Economic Council, Robert Rubin:** Phillips, Kevin, *Arrogant Capital*, Little, Brown, 1994.

46 **When I say I don't think legislation is needed:** Lipin, Steve and Raghavan, Anita, 'GAO to join hot debate on derivatives', *Wall Street Journal*, 18 May 1994, and Peltz, Michael, 'Congress's lame assault on derivatives', *Institutional Investor*, 1 December 1994.

CHAPTER THREE

50 **'Funnily enough,' she told a reporter:** Fredrickson, Tom, 'Blythe Masters, 34', *Crain's New York Business*, 26 January 2004.

53 **Moreover, the credit derivatives concept did not seem sufficiently profitable:** For details of why Freund and Crystal experimented with the idea, then dropped it, see Guill, Gene, *Bankers Trust and the Birth of Modern Risk Management*, Wharton Financial Institutions Centre, 2007, p. 30.

57 **Sure enough, in August 1996, the Fed issued a statement:** see Supervisory Guidance for Credit Derivatives, Washington Federal Reserve, 12 August 1996 <http://www.federalreserve.gov/BOARDDOCS/SRLetters/1996/sr9617.htm>.

63 **Demchak's team worked stealthily:** for details of how this structure
worked, see *The J.P. Morgan Guide to Credit Derivatives*, Risk
Publications, 1999. See also Das, Satyajit, *CDOs and Structured Credit
Products*, Wiley, 2005, pp. 322–44, for a very extensive discussion of
the significance of Bistro in relation to the structures that proceeded
from it, and the subsequent impact on the industry.

65 **Five years hence, commentators will look back:** 'Credit
Derivatives – Five Years Out', Derivativessrategy.com. July/August
1997 <http://www.derivativesstrategy.com/magazine/archive/
1997/0797rtbl.asp>.

CHAPTER FOUR

66 **Bistro-style CDS trades took off fast:** For general discussions of
that, see Das, Satyajit op. cit., pp. 322–44

68 **The pace of change in the way banks manage credit risk:**
Asarnow, Elliot, *The Journal of Lending and Credit Risk Management*,
September 1998, p. 13.

68 **Blythe Masters still looks more like a J.P. Morgan intern:** Ibid.,
p. 8.

70 **But they were also uneasy:** For a debate about the problems of fit-
ting existing regulations to securitizations and the Fed and OCC
response, see *Capital Interpretations, Synthetic Collateralized Loan
Obligations*, 15 November 1999 <http://www.occ.treas.gov/ftp/
bulletin/99-43a.pdf> and *Supervisory Guidance for Credit Derivatives*,
Washington Federal Reserve, 12 August 1996 <http://www.feder-
alreserve.gov/BOARDDOCS/SRLetters/1996/sr9617.htm>.

72 **Cassano happily agreed:** See details about this, and comments from
Cassano, in Conference Call Transcript, AIG Financial Services
Group presentation, 8:30, 31 May 2007, *Thomson Street Events*, p. 23.

73 **Capital reserves could only be cut:** See *Capital Interpretations,
Synthetic Collateralized Loan Obligations*, 15 November 1999
<http://www.occ.treas.gov/ftp/bulletin/99-43a.pdf>.

80 **As the audience filed into the Cipriani:** *The J.P. Morgan Guide to
Credit Derivatives*, Risk Publications, 1999.

CHAPTER FIVE

85 **The fate of the hedge fund maverick Long Term Capital Management:** For an excellent account of this, see Lowenstein, Roger, *When Genius Failed*, HarperCollins, 2002.

86 **In 1999, the year after LTCM imploded:** The study in question was *Improving Counterparty Risk Management Practices* by the Counterparty Risk Management Policy Group, July 1999.

86 **The fact that the OTC markets function:** Remarks by Alan Greenspan before the Futures Industry Association, Boca Raton, Florida, 19 March 1999.

87 **Congress nailed the door shut:** Brickell, Mark, 'Zero to $200 trillion', *ISDA and Risk*, op. cit., p. 25.

89 **Beyond that, the advantages are less compelling:** Santoli, Michael, 'Land of the Giants: Next in line: How would Chase meld with Merrill? Time to reunite the House of Morgan?', *Barron's*, 13 April 1998.

89 **The so-called 'non-interest income':** Michael, Nancy, 'Banking's top performers', *ABA Banking Journal*, 1 June 2000. Data from SEC filings and the magazine's calculations.

89 **From a standing start in 1980:** Frank, Stephen E., 'After Embracing Change, J.P. Morgan is Struggling to Boost its Bottom Line', *Wall Street Journal*, 27 May 1998.

89 **In 1999, the median ROE for the top 100 banks was 18 per cent:** Frank, Stephen E., 'After embracing change, J.P. Morgan is struggling to boost its bottom line', *Wall Street Journal*, 27 May 1998.

93 **As Clayton Rose, one of the senior J.P. Morgan bankers, observed:** Ibid.

94 **But such has been the pace of change in global finance:** anonymous, 'Wall Street's old order changes (Chase Manhattan acquires J.P. Morgan)', *The Economist*, 16 September 2000.

97 **I believe we handled everything with integrity:** Chaffin, Joshua, 'Companies and finance: The Enron collapse – J.P. Morgan had too much exposure, says chairman', *Financial Times*, 7 February 2005.

97 **We did it according to accounting conventions:** Interview: William Harrison, chairman and CEO of JPMorgan Chase, discusses his firm's involvement in the Enron scandal, *CNBC: Market Week with Maria Bartiromo*, 5 August 2002.

98 **It's unnerving how the bad news keeps piling up at J.P. Morgan:** Timmons, Heather and Palmeri, Christopher, 'The perils of J.P. Morgan', *BusinessWeek*, 21 January 2002.

98 **Or as the *Evening Standard* of London tartly declared:** Chambliss, Lauren, 'How a banking giant was laid low', *Evening Standard*, 16 October 2002.

99 **Credit derivatives are a mechanism for transferring risk:** Westlake, Melvyn 'Investment banking – surviving the credit crisis', *The Banker*, 1 May 2002.

CHAPTER SIX

107 **There was a greater need for the derivatives market:** Moulds, Josephine, 'Tim Frost says credit derivatives can solve the crisis in pensions', *Daily Telegraph*, 5 June 2006.

107 **The legal and shareholder framework:** Ibid.

108 **We can promote outstanding people quickly:** Chambers, Alex, 'How JPMorgan survived the loss of a generation,' *Euromoney*, 1 May 2006.

108 **It is unlikely that the sector would have grown:** Ibid.

109 **In 2003, *Risk* magazine designated Deutsche Bank:** *Risk* magazine awards, January 2003 <http://www.risk.net/public/showPage.html?page=9109>.

109 **Pension funds were now targeting:** Hughes, Jennifer, Beales, Richard and Tett, Gillian, 'Investment – even governments are putting money into higher-yielding instruments', *Financial Times*, 17 June 2005.

110 **The product development now is incredibly fast:** van Acoleyen, Katrien, comments to ESF and IMN conference, Nice, April 2005.

112 **Remarkably, that meant that almost half of all mortgage-linked bonds:** BIS Annual Report, June 2007, p. 146.

117 **Each player had its own twist on modelling:** Comment made by Terri Duhon to ESF and IMN conference, Nice, April 2005.

118 **People who are focused on ratings alone are prime fodder:** Comment made by Charles Pardue to ESF and IMN conference, Nice, April 2005.

118 **We are very transparent in everything we do:** Unpublished interview with the *Financial Times*, May 2005.

120 **The purest information to use is data on [historic] defaults:** Unpublished interview with the *Financial Times*, in May 2005.

120 **In March 2000, David Li, a researcher at J.P. Morgan:** The paper in question was David Li, 'On Default Correlation: A Copula Function Approach', *Journal of Fixed Income*, vol. 9, no. 4, March 2000.

121 **As Alex Veroude, the manager of a CDO for Gulf International Bank:** Comment to ESF and IMN conference, Nice, April 2005.

122 **As David Li himself said about the model he had fashioned:** Whitehouse, Mark, 'Slices of risk: How a formula ignited market that burned some big investors', *Wall Street Journal*, 12 September 2005.

122 **The revenues of the largest investment banks grew 14 per cent between 2003 and 2004:** Data taken from Investment banking and capital markets report; Q4 2005, Boston Global Consulting.

CHAPTER SEVEN

124 **The two leaders were near opposites:** Tully, Shawn. 'The deal maker and the dynamo', *Fortune*, 9 February 2004.

125 **Does it bother you:** *CNBC* interview: William Harrison and Coach Dean Smith discuss business and basketball, *Special Report with Maria Bartiromo*, 23 February 2004.

134 **Instead of heading first to the headquarters in the City of London:** Farrell, Greg, 'Dimon adds sparkle to JPMorgan Chase: Ousted Citigroup banker fights his way back to top', *USA Today*, 29 November 2005.

136 **Yond Cassius has a lean and hungry look:** Stires, David. 'At J.P. Morgan, look out for No. 2', *Fortune*, 18 October 2004.

CHAPTER EIGHT

139 **His huge banking merger is not yet delivering:** 'Waiting game – The Lex Column', *Financial Times*, 22 August 2005.

140 **He knows where all the bodies are buried in that monster derivatives portfolio:** Kerr, Ian, 'Jamie Dimon and his "terrible" results', *Euroweek*, 29 October 2004.

142 **Given the profile of JPMorgan as an institution:** Chambers, Alex, 'How JPMorgan survived the loss of a generation', *Euroweek*, 1 May 2006.

144 Onlookers 'should [not] be concerned that home prices are
     rising: Housing Bubble Prospects Q&A, National Association of
     Realtors, August 2005 <http://www.realtor.org/research.nsf/files/
     bubbleq&a.pdf/$file/bubbleq&a.pdf>.

144 House prices have risen nearly 25 per cent over the past two
     years: The Economic Outlook, Ben S. Bernanke, 20 October 2005,
     as cited in Schiller, Robert J., The Subprime Solution, Princeton
     University Press, 2008.

145 In 2005 American households extracted no less than $750 bil-
     lion: 'Sources and Uses of Equity Extracted from Homes', US
     Federal Reserve, March 2007.

146 In mid-2005, though: Schiller, Robert J., op. cit., p. 35.

146 From early 2002 to early 2005: BIS Annual Report, June 2007,
     p. 126.

147 Then, in January 2006, an index for tracking these offerings and
     their values was launched: For details of how the ABX works, see
     <http://www.markit.com/information/products/category/indices/
     abx/about_abx.html>.

CHAPTER NINE

152 By mid-2005 there were $12 trillion CDS contracts: Estimates
     on the size of the CDS market are usually reached by surveying the
     biggest deals. These estimates have varied considerably over time,
     depending on what process is used to collect the surveys. The British
     Bankers Association, for example, has different figures from ISDA. It
     should also be noted that there is a stark difference between the level
     of gross outstanding CDS contracts and the level of net market risk,
     since many outstanding contracts should cancel (or 'net') each other
     out. Net risk, or the replacement cost of contracts, is often a tenth of
     the size of gross outstanding risk. Figures on the gross outstanding
     size of the CDS market here and subsequently, unless otherwise
     stated, are drawn from ISDA data. See <http://www.isda.org/statis-
     tics/pdf/ISDA-Market-Survey-annual-data.pdf>.

152 There is a type of euphoria: Comments by Terri Duhon and
     Cynthia McNulty to the ESF and IMN conference, Nice, April 2005.

155 Those who are successful know this: Brown, Mark and Currie,
     Antony, 'Yield hunger drives structured credit', Euromoney,
     September 2004.

157 **Banks now face the challenging task:** Boston Global Consulting, 'Succeeding with Growth', Report on the 2004 global banking industry.

158 **He decided to bring Merrill into the securitization business with a vengeance:** See Pulliam, Susan, Ng, Serena, Smith, Randall, 'Merrill upped ante as boom in mortgage bond fizzled – fresh $6 billion hit is expected as toll of CDO push rises', *Wall Street Journal*, 16 April 2008. Also Gregory, Michael and O'Connor, Collen, 'Merrill Lynch reinvesting in SanFran', *Private Placement Letter*, 7 July 2003. This account has also drawn on the author's interviews with Merrill Lynch employees.

158 **By 2006, Merrill topped the league table:** Data supplied by Dealogic.

158 **One corner of the AIG empire:** See transcript of AIG Investor Group meeting, 8:30, 5 December 2007, *Thomson StreetEvents*, p. 5; Guerrera, Francesco and Felsted, Andrea, 'Inadequate cover', *Financial Times*, 6 October 2008; Pullman, Ng and Smith, 'Merrill upped ante', op. cit. This account has also drawn on the author's interviews with AIG employees.

160 **Citi's CDO machine began running with such a frenetic speed:** See the 10-Q filing by Citigroup to the SEC, for the third quarter of 2007, p. 9, for details of the super-senior holdings that came back on to its balance sheet as a result of the liquidity puts. These related to CDO of ABS. See also the comments that Barney Frank made about his meeting with Chuck Prince, CEO of Citi in Syre, Steven, 'Frank talk about rules', *Boston Globe*, 20 March 2008. This account has also drawn on the author's interviews with Citi employees.

161 **Arguably the most aggressive player of all in Europe was UBS:** Details on this, excluding extensive numbers, can be found in Shareholder Report on UBS's Writedowns, UBS, 18 April 2008 <http://www.ubs.com/1/e/investors/shareholderreport.html>. This account has also drawn on the author's interviews with UBS employees.

163 **Frankly, most of us had not even heard the word 'super-senior':** Interview with the *Financial Times* in April 2008. See also Hughes, Chris, Simonian, Haig and Thal-Larsen, Peter, 'Corroded to the core: How a staid Swiss bank let ambitions lead it into folly', *Financial Times*, 21 April 2008.

CHAPTER TEN

168 **In October 2006, Bill King, the man:** Tully, Shawn, 'Jamie Dimon's Swat Team', *Fortune*, 15 September 2008. Supplemented with author interviews.

168 **A house crisis approaches:** Witter, Lon, 'The no-money-down disaster', *Barron's*, 21 August 2006.

169 **Builders that built speculative homes:** editorial comment '"Pop!" goes the US real estate bubble', *Toronto Star*, 6 September 2006.

169 **When even Toll Brothers, the high-end builder:** Shilling, A. Gary, 'Implosion; When even Toll Brothers, the high-end builder, suffers cancelations, you know the real estate boom is over'. *Forbes*, 19 June 2006.

169 **The delinquency rate on subprime mortgages rose:** BIS Annual Report 2007, p. 126.

169 **Between October and December 2006 alone:** Ibid., p. 110.

169 **One particularly fast area of growth was so-called 'mezzanine structured finance' CDOs:** Date from internal calculations by JPMorgan.

170 **Over at Deutsche Bank a group of traders:** Based on author interviews. See also Pittman, Mark, 'How stage was set for meltdown: Subprime market began with talk over Chinese takeout', *Bloomberg*, 23 December 2007.

170 **Goldman Sachs was also rolling the dice:** Based on author interviews with Goldman employees. See also Kelly, Kate, 'How Goldman won big on mortgage meltdown', *Wall Street Journal*, 14 December 2007.

171 **The market has overreacted:** Kelly, Kate, 'Behind a subprime call – Bear Stearns analyst dismissed the fears and now feels heat', *Wall Street Journal*, 12 July 2007.

172 **We are responding to the new business environment:** Lambe, Geraldine, 'Dow Kim, the co-president of global markets and investment banking at Merrill Lynch assures Geraldine Lambe that a spate of diversified acquisitions is all part of a disciplined strategy to reshape the company', *The Banker*, 1 February 2007.

172 **When the Boston Consulting Group:** Investment Banking and Capital Markets, Markets Report – Fourth Quarter 2006, Boston Consulting Group, 20 March 2007.

174 **So intense was the mania:** BIS Annual Report 2007, p. 106.

174 **As long as the music is still playing:** Nakamoto, Michiyo and Wighton, David, 'Bullish Citigroup is "still dancing" to the beat of the buy-out boom', *Financial Times*, 10 July 2007.

178 **However, as Basel's BIS noted:** 'The recent behavior of financial market volatility', BIS Paper no. 29, 2006.

179 **Such dispersion, it added, would help to 'mitigate and absorb shocks to the financial system':** IMF's Global Financial Stability Report, April 2006.

180 **In particular, the current environment may be more vulnerable:** Borio, C. and White, W, 'Whither monetary and financial stability?', Paper presented to Reserve Bank of Kansas City Economic Symposium, Jackson Hole, 30 August 2003, and later published in various economic journals.

180 **Alan Greenspan commanded such formidable respect and power:** Author interview. See also similar comments express in Cassidy, John, 'Anatomy of a meltdown', *New Yorker*, 1 December 2008.

181 **What worries me is what might happen if – or when – the system start to *de*-leverage:** Unpublished *Financial Times* interview, spring 2007.

181 **These developments have clear benefits but they may also have side effects:** BIS Annual Report 2007, p. 151.

181 **We are currently seeing elements in global financial markets:** Tett, Gillian, 'Prepare for asset repricing, warns Trichet', *Financial Times*, 29 January 2007.

183 **In April 2007, the Bank pointed out in its Financial Stability Report:** Bank of England Financial Stability Report, April 2007, p. 9. See chart 10 in particular.

184 **In ten years' time, we may therefore . . . be better informed:** Speech by Paul Tucker, executive director and member of the Monetary Policy Committee of the Bank of England, at Merrill Lynch Conference, 'A perspective on recent monetary and financial system developments', London, 26 April 2007

185 **A number of fundamental changes in the US financial system:** Remarks at the New York Bankers Association Financial Services Forum Chairman's Reception, New York, 5 April 2006.

187 **I want to call your particular attention to [our recommendations] which call for urgent industry-wide efforts:** 'Toward

greater financial stability: A private-sector perspective', *The Report of the CRMPG II*, 27 July 2005.

188 **Often it takes a crisis to generate the will and energy:** Geithner, Timothy, McCarthy, Callum and Nazareth, Annette, 'A safer strategy for the credit products explosion', *Financial Times*, 28 September 2006.

189 **If nothing else, that would show that global leaders:** For a summary of the views that Peer Steinbrueck, the German finance minister, expressed to the meeting see the BBC report on the interview between *Die Welt* and Steinbrueck, reported as 'Germany's Steinbrueck interviewed on hedge funds, industry policy', *BBC Monitoring European*, 9 May 2007. In this he said: 'I fear the effects on the stability of the international financial system if hedge funds get into heavy water and their creditors take excessive risks because of lack of transparency. In this respect, I am in agreement with a number of international institutions . . . all are worried about these dangers that could result from insufficient transparency.'

197 **Hard hit by turmoil:** Kelly, Kate and Ng, Serena, 'Bear Stearns fund hurt by suprime loans', *Wall Street Journal*, 12 June 2007.

198 **I'm fearful of these markets:** Quotation taken from indictment filed by prosecutors in New York State law courts against Cioffi and Tannin. For details see <http://fl1.findlaw.com/news.findlaw.com/nytimes/docs/crim/uscioffitannin61808ind.pdf>. See also Landon, Thomas, 'Prosecutors build Bear Stearns case on emails', *New York Times*, 20 June 2008, or Hurtado, Patricia and Scheer, David, 'Former Bear Stearns fund managers arrested by FBI', *Bloomberg*, 19 June 2008.

200 **Another illustration of the danger facing funds that borrow:** Goldstein, Matthew, 'Bear Stearns subprime bath', *BusinessWeek*, 12 June 2007.

202 **Moody's announced it was cutting its ratings on 131 bonds:** See Ng, Serena and Kelly Kate, 'Ills deepen in subprime-bond arena, *Wall Street Journal*, 18 June 2008.

203 **In late June, Bear Stearns publicly announced:** See Creswell, Julie and Bajaj, Vikas, '$3.2 billion move by Bear Stearns to rescue fund', *New York Times*, 23 June 2007; Mackintosh, James, Scholtes, Saskia and White, Ben, 'Bear hits other banks by raising exposure to subprime mortgages', *Financial Times*, 23 June 2007.

206 **Another was the downgades that the ratings agencies were themselves were starting to make:** For a good timeline of those events, see BIS Annual Report 2008, pp. 95–9.

207 **The problem is that people just don't know quite what to trust:** Unpublished interview with Donald Aiken by the *Financial Times*, August 2007.

207 **Thus while the IKB funds held more than $20 billion in assets:** For accounts of this see Gumbel, Peter, 'Subprime on the Rhine', *Fortune*, 2 September 2007; Mollenkamp, Carrick, Taylor, Edward and McDonald, Ian, 'Impact of mortgage crisis spreads – how subprime mess ensnared German bank', *Wall Street Journal*, 10 August 2007.

CHAPTER TWELVE

211 **I see striking similarities with the early stages of our own financial crisis:** Author interview. See also Tett, Gillian, 'Financial faith found wanting – Japan offers a salutary tale in banking crises', *Financial Times*, 2 January 2008; Tett, Gillian, 'The big freeze: A year that shook faith in finance', *Financial Times*, 3 August 2008.

211 **Bernanke observed in a speech before the Federal Reserve of Chicago:** Chairman Ben S. Bernanke at the Federal Reserve Bank of Chicago's 43rd Annual Conference on Bank Structure and Competition, Chicago, 17 May, 2007.

212 **In the order of $50 billion to $100 billion:** See Del Bruno, Joe, 'Subprime fallout overblown?', Associated Press, 21 July 2007; Aversa, Jeannine, 'Fed boss reacts to subprime situation', Associated Press, 20 July 2007.

212 **Or as Bill Dudley, a senior figure at the New York Federal Reserve:** Speech by Dudley to a SIFMA Legal and Compliance conference, New York, 13 June 2007.

212 **In truth only a third of those structures were thought to be linked to mortgages:** See Bank of England Financial Stability Report, October 2007, p. 19.

214 **Quite honestly, the funding never ordinarily kept us awake at night:** 'Deal of the Year: Cairn High Grade SIV-lite Restructuring', *Risk*, January 2007.

219 **We are certainly not going to protect people from unwise lending decisions:** Duncan, Gary, 'Governor warns careless lenders "the Bank will not bail you out"', *The Times*, 9 August 2007.

221 **There are a lot of investors who invested on a leveraged basis:** Comment taken from proceedings of Jackson Hole conference, session on General Discussion: Housing and Monetary Policy, p. 480.

221 **What we are seeing right now is a total overreaction:** Ibid, p. 483.

222 **The real issue right now is a run:** Ibid, p. 485.

222 **It is stunning how little many policymakers know:** Tannenbaum, Carl, blog on real-time economics, *Wall Street Journal*, 4 September 2007 <http://blogs.wsj.com/economics/2007/09/04/economists-react-views-from-jackson-hole/>.

225 **At the start of 2007, the rate of default on subprime mortgages:** See Bank of England Financial Stability Report, October 2007, p. 17, drawing from data from Mortgage Bankers Association and Thomson Financial.

226 **The average rate on an adjustable mortgage rose from 3.5 per cent in late 2005:** Calculation by Citigroup based on Bloomberg data, from Opportunities in Dislocation, Citigroup, October 2007.

226 **There's no model for what's happening now:** Ivry, Bob, 'Bernanke was wrong – subprime contagion is spreading', *Bloomberg*, 10 August 2007.

226 **Owning a home has always been at the center of the American dream:** President Bush discusses home ownership in financing, Department of the US White House FDCH Regulatory Intelligence Database, 31 August 2007.

228 **Although the firm remains profitable:** Robert Peston on *BBC News 24*, 8.30 p.m., 13 September 2007.

229 **At the turn of the century the bank had embraced securitization with a vengeance:** For data on this see 'The funding crisis at Northern Rock', Bank of England Financial Stability Report, October 2007, pp. 10–11.

229 **At the start of the year its website:** Tett, Gillian, 'Elaborate debt deals spread risk but distort the data', *Financial Times*, 15 January 2007.

233 **I don't know how anyone could characterize it as a bailout:** Holzer, Jessica, 'Steel downplays government's role in "superfund" aimed at calming markets', *The Hill*, 16 November 2007.

234 **The performance, particularly in the US housing [and] mortgage sector:** Freeland, Chrystia and Scholtes, Saskia, 'View from the

top: Ray McDaniel, chief executive of Moody's Investors Service',
Financial Times, 12 October 2007.

234 **By September 2007, more than 30 per cent of the subprime
mortgage loans issued in late 2005 by Fremont:** See Bank of
England Financial Stability Report, October 2007, p. 17, sourced to
Bloomberg.

237 **Whereas in a CLO . . . it is unlikely that all the loans default
simultaneously:** King, Matt and team, 'Estimating CDO of ABS
writedowns', Citigroup Fixed Income Quantitative Research, 6
November 2007.

239 **One clue to what had gone wrong could be found in the dry,
technical details:** See the 10-Q filing by Citigroup to the SEC for
the third quarter of 2007, p. 9, for details.

241 **The losses at UBS were arguably even more shocking:** See
Shareholder Report on UBS's Writedowns, 18 April 2008 <http://
www.ubs.com/1/e/investors/shareholderreport.html>.

243 **We had seen what had happened after Enron:** Author interview
with senior auditors and bankers.

243 **In the first half of 2007, large Western banks had posted:** See
Bank of England Financial Stability Report, October 2008, p. 14, for
data on capital. Notes that global banks before the crisis had tier-one
capital of $3.4 trillion.

246 **Huge quantities of money from the emerging world:** HSBC
report cited in Elliot, Larry, 'Global economy: Oil money is
coming – and there is little the West can do about it', *Guardian*, 1
March 2008.

250 **This is a relatively small transaction, representing around 2 per
cent:** Official release and statement, 'Northern Rock sells mortgage
assets to JPMorgan for £2.25 billion', *Citywire*, 11 January 2008

252 **In early 2008, Steve Black repeatedly told analysts that the bank
was not actively pursuing mergers:** In fact at the bank's investor
day in February 2008, when he was asked if he would do a large
overlapping investment bank transaction, he said, 'The only way we
would do it would be if you could find something that filled some
strategic gaps where you got the overlapping businesses for free.'

254 **As the financial woes intensified in early 2008:** This section is
drawn from interviews with key participants. See also Kelly, Kate,
'The fall of Bear Stearns (part 1): Lost opportunities haunt final days

of Bear Stearns', 'The fall of Bear Stearns (part 2): Fear, rumors touched off fatal run on Bear Stearns', 'The fall of Bear Stearns (part 3): Bear Stearns neared collapse twice in frenzied last days', *Wall Street Journal*, 27, 28, 29 May 2008; Burrough, Bryan, 'Bringing down Bear Stearns', *Vanity Fair*, 1 August 2008; Bamber, Bill and Andrew Spencer, *Bear Trap: The Fall of Bear Stearns and the Panic of 2008*, Brick Tower Press, 2009.

255 **On 5 March Bear's cash holdings, on paper, topped $20 billion:** Data on liquidity levels from SEC, as cited in Bank of England Financial Stability Report, April 2008, p.11.

260 **We had been on the brink of the biggest financial meltdown:** Quotes taken from Gruen, Abby, 'Wall St. dances at news of Fed's interest rate cut – some fear relief won't be long-term', *Star Ledger*, 19 March 2008.

261 **With that one jaw-dropping deal . . . Dimon:** Dash, Eric, 'Chief lives up to the Morgan tradition: In purchasing Bear Stearns, Dimon emerges as a major winner', *New York Times*, 19 March 2008.

263 **By 2007 the New York Fed calculated that the combined assets of all of the SIVs:** See 'Reducing Systemic Risk in a Dynamic Financial System', Timothy F. Geithner, President and Chief Executive Officer, New York Federal Reserve, remarks at the Economic Club of New York, New York, 9 June 2008.

CHAPTER 15

266 **Also in the spring of 2008, the Institute of International Finance:** Final Report of the IIF Committee on Market Practices: Principles of Conduct and Best Practices Recommendations, IIF Washington, 17 July 2008.

266 **As Brickell stood on the podium in the ballroom of the Vienna Hilton:** Speech to ISDA annual conference, Vienna, 16 April 2008.

267 **Costly as those reforms will be, those costs will be minuscule:** Covering letter from E. Gerald Corrigan and Douglas Flint to Secretary Paulson and Governor Draghi, 6 August 2008 <http://www.crmpol-icygroup.org/docs/CRMPG-III-Transmittal-Letter.pdf>.

268 **We face a race:** Tucker, Paul, 'The New Financial Frontiers', speech to Chatham House, London, 13 June 2008, at <http://www.bankofeng-land.co.uk/publications/speedres/2008/ speech348.pdf>.

268 **Though some argued that those ABX price falls had gone too far:** See Bank of England Financial Stability Report, May 2008, p. 18.

276 **On 16 September the $62 billion Reserve Primary Fund:** <http://www.reservefunds.com/pdfs/Press%20Release%202008_09 16.pdf>.

276 **By the summer of 2007 AIG was holding around $540 billion super-senior risk:** The account about AIG is drawn from interviews with financiers previously at the group, supplemented by material drawn from transcripts of AIG's conference calls with investors on 31 May and 5 December 2007. See also Guerrera, Francesco and Felsted, Andrea, 'Inadequate cover', *Financial Times*, 6 October 2008; Morgenson, Gretchen, 'Behind crisis at AIG, a fragile web of risks', *New York Times*, 29 September 2008; O'Harrow, Robert and Dennis, Brady, 'Downgrades and downfall: How could a single unit of AIG cause the giant company's near-ruin and become a fulcrum of the global financial crisis? Straying from its own rules for managing risk and then failing to anticipate the consequences', *Washington Post*, 31 December 2008.

284 **On Sunday, 13 October 2008, Jamie Dimon received an urgent phone call:** This is drawn from author interviews, supplemented with Landler, Mark and Dash, Eric, 'Drama behind a banking deal', *New York Times*, 15 October 2008. Under the scheme the government initially agreed to invest $250 billion in senior preferred bank stock, half of which was earmarked for nine large banks; half would be available to thousands of small and regional banks. The investments counted towards each bank's base, or tier-one, capital ratio. Under the original plan, the minimum investment was supposed to be 1 per cent of risk-weighted assets; the maximum up to $25 billion or 3 per cent of risk-weighted assets, whichever was less.

EPILOGUE

288 **Mark-to-market losses had almost reached $3 trillion:** See Bank of England Financial Stability Report, October 2008, p. 14. The estimate covers all three main currency areas, and refers to mark-to-market losses on financial assets. These totalled $2.85 trillion in October, but were believed to have risen further in the subsequent two months.

288 **Banks and insurance companies had already written down more than $1 trillion:** See *Capital Markets Monitor*, February 2009, Institute of International Finance, Washington. Banks accounted for more than $800 billion of write-downs, insurance companies for the rest.

288 **The *Financial Times* calculated:** Giles, Chris, 'Public debt surges towards £1200 billion mark', *Financial Times*, 20 February 2009.

290 **When an industry dinner was held in London to hand out banking prizes:** IFR awards for 2008, presented in January 2009. J.P. Morgan won six out of the nine main categories, considerably more than any other bank had ever done.

293 **What we think of as the traditional hedge fund will shrink:** Freeland, Chrystia, MacIntosh, Julie, 'View from the top: Andrew Feldstein, chief executive of BlueMountain Capital', *Financial Times*, 19 December 2008.

295 **One British newspaper dubbed her:** Teather, David, 'Blythe Masters: The woman who built financial "weapons of mass destruction"', *Guardian*, 20 September 2008.

295 **Angry postings on the the internet:** See <http://www.blogher.com/blame-game-global-financial-collapse-fingers-are-pointing-one-woman-blythe-masters#comments> <http://zionistgoldreport.wordpress.com/2008/11/10/scam-artist-blythe-masters-speaks>.

295 **When she addressed a meeting of SIFMA in late 2008:** Opening comments, 'Through the turmoil', address to SIFMA Annual Meeting, New York, 28 October 2008 <http://events.sifma.org/2008/292/event.aspx?id=8566>.

Glossary

Asset-Backed Commercial Paper (ABCP)
A short-term security that commonly lasts between overnight and 180 days. It is typically issued by a bank or other financial institution, backed by physical assets such as trade receivables, commercial loans or holdings of bonds. Until 2007 it provided cheap funding.

Asset-Backed Security (ABS)
A security that is backed by portfolio of assets or cash flows from assets that are normally placed in a specially designated vehicle. The assets are often (but not always) loans. The assets are usually diversified, ideally to help reduce risk.

Bank Capital
The margin by which creditors are covered if the bank's assets are liquidated. A measure of a bank's financial health is its capital/asset ratio, which bank regulations require to be above a prescribed minimum.

Basel Accord
A set of regulations that established levels of bank capital, drawn up by the Basel Committee on Banking Supervision (BCBS), a committee of international central bankers and supervisors. The first accord, known as Basel I was drawn up in 1988. In 2004 a Basel II accord was published that was designed to align bank capital with risk in a closer manner. The secretariat for the committee is in the Bank of International Settlements in the Swiss town of Basel.

Bistro (Broad Index Secured Trust Offering)

J.P. Morgan's proprietary name for the idea of creating CDOs out of credit derivatives. It was first launched in 1997 and was the forerunner for the synthetic CDO structure that later became widespread.

Collateralized Debt Obligations (CDOs)

A form of asset-backed security. They are typically created by bundling together a portfolio of fixed-income debt (such as bonds) and using those assets to back the issuance of notes. Such notes usually carry varying levels of risk. Cash CDOs are created from tangible bonds, bonds or other debt; synthetic CDOs are created from credit derivatives.

Collateralized Debt Obligations of Asset Backed Securities (CDO of ABS)

CDOs built out of asset-backed securities, which are usually (but not always) types of mortgage-backed bonds.

Collateralized Loan Obligations

CDOs built out of loans, which are usually 'leveraged loans' (those extended to companies whose debt is rated non-investment grade).

Conduit

An entity that funds itself by issuing short-term debt and invests in assets such as trade receivables, commercial loans or bonds. It is backed up by credit lines from a bank and closely affiliated with a bank, but it does not always appear on a bank balance sheet. Structured investment vehicles (SIVs) are closely related to conduits.

Correlation

The degree to which asset prices, events or risks move in the same manner.

Credit Default Swap (CDS)

A contract between two parties, where the buyer pays a regular fee to the seller in exchange for a guarantee that they will be compensated in the case of any default on a stipulated piece of debt. CDS contracts are similar to insurance in some senses, but they are not regulated in the same manner, can be freely traded, and can be struck even if the buyer does not own the debt they wish to 'insure'.

Credit Derivatives
A bilateral contract between a buyer and seller whose value derives from the credit risk attached to an underlying bond, loan or other financial asset. Typically, they are designed to compensate one party, if that underlying asset goes into default. CDSs (credit default swaps) are one form of credit derivatives, but not the only one.

Derivative
A financial instrument whose value derives from an underlying asset, most normally commodities, bonds, equities or currencies.

Gaussian Copula
A statistical technique developed by David Li, a former J.P. Morgan analyst, for measuring the level of correlation and default probabilities in CDOs.

Leverage
Techniques that can magnify returns (or losses). The phrase is most commonly used to refer to debt, since the application of debt to a financial structure or strategy can magnify returns and losses. However, less commonly, the phrase can also be used to describe the manner in which the structure of a CDO, or other derivative, magnifies investor exposure to price swings.

Leverage Ratio
Most commonly used to describe the ratio between equity and debt, or earnings and debt.

Leveraged Finance
Funding for companies that carry a rating below investment grade. This includes high-yield bonds (bonds to companies rated below investment grade), and leveraged loans (loans to the same category of companies). In this decade it has been widely used to fund private equity bids, also known as leveraged buyouts.

Liquidity
The degree to which assets can be traded freely, or not.

Mortgage-Backed Bond Security
Bonds that are issued from a special-purpose vehicle that holds a portfolio of mortgages. These bonds are often issued in several tranches of riskiness.

Repurchase, or 'Repo' Market
A market where two participants agree that one will sell securities to another and make a commitment to repurchase equivalent securities on a future specified date, or on call, at a specified price. In effect, it is a way of borrowing or lending stock for cash, with the stock serving as collateral.

Special Purpose Vehicle
A shell company that is created to hold a portfolio of assets, such as bonds or derivatives contracts, and then issue securities backed by those assets. It may be created by a bank, but is a separate legal entity.

Structured Investment Vehicle (SIV)
An entity that operates in a manner similar to a conduit, but which does not enjoy complete credit support from a bank, and is often run in a manner that is more independent.

Super-Senior Risk
The most senior part of the capital structure of a CDO, which is the least exposed to the risk of default. Such risk always used to carry triple-A designations from the credit-ratings agencies.

Tranche
A class of securities that are issued by a collateralized debt obligation or asset-backed security that carries a certain level of risk. Normally, CDOs issue several different tranches of securities including a senior tranche (least risky), junior tranche or equity tranche (most risky) and mezzanine tranche (in between).

Acknowledgements

This book could not have been written without the help of a vast number of people, on both sides of the Atlantic, who have generously given their time over many years to help me understand how the financial world works (and, more recently, how it ceased to function). These thoughts and conversations have entwined to create the tapestry of this book. Many of the bankers, regulators and investors who have provided inspiration for it have asked to remain anonymous. That is no surprise, given the current political climate. But while I have not cited their names, they know who they are, and I wish to stress that I am truly grateful for their time. Thanks should also be given to the numerous former and current staff of J.P. Morgan who have talked to me on many occasions since early 2005. The bank did not initiate this project and it has not approved this book. On the contrary, some J.P. Morgan employees were extremely uneasy when they found out that I planned to write a book and a few actively tried to dissuade me. In the end, though, almost all graciously responded to my questions, and some devoted many hours to trying to explain their story. If I have misunderstood their tale, the mistakes are entirely mine.

My employer, the *Financial Times*, generously allowed me to take time off to pursue this project, even in the middle of a credit crisis. I am most grateful to Lionel Barber and Martin Dickson, respectively editor and deputy editor. I first started trying to wade through the alphabet soup of the credit world back in 2005, in tandem with my *FT* colleagues, and along the way I have benefited enormously from their insights and help. Particular thanks are due to Richard Beales, Chris Brown-Humes, Joanna Chung, Paul J. Davies, Aline Van Duyn, Francesco Guerrera, Jennifer Hughes, Michael Mackenzie, Sam Jones, David Oakley, Anousha Sakoui,

Saskia Scholtes, Henny Sender, Gary Silverman and Peter Thal-Larsen. Janet Tavakoli, Satyajit Das and Arturo Cifuentes were some of the few mavericks who were willing to speak openly to the *FT* about the looming credit dangers at an early stage. In various stages of writing, Adam Ridley, Charles Morris, Henry Fajemirokun, Keith Hart and Satyajit Das read various drafts and offered extremely helpful comments. Henny Sender also offered very kind logistical support. Pascal Spreen, Shannon Gitlin and Madhavi Pulapaka conducted research. Merryn Somerset Webb has been a wonderful source of support over the years. Sophia Arnold and Martha Mehta provided intellectual inspiration and welcome laughter. I am also very grateful to Keith Hart and other senior anthropologists for advice. The postgraduate work I did fifteen years ago in the social anthropology department of Cambridge University, under Ernest Gellner and Caroline Humphrey, instilled an analytical framework that deeply influences me, even today. More recently, I have also greatly benefited from debates at the London School of Economics and the University of Westminster.

My agent, Amanda Urban (Binky) at ICM in New York, was endlessly supportive about the book project, even back in early 2007, when it was wildly unfashionable to talk about CDOs and CDS. Karolina Sutton, at Curtis Brown in London, was very helpful too. Emily Loose at Free Press in New York worked extremely hard under brutally tight deadlines to turn my text into a book that would be readable by a wide audience. She did a truly remarkable job. I am thankful to them all. Many thanks also to Tim Whiting and Zoë Gullen of Little, Brown in London for turning the copy into a book that would make sense for a British audience with great aplomb.

At critical junctures, Cynthia Fajemirokun, Esmond Naylor, Peter and Romaine Tett all offered valued domestic support. Priya Patel and Julie Philips provided help with childcare. The biggest thanks, though, must go to Henry Fajemirokun whose profound insight and determination to challenge the accepted wisdom have been a central source of intellectual inspiration for me over the years, in relation to this book and much else. I am also very grateful for his support during the frenzied writing process. Saying 'thank you' sounds glib, but I mean it.

Index

AFTERSHOCK

Philippe Legrain

The financial crisis brought the world to the
brink of economic breakdown. As bubble turned to bust,
depression loomed. Now bankers' bonuses are back, house
prices are rising again and politicians promise recovery while
unemployment rises, frictions with China grow and the
planet overheats. Is this really sustainable – or do
we need to change course?

In this incisive assessment of the post-crisis world,
Philippe Legrain – economist, journalist and author – looks
at what went wrong, and how the world's leaders and financial
institutions can learn from their disastrous mistakes. Reporting
first-hand from around the world, he explains how the world's
economy is being reshaped and what it means for jobs and
our future prospects. He sets out the huge dangers
ahead – and the opportunities to craft a fairer,
safer, richer and greener world.

Wide-ranging, brilliant and impassioned, *Aftershock*
could not be more timely; it is at once a warning from history
and a compelling call to arms for the future.

LITTLE, BROWN
978-1-4087-0223-9

THEM AND US

Will Hutton

The suddenness and depth of the current recession
has raised questions about the workability of capitalism not
discussed since the 1930s. One of the constraints on recovery
is the growing belief that if the old model did not work,
there is no new one on offer.

In *Them and Us*, Will Hutton sets out to provide one,
arguing that reconstructing a bust financial system is not just a
technical question. It cannot be done without a full scale revision
of the wider values on which the system is based. And fairness
and equality must be placed at the heart of the new
capitalism for society's future wellbeing.

An incisive and indispensable look at how our society
has fragmented into inequality, and how to address this blight
on our times, *Them and Us* musters brilliant, convincing
arguments that will find favour on both right and left.

LITTLE, BROWN
978-1-4087-0151-5

Now you can order superb titles directly from Abacus

☐ Aftershock   Philippe Legrain   £12.99
☐ Them and Us   Will Hutton   £20.00

The prices shown above are correct at time of going to press. However, the publishers reserve the right to increase prices on covers from those previously advertised, without further notice.

──────────── ⬭ABACUS ────────────

Please allow for postage and packing: **Free UK delivery.**
Europe: add 25% of retail price; Rest of World: 45% of retail price.

To order any of the above or any other Abacus titles, please call our credit card orderline or fill in this coupon and send/fax it to:

Abacus, PO Box 121, Kettering, Northants NN14 4ZQ
Fax: 01832 733076   Tel: 01832 737526
Email: aspenhouse@FSBDial.co.uk

☐ I enclose a UK bank cheque made payable to Abacus for £ . . . . .
☐ Please charge £ . . . . to my Visa/Delta/Maestro

Expiry Date   ☐☐☐☐   Maestro Issue No.   ☐☐

NAME (BLOCK LETTERS please) . . . .

ADDRESS . . . .

. . . .

. . . .

Postcode . . . . Telephone . . . .

Signature . . . .

Please allow 28 days for delivery within the UK. Offer subject to price and availability.